IT Resilience

IT Resilience

Cloud's Vital Role

RAFEAL MECHLORE

Readers Publications

CONTENTS

INDEX 1

INTRODUCTION 3

1 | Chapter 1 17

2 | Chapter 2 47

3 | Chapter 3 71

4 | Chapter 4 105

5 | Chapter 5 130

6 | Chapter 6 160

7 | Chapter 7 183

8 | Chapter 8 213

9 | Chapter 9 234

10 | Chapter 10 254

INDEX

Introduction

1. The Growing Importance of IT Resilience
2. The Role of Cloud Technology
3. Purpose and Scope of the Book
4. Overview of Chapters

Chapter 1 : Understanding IT Resilience
1.1 Defining IT Resilience
1.2 The Business Impact of Downtime
1.3 Key Components of IT Resilience
1.4 Resilience vs. Redundancy

Chapter 2 : The Evolution of Cloud Technology
2.1 Historical Context of Cloud Computing
2.2 Types of Cloud Services (IaaS, PaaS, SaaS)
2.3 Cloud Deployment Models (Public, Private, Hybrid)
2.4 Benefits and Challenges of Cloud Adoption

Chapter 3 : Cloud's Role in IT Resilience
3.1 Cloud as a Scalability Solution
3.2 Cloud for Disaster Recovery and Backup
3.3 Cloud for Data Redundancy and Replication
3.4 Cloud-Based Monitoring and Automation

Chapter 4 : Cloud Security and Compliance
4.1 Addressing Security Concerns in the Cloud
4.2 Regulatory Compliance and Data Governance
4.3 Best Practices for Securing Cloud-based Resilience

Chapter 5 : Cloud Migration Strategies
5.1 Planning and Assessing Your IT Infrastructure
5.2 Lift-and-Shift vs. Re-architecture
5.3 Managing Data Migration
5.4 Cost Considerations in Cloud Migration

Chapter 6 : Building Resilient Applications
6.1 Developing Cloud-Native Applications
6.2 Microservices, Containers, and Serverless Computing
6.3 Designing for Failure and Recovery

Chapter 7 : Monitoring and Testing
7.1 Continuous Monitoring and Alerting
7.2 Simulating Failure Scenarios
7.3 Regularly Testing Resilience Plans
7.4 Incident Response and Recovery Procedures

Chapter 8 : Cloud Providers and Services
8.1 Leading Cloud Providers (e.g., AWS, Azure, GCP)
8.2 Cloud Services for Resilience
8.3 Vendor Lock-in Considerations

Chapter 9 : Cost Optimization
9.1 Managing Costs in the Cloud
9.2 Cost vs. Resilience Trade-offs
9.3 Cost Optimization Strategies

Chapter 10 : The Future of IT Resilience and Cloud
10.1 Emerging Technologies and Trends
10.2 AI and Machine Learning in Resilience
10.3 Sustainability and Resilience
10.4 Ethical and Societal Considerations

INTRODUCTION

The need of having resilient information technology has gone to the top of the list of objectives for most organizations in today's increasingly digital and technologically dependent society. Technology influences practically every facet of both our personal and professional life. This book, titled "IT Resilience: Cloud's Vital Role," takes the reader on an in-depth excursion through the ever-changing environment of IT resilience and the pivotal role that cloud technology plays in assuring the continuous operation of enterprises and their longevity in the face of adversity.

The digital transformation that has been sweeping through sectors over the past few years has brought out opportunities and challenges that have never been seen before. It has completely altered the ways in which companies conduct their operations, interact with their clients, and manage their internal procedures. However, as a result of this, they are now extremely dependent on the accessibility, safety, and continuity of their information technology systems. Any kind of interruption, whether it be a problem with the hardware, an online attack, or a natural disaster, can have severe repercussions, including monetary losses, reputational harm, and even the possible destruction of a company.

Because of their increased susceptibility to disruptions caused by information technology, firms are being forced to embrace resilience as a strategic goal. The ability to resist disruptions and recover quickly and effectively from them is what is meant by the term "IT resilience," which is defined within these pages. It goes beyond merely being redundant because it also involves the capacity to progress while being challenged, learn from one's previous experiences, and improve as a result of those experiences.

This book starts off by laying a solid groundwork in the idea of IT resilience and its many applications. We are going to look into the essential components that support resilience, investigate its significance in the contemporary environment of business, and distinguish it from the more well-known idea of redundancy. Readers will be able to obtain a clear view of the problems and opportunities that lie ahead of them after they have a solid understanding of the complexities of resilience.

The historical backdrop of IT resilience will be revealed, with an emphasis placed on the central role played by cloud technology in the process of sculpting the landscape of resilience. We will investigate the various cloud deployment strategies as well as the many kinds of cloud services, such as Infrastructure as a Service (IaaS), Platform as a Service (PaaS), and Software as a Service (SaaS).

It will be explored both the benefits and the challenges of adopting cloud technology, which will equip readers with the knowledge they need to make decisions based on accurate information.

The examination of how the use of cloud technology might change the resilience capacities of an organization constitutes the meat and potatoes of this book. The inherent scalability and flexibility of the cloud are utilized to bolster automated processes, data redundancy, and disaster recovery capabilities. Readers will be provided with concrete examples of how prominent firms have successfully incorporated cloud technologies into their resilience strategies through the use of real-world case studies. These case studies will serve as a source of inspiration as well as practical insights, showing the opportunities that await those who are able to grasp the potential of the cloud.

As we move through the chapters, we will discuss the most important components of cloud security and regulatory compliance. This book will provide a comprehensive guide on securing data in the cloud and navigating the complex world of compliance, which varies greatly depending on the type of business and where it is located. In this section, we will lay out in full the best practices and techniques for reducing potential security threats and conforming to the applicable regulatory requirements.

Migration techniques to the cloud will be front and center, providing readers with a road map for planning, evaluating existing IT infrastructure, and making strategic decisions. During the debate, topics such as "lift-and-shift" versus re-architecture, managing data migration, and the all-important cost aspect will be brought up.

In parallel, the art of developing resilient apps will be investigated in this book, with an emphasis placed on cloud-native techniques and strategies. Microservices, containers, serverless computing, and the fundamentals of designing applications that anticipate and respond gracefully to failure will all be covered in depth during this session.

In addition to this, continuous monitoring and testing will be highlighted as essential components of a resilient IT strategy. The book will shed light on the need of real-time monitoring, the benefits of simulating failure situations, and the requirement of regular testing and the continual refinement of resilience strategies. A well-structured incident response and recovery plan will serve as a lifeline in the case of an incident, allowing you to minimize the effects of disruptions and keep operations running smoothly.

This book will present readers with an in-depth view of top cloud providers such as Amazon Web Services (AWS), Microsoft Azure, and Google Cloud Platform

(GCP), as well as the services that each of these cloud providers offers. Readers will be able to traverse the complexities of the cloud ecosystem as a result of the fact that it will also discuss the potential issues and considerations around vendor lock-in.

This investigation will focus heavily on finding effective ways to control expenses incurred when utilizing cloud computing. This book will offer advise on how to reconcile the financial consequences of cloud technology with the need for business continuity. It will include ideas for optimizing costs without compromising resilience.

Finally, we will examine the future of IT resilience and the cloud with an open mind. Emerging technologies, the role of artificial intelligence and machine learning, concerns regarding sustainability, as well as the ethical and societal considerations that are inherent in our digital future will be investigated. Organizations who want to stay ahead of the curve in the rapidly advancing field of IT resilience need to understand these patterns in order to be successful.

This book is more than just a helpful guide; rather, it is a rallying cry to get people to take action. The concluding chapters will equip readers with the knowledge and skills necessary to evaluate the resilience of their own companies, formulate a strategic plan, and prevail over widespread obstacles. When you have completed this trip, you will be equipped with the knowledge and tools necessary to begin a robust IT transformation, one in which the cloud's important role is firmly integrated into your strategy. This transition will allow your IT infrastructure to better withstand disruptions.

This book is your essential companion on the path to a more resilient and digitally thriving future. Whether you are an IT professional seeking to enhance your organization's resilience, a business leader looking to safeguard your company's future, or simply an individual intrigued by the dynamic intersection of IT resilience and cloud technology, this book will guide you to a more resilient and digitally thriving future.

1. **The Growing Importance of IT Resilience**

   It is impossible to overestimate the growing significance of IT resilience in the dynamic environment of modern business, which is always changing. The capacity of an organization to resist and recover from disruptions has emerged as a strategic priority in light of the growing reliance that businesses place on technology to power their operations, provide for the needs of their consumers, and propel innovation.

   This article investigates the elements that have led to the increased significance of IT resilience, the variables that are driving this demand, and the fundamental concepts that are supporting it.

   The Era of Digital Disruption and Transformation

   In the course of the last several decades, we have been able to observe a significant shift in the manner in which enterprises are run. The emergence of the digital age has brought about a profound change in the manner in which businesses perform their operations, communicate with their clients, and organize their internal workflows. Businesses now have the ability to be more nimble, efficient, and customer-focused as a result of the widespread use of digital technologies, which has ushered in a new world of possibilities. However, as a result of this digital revolution, firms are now more susceptible to disruptions in their IT systems.

In current age of digitization, information technology serves as the foundation for almost every sector of the economy. It makes it possible for businesses to connect with markets all over the world, to simplify their supply chains, to tap into the power of data analytics, and to provide personalized experiences for their customers. The reliance on information technology systems has reached a point where any disruption, regardless of whether it was caused by a failure in the hardware, a breach in cybersecurity, a natural disaster, or human mistake, can have fatal implications. The cost of downtime and data loss can now be evaluated not only in terms of financial terms but also in terms of harm to a company's reputation and the loss of trust from its customers. This presents a complex terrain for organizations, which must now navigate it.

The Repercussions of Interruptions in Information Technology

When information technology systems malfunction or are breached, the repercussions can have far-reaching effects. The financial repercussions are those that manifest themselves first and are felt almost immediately. An interruption in service can result in a loss of revenue, higher costs associated with operations, and even penalties for violating service level agreements. According to a survey that was published by Gartner, the typical cost of downtime in information technology is around $5,600 per minute. This number can equate to more than $300,000 per hour for some businesses. The cost of downtime can be much higher for companies operating in industries such as online commerce, the financial industry, or healthcare.

In addition, the loss of data or a breach in security might have equally significant effects. The leaking of confidential information, regulatory fines, legal obligations, and long-term damage to an organization's reputation are all potential outcomes of these types of incidents. When a corporation's security for customer information is breached, the trust that customers invest in that company can suffer significant and often irreparable damage.

Consider the scenario of a multinational retailer whose e-commerce platform being hit by a cyberattack during the busiest time of year for retail, leading to a substantial outage of the website and the theft of customer data. There is a potential for damages amounting to millions of dollars due to the erosion of client trust, financial losses, and regulatory fines. In addition, the effects of the incident on the company's brand may continue to be felt for a number of years.

The Necessity of a Robust IT Infrastructure

The imperative of IT resilience has arisen as a major issue for companies all over the world as a result of the growing dependence on technology and the potentially catastrophic implications of disruptions to IT. The term "IT resilience" refers to an organization's capacity to maintain its operations despite the occurrence of unfavorable circumstances. This is accomplished by ensuring that essential IT systems are accessible and that data is safeguarded.

The traditional method of redundancy in information technology, which often entails making duplicates of systems or data to reduce the risk of having a single point of failure, is not sufficient for achieving IT resilience. A holistic approach, resilience is a strategy that not only seeks to minimize disruptions but also focuses on an organization's capacity to recover from them, adapt to new circumstances, and gain knowledge from the experience. It comprises the strategies, technology, and best practices that make it possible for enterprises to keep a high level of service availability even in the face of unforeseen occurrences.

The Importance of IT Resilience and the Factors That Drive It

The danger of interruptions increases along with the complexity of IT ecosystems, which often include a combination of on-premises infrastructure, cloud services, and applications provided by third parties. It is absolutely necessary, given the complexity of the environment, to manage and provide resilience.

Threats to Cybersecurity The proliferation of complex online attacks has made enterprises increasingly vulnerable to data breaches and ransomware assaults. Resilience in information technology is essential for minimizing the effects of such attacks and rapidly recovering lost data.

Regulatory Requirements Numerous sectors are subject to stringent regulations that mandate the preservation of data and the recovery of information in the event of a disaster. Should you fail to comply with these regulations, you risk incurring significant penalties.

Customer Expectations Customers in today's world anticipate uninterrupted access to the services they pay for and very little downtime.

Because clients may look for other options in the event of any interruption or data loss, resilient operations are an important competitive differentiation. Organizations that operate on a worldwide scale are required to maintain their resilience across a variety of geographical locations and time zones as a result of globalization. A crucial component of IT resilience is ensuring business continuity in the case of natural disasters or events with geopolitical repercussions.

Dependencies on Third-Party Suppliers and Partners Many organizations are reliant on the services of third-party suppliers and partners for essential operations. The degree to which these external entities are resilient can have a direct bearing on an organization's ability to withstand adversity.

Evolving Technologies: New technologies, such as the Internet of Things (IoT) and artificial intelligence, are becoming increasingly important to the operations of businesses. Maintaining a competitive advantage is dependent on taking the necessary steps to ensure the robustness of these technologies.

Natural Catastrophes The frequency and severity of natural catastrophes have both grown as a result of climate change and other environmental causes. Resilience in information technology is essential for businesses located in locations prone to natural disasters.

Preparedness for Pandemics: The COVID-19 pandemic brought to light the importance of resiliency in the face of global catastrophes. Working remotely and having access from a distance to essential computer systems grew increasingly important.

Concepts Crucial to the Resilience of IT

Availability: The concept of maintaining high availability is essential to the concept of resilience as a whole. This entails making certain that vital information technology (IT) systems and services are always available to users, even in the event that there are disruptions.

The term "Recovery Time Objective" (RTO) refers to the maximum amount of time that a system or service is allowed to be down after an incident. A higher amount of resilience can be deduced from an RTO that is lower.

Recovery Point Objective (RPO) is a term that describes the greatest quantity of data that a company is willing to lose in the event of an incident. RPO is defined by the phrase "recovery point." A lower RPO suggests that there will be less data loss overall.

The creation of duplicate systems or components is an example of redundancy. The goal of redundancy is to ensure that business operations can continue normally in the event that one of the systems or components fails.

Backup and Restore: Having regular backups of your data and systems is really necessary in order to have a speedy recovery. This entails making copies of both the data and the systems so that they can be restored in the event of a malfunction.

Recovery from Disaster: Plans for disaster recovery include methods and procedures for recovering information technology (IT) systems and data in the event of a catastrophe. This often comprises procedures for data backup and restoration, alternative data centers, and the testing of recovery strategies.

Business Continuity: Business continuity is a broader strategy that not only focuses on IT systems but also on the organization's capacity to continue key business functions even in the face of adversity. This strategy is included in the definition of business continuity.

Response to Incidents The process of responding to incidents requires taking a methodical, organized approach to resolving and controlling disturbances. It involves recognizing and categorizing incidents, beginning the process of developing response plans, and gaining knowledge from past incidents in order to increase future resilience.

Testing Your Resilience It is essential to test your resilience plans on a regular basis. As part of this process, it may be necessary to simulate disruptive occurrences in order to evaluate the efficacy of recovery techniques.

2. **The Role of Cloud Technology**

   Cloud computing has become an influential force in the corporate world, altering the ways in which firms run their operations, store data, and provide services to customers. In this era of digital transformation, the role that cloud technology plays in enabling businesses to adapt, develop, and grow is more important than ever before.

   This article goes deeply into the multidimensional function that cloud technology plays and investigates the impact that it has on numerous aspects of modern business, including the IT infrastructure, innovation, and other areas.

   The Development of Technology Based on the Cloud

   It is essential to have a solid understanding of the development of cloud technology before delving into its contemporary applications. The idea behind cloud computing, in which information technology resources are made available to users over the internet, has roots that go all the way back to the 1960s. However, it wasn't until the early 21st century that cloud technology became well-known and was used by a significant number of people.

   Grid computing, utility computing, and application service providers (ASPs) can be traced back to the beginnings of cloud computing technologies. These forerunners were crucial in laying the groundwork for the development of cloud computing, which eventually developed as an all-encompassing strategy for providing computing services through the use of the internet. The debut of Amazon Web Services (AWS) in 2006, which popularized Infrastructure as a Service (IaaS), and the release of platforms such as Microsoft Azure and Google Cloud Platform (GCP) are key milestones in the history of cloud technology. Amazon Web Services (AWS) was one of the companies that popularized IaaS. These days, "cloud technology" refers to a wide variety of services, such as "Infrastructure as a Service," "Platform as a Service," and "Software as a Service," respectively. Each of these many service models contributes in its own unique way to the success of various parts of today's businesses.

   IaaS Is the Basic Building Block of Cloud Infrastructure

   Cloud computing relies heavily on a component known as Infrastructure as a Service, or IaaS for short. It delivers through the internet virtualized computer resources to enterprises, such as servers, storage, and networking. These resources can be used by organizations. IaaS is designed to act as the foundation for IT infrastructure, which enables businesses to scale the amount of computing resources they use up or down depending on their requirements.

There are numerous advantages to using IaaS. It eliminates the necessity for companies to

purchase and maintain physical hardware, which results in a reduction in the cost of capital. Because of the elasticity of infrastructure as a service (IaaS), organizations are able to respond to varying workloads while still only paying for the resources they really utilize. IaaS also makes it easier to implement solutions for data backup and disaster recovery, which increases the robustness of IT systems.

PaaS: Putting Application Development in Your Hands.

Platform as a Service, also known as PaaS, is a kind of cloud computing service that is intended to facilitate the process of application development and deployment. PaaS makes available to developers the tools, frameworks, and infrastructure required to build, test, and launch software applications. PaaS's purpose is to simplify the development process by freeing developers from the burden of managing the underlying infrastructure so they can instead concentrate on writing code.

The development process is sped up by PaaS, which also encourages teamwork and collaboration among the many development teams and makes it easier to deliver apps. Scalability is another feature offered by the platform, and it ensures that applications can expand in response to rising demand from end users. In addition, PaaS provides support for a wide range of programming languages and development frameworks, which makes it a flexible option for developing contemporary software applications.

Delivering Software Solutions Is What SaaS Stands For

Software as a Service, sometimes known as SaaS, is one of the cloud computing industry's most well-known and popular deployment models. SaaS is short for software as a service, and it refers to the delivery of software applications and services over the internet. This removes the requirement that users install and maintain software on their own devices. Individuals as well as businesses can benefit from the simplification of the software deployment, update, and maintenance processes that SaaS provides.

SaaS applications cover a wide range of different purposes, from customer relationship management (CRM) software like Salesforce to productivity tools like Microsoft 365 and Google Workspace. Salesforce is one example of a SaaS application. Applications delivered as a service (SaaS) are great for enterprises of any size because of their scalability and accessibility. In addition, software as a service (SaaS) typically comes with subscription-based pricing models, which reduces initial expenses and improves cost predictability.

IT RESILIENCE

The Importance of Cloud Computing in Today's Modern Businesses
Businesses can save money by reducing their need to invest in and maintain on-premises infrastructure thanks to cloud technology's ability to eliminate this requirement. This transition from capital expenses (CapEx) to operating expenses (OpEx) enables firms to allocate resources more effectively, with the flexibility to scale up or down depending on the demand for those resources. Cloud computing provides a level of scalability that is unmatched by other methods. Companies are able to swiftly make available additional resources in order to meet peaks in demand, and they can scale back their operations during times of lesser utilization. This adaptability is especially important for companies that have workloads that are prone to fluctuations.

Cloud computing enables a global presence through the use of distributed data centers that can be situated in virtually any part of the world. As a result, businesses are able to provide their services and information to an audience located anywhere in the world with far less delay, which improves the user experience.

Cloud technology offers a safe and economical alternative for the storing and backup of data, and it is becoming increasingly popular in recent years. It ensures data redundancy and resilience, which in turn reduces the risk of data loss due to faults in the hardware or natural disasters.

Security and Compliance: Cloud service providers make significant financial investments in the implementation of security protocols and compliance certifications. They provide businesses with a comprehensive array of products and services in order to assist those businesses in satisfying their security and compliance obligations.

Planned Continuity of Business Operations and Recovery from Catastrophe Cloud computing is an essential component of business continuity and emergency preparedness plans. It enables businesses to quickly recover from disturbances, create data backups, and create redundancies in their systems.

Collaboration and Productivity: Software as a service (SaaS) solutions, such as office productivity suites and communication tools, improve collaboration and productivity by allowing users to have remote access to mission-critical applications and data. During the COVID-19 pandemic, when working from a remote location became the norm, this came in quite handy.

Due to the freedom offered by the cloud, businesses are now able to experiment with new ideas and evolve at a much quicker rate. In today's fast-paced digital landscape, it is crucial for businesses to have the ability to swiftly spin up environments in order to test new ideas.

Artificial Intelligence and Machine Learning Cloud providers offer AI and machine learning services, which enables businesses to utilize cutting-edge technologies without the requirement for specialized skills or infrastructure. In other words, organizations may take advantage of these services with little to no investment.

Integration of the Internet of Things (IoT): Cloud technology is able to accommodate the massive volumes of data that are produced by Internet of Things (IoT) devices. This makes it possible to analyze this data and gain insights from it.

Advantage competitive: Businesses who adopt cloud computing immediately put themselves in a position to obtain a competitive advantage. They are able to respond rapidly to shifting market conditions, better satisfy the requirements of their customers, and innovate in ways that were not possible in the past.

3. **Purpose and Scope of the Book**

The intention for writing a book and the breadth of its coverage are the compass points that point the author in the right direction while they work on the project. This principle is adhered to by "Unveiling the Human Psyche" without exception. As part of this in-depth investigation of the human psyche, we will set out on a quest to unravel the mysterious workings of the human mind's myriad complexities. The goal of this book is to decipher the intricate workings of the human mind, illuminating the profound secrets that underlie our thoughts, feelings, and actions. It is a journey into the inmost recesses of the human psyche, during which we investigate the fundamental aspects of what it is that makes us who we are.

The purpose of this research is to expose previously concealed aspects of the human psyche

The fundamental objective of this book is to investigate the psychology of human beings and bring to light the concealed realities that are buried under the surface. It is written with the intention of shedding light on the complex inner workings of the human mind, with the goal of providing readers with a thorough understanding of their own ideas, feelings, and behaviors. We hope that through diving into the intricacies of the human psyche, we will be able to discover the fundamental forces that form both our personal and communal experiences.

One of the most important aspects of one's own personal growth and development is gaining an understanding of the human psyche. It gives people the ability to make choices based on more accurate information, cultivate healthier relationships, and manage the difficulties of life with greater clarity and purpose. The information that is shared in this book gives readers invaluable insights into their own thoughts, which enables them to set off on a path toward self-discovery and personal growth.

In addition, a thorough investigation into the human psyche might provide insights into the more general human experience. It has the capability of shedding light on the factors that drive society trends, influence cultural dynamics, and form historical events. This book seeks to contribute to a greater knowledge of human nature and the complicated interaction of human ideas, feelings, and behaviors by exploring the human psyche on both an individual and collective level. It does so by examining the human psyche in both its individual and collective forms.

Understanding the Complicated Landscape of the Human Psyche is the Goal of This Project.

This book examines the most recent discoveries made in the realms of psychology and neuroscience. Both of these disciplines are covered in depth. It investigates the neurological and psychological processes that are the foundation of human thought, emotion, and action. The goal of this article is to offer readers with a full grasp of the scientific basis of the human psyche by drawing from the most recent research that has been conducted.

Emotional Intelligence and Mental Health: Emotional intelligence is a crucial component in the process of decoding the human psyche. We take a look at the numerous feelings that play a role in the formation of our experiences and share some views on how emotional health can be maintained and improved. In addition, the book delves into the complexities of mental health, covering topics such as stress, anxiety, and depression, and offering advice on how to strengthen one's emotional fortitude in the process.

Personality and Identity: The documentary "Unveiling the Human Psyche" delves into the idea of a person's personality and the ways in which it affects their conduct and the relationships they have with other people. The reader will get an understanding of the processes that lead to the formation of personality traits, self-identity, and the ways that personality can change throughout the course of one's lifetime. In addition to this, we discuss the influence that things like culture and one's surroundings have on an individual's sense of self.

Connections and Communication: The book dives into the area of human connections, studying how the human mind influences communication and the dynamics of interpersonal relationships. Readers can improve their capacity to connect with people, communicate with others, and develop healthy relationships by gaining an awareness of the psychological foundations around which our interactions with others are built.

Impact on Cultures and civilizations The human psyche is not merely confined to the realm of the individual; rather, it plays a critical part in the formation of cultures and civilizations. The documentary "Unveiling the Human Psyche" examines the communal features of the human mind, discussing how group psychology, norms, and values influence the dynamics of society.

We investigate the various ways in which the human mind influences cultural occurrences as well as the development of societies.

Self-Discovery and Personal Development: This book goes beyond academic exploration to offer practical advise on self-discovery and the development of one's personality. The activities, tactics, and real-life examples that are provided for the readers in this book will help them on their journey toward a more profound understanding of who they are and the advancement of their personal growth.

4. **Overview of Chapters**

This book, which is titled "Unveiling the Human Psyche," is an in-depth investigation into the complexities that are associated with the human mind. Within this section, we will provide an overview of the chapters that are contained within the book, outlining the primary ideas and insights that are presented within each chapter. The voyage into the intricacies of the human psyche is a fascinating one, and this roadmap will lead readers on that journey.

Chapter 1 :The fundamentals of human psychology are covered

In the first chapter, we will build the framework for the examination of the human psyche that will follow in subsequent chapters. We go into the fundamentals of human psychology, discussing important ideas, providing historical context, and outlining the fundamentals of how the mind functions. The reader will come away with a profound comprehension of the essential components that shape human cognition, emotion, and action. This chapter will serve as the cornerstone upon which the succeeding chapters will develop, so establishing a solid foundation for the voyage that lies ahead.

Chapter 2 :The neurological terrain of the mind is discussed

In the second chapter, readers are introduced to the complex field of neurology. In this section, we investigate the neurological mechanisms that support the human psyche by analyzing the structure and operation of the brain. Readers will get a deeper understanding for the biological basis of human psychology as they gain insights into the many regions of the brain and their functions in generating ideas, emotions, and actions through the course of this book. In addition to this, we look at the most recent findings in brain research and discuss what those findings mean for our knowledge of the mind.

Chapter 3 :The Hidden Face of Emotions: Understanding the Core of the Human Experience

Emotions are at the center of the human experience, and the purpose of this chapter is to dissect the many facets of these experiences. We investigate the full gamut of human feelings, from happiness to sadness, rage to love, and everything in between. Readers will obtain a profound grasp of how emotions influence our decisions, relationships, and overall well-being. In addition, this chapter gives readers actionable advice on how to manage and improve their emotional health, which enables them to navigate the emotional terrain with better resilience and self-awareness.

Chapter 4 : The Mysterious Nature of Personality is Discussed

The fascinating subject of personality is the focus of the fourth chapter. In this section, we will discuss the enduring characteristics that give each person their own identity. Readers will investigate many theories of personality development and learn about the factors that have a lasting influence on an individual's personality. We also go into the idea of self-identity and how it changes as a result of the things that happen to us during our lives. Those who are interested in gaining a deeper understanding of both themselves and others may find this chapter to be a source of helpful information.

Chapter 5 : Building Stable Relationships is the Topic

The human psyche has a significant impact on the dynamics of interpersonal relationships, which is the topic of discussion in Chapter 5 of this book. The art of communication, the resolution of conflict, and the psychological foundations of a variety of relationship types, ranging from familial ties to friendships and romantic partnerships, are all topics that are covered in this course. Readers can improve their interpersonal skills, build healthier relationships, and foster greater empathy and understanding by developing an awareness of the psychological components of human connections.

Chapter 6 : The cultural tapestry of the human psyche is discussed

The human mind is more than the sum of its individual experiences; it also weaves a significant thread into the intricate fabric of culture and society. The communal features of the human mind are investigated in Chapter 6, which also provides some illumination on group psychology, cultural standards, and societal ideals. The reader will come away with a better understanding of how the human brain produces cultural phenomena, how it affects society patterns, and how it drives historical events. This chapter presents an insightful and original viewpoint on the dynamic relationship that exists between individual and collective psychology.

Chapter 7 : The potency of coming into one's own

The theoretical investigation is brought to a close in Chapter 7, which ushers in the practical application section. In this section, we provide the readers several tools and tasks that might help them discover themselves and grow personally. Readers can get insight into their own strengths, flaws, and goals by engaging in self-reflection and doing an honest appraisal of themselves. This chapter gives readers the tools they need to go on a life-altering path toward increased self-awareness, self-improvement, and personal fulfillment.

Chapter 8 : The benefits of mindfulness on one's mental health are discussed

In this fast-paced world, maintaining a healthy mental state is an essential component of living a life that is rewarding. The practice of mindfulness is examined in Chapter 8, along with its significant influence on a person's mental health. The readers will gain an understanding of how the practice of mindfulness can assist alleviate symptoms of stress, anxiety, and depression while also improving general psychological well-being. This chapter offers a variety of exercises and suggestions that might help you incorporate mindfulness into your day-to-day life.

Chapter 9 : Understanding the Human Psyche in the Future Topic

The final chapter of the book delves into the possibilities for the future of psychological research on humans. Our investigation delves into developing tendencies in the fields of psychology and neuroscience, such as the application of innovative technologies to increase our understanding of the mind, such as artificial intelligence (AI) and virtual reality (VR). In addition, we take into consideration the moral issues that are raised by the research conducted on the human psyche as well as the implications that any future findings may have for society.

Chapter 1

Understanding IT Resilience

In the fast shifting digital landscape of today, the resilience of a company's information technology infrastructure has emerged as an essential component of corporate operations. Because of their ever-increasing reliance on technology for a variety of business operations, as well as the ever-increasing complexity of IT systems, businesses are increasingly susceptible to a wide variety of interruptions. These include everything from natural catastrophes to cyberattacks and hardware failures. Resilience in information technology is essential to maintaining corporate operations in the face of these obstacles.

This article goes further into the idea of IT resilience, providing an explanation of what it is, why it is important, and how businesses may attain and keep it. We will investigate the fundamental ideas behind IT resilience, as well as the technology, tactics, and business practices that underpin it, and the practical advantages it affords to companies. At the end of this, you will have a complete grasp of the resilience of information technology and the vital role it plays in the operations of modern businesses.

What exactly does "IT Resilience" mean?

In the field of information technology (IT), "IT resilience" refers to an organization's capacity to keep its IT services and activities running smoothly and continuously despite interruptions or breakdowns. These disturbances can originate from a wide number of causes, including malfunctioning gear or software, cyberattacks, natural disasters, or even human mistake. In its most basic form, information technology (IT) resilience refers to the process of constructing an IT infrastructure that is both resilient and adaptable, with the ability to adjust to unforeseen difficulties without compromising the availability, performance, or security of essential systems and data.

Resilience in information technology is separate from redundancy in information technology and recovery from disaster in information technology. IT resilience goes beyond the notions of redundancy and disaster recovery, which both focus on the capacity to recover data and systems following an incident. Redundancy includes having multiple components or systems in place to assure uptime, while disaster recovery centers on the ability to recover data and systems after an incident. It requires not only recovering from an incident but also withstanding the impact of the incident in the first place and reducing the amount of damage caused by the incident.

Why Maintaining IT Resilience Is So Crucial

Understanding the various factors that contribute to the necessity of IT resilience can shed light on the importance of this concept in the context of the present corporate environment.

1. **Continuity of Business Operations**
   The ability to keep operating normally is one of the most important reasons why IT resilience is
   so important. Businesses are dependent on their information technology systems for day-to-day operations in this increasingly digital world. A large amount of financial loss as well as damage to the organization's reputation might be the consequence of downtime. By guaranteeing the resilience of their information

technology systems, businesses may reduce the amount of disruptions they experience and maintain uninterrupted service to their consumers.

2. **Methods for Avoiding Danger**

    IT resilience is a potent method for risk reduction that may be utilized in response to a wide variety of threats, including data breaches, cyberattacks, and natural disasters. It assists organizations in preparing for and mitigating the possible impact of these occurrences, which in turn reduces the possibility of catastrophic damage and the loss of data.

3. **Observance of the Requirements**

    There are numerous sectors that are subject to stringent rules and compliance requirements in relation to the security of data and the continuation of business. With the support of IT resilience measures, businesses can meet their legal and regulatory duties, thereby avoiding potentially expensive penalties and other legal repercussions.

4. **Confidence from the Clients**

    Customers have come to expect businesses to be accessible and responsive at all hours of the day and night. The trust and confidence of customers might be damaged by any downtime or loss of data. Resilience in information technology ensures that firms can live up to the standards set by their customers and continue to earn their trust.

5. **An Advantage over Competitors**

Businesses who are able to recover quickly from technological setbacks have a significant advantage in the marketplace. They are able to recover from disturbances more quickly, adapt more effectively to shifting conditions, and continue to serve clients even when competitors may stumble. Given the frenetic nature of the modern business world, this confers a substantial competitive edge.

Critical Elements of IT Disaster Recovery

In order to achieve IT resilience, one must adhere to a number of fundamental concepts and practices that serve as a roadmap for the creation and upkeep of a resilient IT infrastructure. These guiding concepts are applicable to a wide variety of business sectors as well as companies of diverse sizes.

1. **Redundancy and Continuity of Service**
   The concept of redundancy is essential to the resilience of information technology. It entails
   creating several copies of essential elements, systems, or data in order to maintain uninterrupted functioning in the case of a malfunction. It is common practice to implement redundancy in server architecture, data storage systems, network connections, and even power supplies. When a primary component fails, failover mechanisms are activated so that the system can automatically switch to using redundant resources.
2. **A Totally Integrated Backup and Recovery System**
   Strategies for data backup and restoration are absolutely necessary for resilient information technology. In the event that data is corrupted, deleted, or the system fails entirely, having regular backups of the data and configurations of the system, both on-site and off-site, ensures that information can be restored. These backups should be tested on a consistent basis to ensure that they are still useful.
3. **Capacity for Growth and Adaptability**
   Scalability and adaptability are two essential qualities of a resilient IT architecture. This indicates that it is able to easily adjust to changes in demand, whether it be an increase in the number of users that access it, the addition of new services, or the incorporation of new technology. Scalability ensures that the infrastructure can accommodate unforeseen spikes in consumption without compromising its performance.

4. **Protection from Dangers and Detection of Dangers**
Resilience in information technology relies heavily on security in many forms. A robust infrastructure needs to be guarded against both the external dangers, such as cyberattacks, and the internal dangers, such as data breaches. It is absolutely necessary to protect IT systems by putting in place stringent security measures, such as firewalls, intrusion detection systems, and performing regular security audits.
5. **The Diverse Geographies of the World**
The distribution of information technology resources over a number of different geographic regions can help improve resilience. An organization can ensure that a localized occurrence, such as a natural disaster, would not result in complete downtime by ensuring that there is not a single point of failure inside the firm. In order to achieve geographic variety, cloud-based technologies are frequently utilized.
6. **Preventative Monitoring and Rapid Reaction to Incidents**
For information technology to be resilient, proactive monitoring tools and incident response procedures are necessities. The continual monitoring of system health and performance provided by these tools enables businesses to identify and resolve issues well in advance of the catastrophic breakdowns they could otherwise cause. Plans for responding to incidents detail the steps that should be performed in the event that an incident occurs. This helps to ensure a prompt and coordinated response.
7. **Training and Awareness for Staff Members**
The robustness of the IT system is directly influenced by the employees. They need to be educated on the most up-to-date best practices, as well as security awareness and incident response protocols. Employees who are well-informed and well-prepared can assist reduce the negative effects of incidents and avoid security breaches.
8. **Testing and simulation on a regular basis**

Testing and simulation exercises should be performed on a regular basis in order to accurately assess the IT resilience of a company. Among these are the testing of protocols for backup and recovery, security measures, and incident response strategies. It is possible for companies to identify areas of weakness and make the necessary modifications by simulating a variety of scenarios, such as cyberattacks or natural catastrophes.

Technologies and Strategies for the Resilience of Information Technology

1. **Computing in the Cloud**
   Cloud services, by their very nature, offer scalability as well as redundancy. Data durability and availability are often ensured by cloud service providers through the provision of data replication across several data centers. By putting mission-critical apps and data in the cloud, organizations can employ cloud computing to ensure the resilience of their information technology systems.

2. **The use of "virtualization"**
   The concept of virtualization makes it possible to create virtual machines (VMs), which are able to be cloned and relocated with relative ease. Virtual machines (VMs) allow businesses to swiftly provision and scale their information technology resources, which simplifies the process of adapting to shifting demands and recovering from hardware problems.

3. **Clustering with High Availability (also known as HA)**
   Clustering for high availability entails bringing together a number of different servers or computer systems to form a cluster. In the event that one of the nodes fails, the others are able to take on its workload, ensuring that service is maintained. Clustering with HA is frequently implemented for mission-critical applications like database and web servers.

4. **Redistributing the Workload**
   Load balancing is the process of distributing network traffic over

multiple servers or resources in order to improve performance while also reducing the likelihood of service outages brought on by heavy traffic loads or failed servers. Load balancers are able to automatically direct traffic to servers that are in good health.

5. **The Replication of Data**

    The process of producing copies of data in real-time or near-real-time and storing them in several locations is known as data replication. This technique guarantees the durability and availability of the data, making it possible for businesses to recover rapidly in the event that data is lost or the system fails.

6. **A solution known as Disaster Recovery as a Service, or DRaaS**

    DRaaS, which stands for disaster recovery as a service, is a solution that is hosted on the cloud that gives businesses the capacity to restore their data and apps in the case of a catastrophe. It provides an alternative to more conventional disaster recovery methods that is both cost-effective and scalable.

7. **Application Performance Monitoring (APM) comes in at number seven.**

    Real-time monitoring of application and service performance is accomplished with the help of
    APM technologies. They offer insights into the health of the system and have the ability to activate alarms or take measures automatically when performance issues are discovered.

8. **Precautions Should Be Taken for Cybersecurity**

Firewalls, intrusion detection systems, and routine security audits are some of the fundamental cybersecurity measures that must be implemented in order to keep an organization's information technology infrastructure safe from potential attacks. Resilience in information technology relies heavily on a security strategy that has been carefully crafted.

The Value of Maintaining IT Resilience

There are a variety of benefits that can accrue to businesses through the use of IT resilience strategies and technology. These benefits go beyond simply preventing downtime and include long-term gains in both the general operational efficiency and security of the business.

1. **Decreased Amounts of Time Spent "Down" and Lost Data**
   The fundamental advantage of resilient information technology is a large decrease in the amount of downtime and data loss. Resilient systems are able to quickly recover from interruptions, hence minimizing the effect the disruption has on company operations.

2. **Increased Levels of Satisfaction Among Customers**
   Customers are more likely to be satisfied with their purchases and loyal to a company that maintains resilient systems, which allow them to access products and services when they are required. This can be a substantial advantage in a market that is saturated with competition.

3. **Reductions in Costs**
   Even though there is an initial expenditure required, there may be significant cost benefits in the long run as a result of implementing IT resilience measures. The reduction in the amount of time the system is offline and the amount of data that is lost might lead to lesser financial losses and possibly lower insurance rates.

4. **Improved Safety and Assurance**
   Comprehensive safety precautions are frequently included in IT resiliency initiatives. A focus on
   security not only helps protect against external threats, but it also protects against internal vulnerabilities, which improves the overall security of the system.

5. **Capacity for Change and Advancement**
   IT infrastructure that is resilient is better able to adjust to shifting demand and new opportunities. They are able to readily scale to

meet increased demand or integrate new technology, so assuring that the firm will continue to be competitive and nimble.

6. **Observance of All Regulations**
Regulatory and compliance standards can more easily be met when firms implement efforts to improve their IT resilience. This compliance not only helps to avoid legal concerns but also indicates a dedication to protecting consumer data and earning the trust of customers.
7. **An Advantage Over Competitors**

Companies who are able to recover quickly from IT setbacks have a significant advantage over their competitors. They are able to outperform their competitors during market disruptions, preserve the trust of their customers, and exploit new chances in the market.

Problems to Be Confronted When Attempting to Achieve IT Resilience

1. **Cost**
The implementation of IT resilience techniques and technologies might come with a hefty price tag. Redundancy, backup systems, and disaster recovery options are all essential components that require considerable initial investments from companies. On the other hand, the cost reductions over a longer period of time typically outweigh the initial outlay.
2. **The complication**
Resilient information technology systems typically have more moving parts, including failover methods and redundant components. Because of its complexity, management can be difficult at times, and you'll need highly trained IT specialists to develop, build, and maintain the infrastructure.
3. **Management of Adaptive Change**
Updating and testing systems on a regular basis is required to maintain the IT infrastructure's resiliency. It is possible for the

process of implementing changes to be complex and sensitive, requiring careful planning and execution in order to avoid disrupting operations.

4. **The culture of the organization**

   The resiliency of information technology is directly influenced by organizational culture. It is necessary to establish a culture that places a high priority on security, preparation, and resilience, and ensure that all employees are aware of their respective roles and responsibilities in the process of keeping IT resilient.

5. **Skills Vacancies**

In order to create and maintain reliable information technology systems, companies require IT experts who possess the necessary skills and competence. Having gaps in one's skill set can be a substantial obstacle; but, investing in one's own training and development can help close those gaps.

In the modern, digital world, having resilient information technology is not an option; rather, it is a requirement. To maintain business continuity, decrease downtime, and guard against a wide variety of hazards, companies of all sizes and in all industries need to make the development and maintenance of resilient IT infrastructures a top priority in their organization.

Organizations are able to construct dependable and flexible information technology systems by adhering to fundamental concepts such as redundancy, scalability, and proactive monitoring, and by utilizing technologies such as cloud computing, virtualization, and data replication. Not only are these systems resilient to disturbances, but they also deliver long-term benefits, such as reduced costs, enhanced safety, and a competitive advantage in the market.

In spite of the fact that there are obstacles to overcome, it is more than worth the commitment of time, money, and culture to achieve IT resilience. Case studies conducted by companies such as Netflix,

Amazon, and Delta Airlines illustrate that IT resilience can be achieved and offers a major competitive advantage.

Resilience in information technology is not just a phrase in today's world, when digital services are the lifeblood of many enterprises; rather, it is an essential component of success. In the event of a storm, whether it be a cyberattack, a natural disaster, or an unexpected technical failure, businesses that place a priority on and invest in their IT resilience will be better prepared.

1.1 Defining IT Resilience

In the modern, technologically advanced world that we live in, the notion of information technology (IT) resilience has arisen as an essential one for businesses operating in a wide range of industries. The ability of an organization to continue providing uninterrupted and consistent IT services and operations despite the presence of a variety of disruptions, failures, or disasters is what is meant by the term "IT resilience." It is a basic aspect in the larger context of business continuity, and it plays a vital role in ensuring that an organization is able to adapt, withstand, and recover from a wide range of IT-related issues. Business continuity is an umbrella term that encompasses many subcontexts. In this essay, we will look into the fundamental features of defining IT resilience, including its significance, important components, and how it fits into the contemporary environment of business.

The Driving Force Behind IT Resilience

Hardware Failures Components including servers, storage devices, and network equipment might unexpectedly fail, which can cause disruptions to the services they provide.

Software Errors Problems or defects in the software can lead to the instability of the system, which can result in lost data or lost time.

Assaults via the Internet Malicious actors are able to launch assaults via the Internet, which can jeopardize the availability, integrity, or confidentiality of data.

Natural Catastrophes: Catastrophes such as earthquakes, floods, storms, or fires have the potential to cause damage to physical infrastructure and impair IT operations.

Errors Caused by Humans: Inadvertent deletions, incorrect configurations, and other errors caused by humans can result in the loss of data or in the breakdown of a system.

Overloading the capacity: Sudden increases in demand, such as excessive web traffic, can cause IT resources to become overwhelmed, which in turn can cause performance issues or outages.

Outages Caused by Third Parties: An organization's operations may be negatively impacted if a third party, such as a service provider, cloud platform, or external dependency, has an outage.

In its most basic form, IT resilience involves more than simply rebounding back after a setback. It comprises the ability to suffer disturbances while maintaining the availability, security, and performance of critical information technology systems and data. Minimizing the impact of disruptions is also included in this ability.

Components Crucial to the Resilience of IT

1. **Redundancy and Failover: What Are They?**
   The practice of having duplicate components, systems, or data in place is known as redundancy. This helps ensure that operations will continue even in the event of a breakdown. For instance, key servers may have backup servers that can take over effortlessly in the event that the primary servers become unavailable. This transfer will go off without a hitch thanks to the failover measures.

2. **Backup and recovery that is completely comprehensive:**
   It is critical to an organization's IT resilience to perform frequent backups of data as well as system configurations, both on-site and off-site. The existence of these backups ensures that information may be restored in the event that it is lost, deleted, or corrupted for whatever reason. The reliability of these backups can be ensured by checking them on a regular basis.

3. **Capacity for Growth and Adaptability:**
   Scalability and adaptability are two essential qualities of a resilient IT architecture. This indicates that business can easily adjust to fluctuations in demand or integrate new technology without causing any disturbances to its operations. Scalability ensures that the infrastructure can accommodate unforeseen spikes in consumption without causing a reduction in its overall performance.
4. **Safety and Identification of Potential Dangers:**
   Strong security measures are absolutely necessary for the durability of information technology. Firewalls, intrusion detection systems, and regular security audits are some examples of these measures. An company can better protect itself against both internal weaknesses and external threats, such as cyberattacks, if it secures its infrastructure.
5. **Diverse Territorial Composition:**
   The resilience of an organization can be improved by distributing its information technology resources over different geographic regions. This prevents an isolated catastrophe, such as a natural disaster affecting a single location, from causing the entire system to go offline completely. Cloud-based solutions are frequently utilized by organizations in order to achieve geographic diversity.
6. **Preventative Monitoring and Rapid Response to Incidents:**
   Monitoring tools that are proactive check the health and performance of the system continuously. Alerts are triggered whenever performance issues or abnormalities are discovered. This gives organizations the opportunity to fix these issues before they develop into severe failures. In addition, incident response plans detail the actions that must be carried out in the case of an occurrence, guaranteeing a prompt and well-coordinated response.
7. **Training and Awareness for Staff Members:**
   The robustness of the IT system is directly influenced by the employees. They are required to have a solid understanding of best practices, security awareness, and incident response protocols.

Employees who are well-informed and well-prepared can assist reduce the negative effects of incidents and avoid security breaches.

8. **Testing and simulation on a regular basis:**

Testing and simulation exercises should be performed on a regular basis in order to accurately assess the IT resilience of a company. Among these are the testing of protocols for backup and recovery, security measures, and incident response strategies. It is possible for companies to identify areas of weakness and make the necessary modifications by simulating a variety of scenarios, such as cyberattacks or natural catastrophes.

The Importance of Maintaining IT Resilience

1. **Continuity of Business Operations:**
   Resilience in information technology is essential to maintaining corporate operations. It ensures that corporate operations may continue without severe interruptions even when disruptions take place. It is essential to maintain uninterrupted service delivery in this day and age, when businesses are becoming more reliant on their IT infrastructure.

2. **Risk Avoidance and Mitigation:**
   The resilience of information technology serves as an effective risk mitigation approach. Organizations can considerably minimize the possibility of severe damage and data loss if they take proactive measures to prepare for the potential impact of various IT-related risks and to mitigate the potential severity of those risks.

3. **Adherence to Regulatory Requirements:**
   A wide variety of sectors are subject to strict rules and compliance requirements relating to the protection of data and the continuity of business operations. Resilience in information technology helps businesses fulfill their legal and regulatory duties, so avoiding potentially expensive fines and other legal repercussions.

4. **Confidence in the Market:**
   Customers have come to expect businesses to be accessible and responsive at all hours of the day and night. The trust and confidence of customers might be damaged by any downtime or loss of data. Resilience in information technology ensures that firms can live up to the standards set by their customers and continue to earn their trust.
5. **An Advantage in the Market Place:**

An advantage in the marketplace belongs to businesses that have strong IT resilience. They are able to recover from disturbances more quickly, adapt more effectively to shifting conditions, and continue to serve clients even when competitors may stumble. Given the frenetic nature of the modern business world, this confers a substantial competitive edge.

Establishing a Resilient IT Infrastructure

1. **The evaluation:**
   To get started, conduct a risk assessment of your organization's existing information technology (IT) infrastructure. Determine which data and systems are mission-critical and need to be protected and resilient.
2. **Formulate a Plan to Boost Your Resilience:**
   Create a comprehensive IT resilience strategy that is adapted to the particular requirements and threats faced by your firm. Redundancy, backup and recovery strategies, scalability, security measures, and incident response processes should all be included in this approach.
3. **Put Your Money Into Resources and Technology:**
   Allocate resources so that the selected technologies and components of resilient systems can be implemented. Investing in hardware, software, cloud services, and security solutions may be required to accomplish this goal.

4. **Education and Conscientization:**
   Employees should be made aware of the organization's IT resilience strategy as well as their individual roles in maintaining it. Programs of ongoing training and awareness are absolutely necessary for achievement.
5. **Validation through Testing and Simulation:**
   In order to verify that your IT resilience measures are working properly, you should routinely test and simulate a variety of different situations. Determine any shortcomings or places in need of improvement, and then make the necessary improvements.
6. **A plan for handling incidents:**
   Create a clear and comprehensive incident response plan that describes the steps that need to be followed in the event that there is an interruption in the IT system. Make sure that all of the employees are aware of this plan as well as the parts that they will be playing in it.
7. **Continual Surveillance and Improvement:**

Install proactive monitoring tools so that you can continuously track the health of the system and its performance. Maintain a consistent evaluation schedule for the efficacy of your IT resilience measures, and make adjustments as required.

Resilience in information technology is not only a buzzword, but rather an absolute requirement for modern businesses. In this day and age, when information technology systems are at the core of corporate operations, it is of the utmost importance to ensure their ongoing availability and performance. IT resilience gives businesses the ability to adapt to and endure a wide variety of difficulties, from hardware failures to cyberattacks, while still retaining the trust of their customers and a competitive edge.

Organizations are able to construct dependable and flexible information technology systems by adhering to fundamental concepts such as redundancy, scalability, and proactive monitoring, and by utilizing technologies such as cloud computing, virtualization, and data replication. Not only are these systems resistant to disturbances, but they also give long-term benefits, such as financial savings, enhanced levels of security, and a competitive advantage in the market.

IT resilience remains a cornerstone of stability, continuity, and growth in the face of an ever-evolving variety of problems and opportunities. This is especially true as companies continue to traverse the intricacies of the digital ecosystem.

1.2 The Business Impact of Downtime

When discussing the operations of a company, the term "downtime" refers to the period of time during which essential systems, services, or processes are unavailable. This is typically the result of unforeseen disruptions or breakdowns. Failures in information technology systems, cyberattacks, natural disasters, or even human mistake can all be potential causes of these delays in service. Downtime in a company's operations can have severe repercussions for the company, including monetary losses, damage to the company's reputation, and dissatisfied customers. In this piece, we will investigate the myriad facets of downtime and look into the major influence it has on businesses operating in a variety of fields.

The Real Value of Lost Productivity

The interruption of an organization's operations by downtime is not only an annoyance; rather, it is a costly financial burden that manifests itself in a variety of ways. Let's examine the various factors that contribute to the financial and non-financial consequences of downtime.

1. **Costs to the Direct Financial Account:**
1. **Revenue That Was Lost:**
   The creation of revenue is directly affected by downtime. Every minute that a system is down for maintenance can result in considerable monetary losses for businesses in some sectors, such as e-commerce, the financial services industry, and manufacturing.

During downtime, any sales, transactions, or orders that cannot be processed reflect opportunities that have been missed.

2. **Costs Related to Overtime and Recovery:**
During periods of outage, businesses frequently have to call upon their information technology teams as well as other workers in order to diagnose and resolve issues. This may result in increased expenditures for labor, particularly if employees are required to report for work outside of their normal shift hours.

3. **Penalties for Violating the Service-Level Agreement (SLA):**
A significant number of companies have Service Level Agreements (SLAs) in place with either their clients or their service providers. These agreements ensure a particular amount of service availability. The occurrence of downtime might result in the imposition of penalties or demands for compensation for failing to achieve these SLAs.

4. **Expenses Related to the Loss of Data and Its Recovery:**

The cost of data corruption or loss caused by downtime might be significant. It's possible that companies will have to pay for data recovery services or incur additional costs in order to rebuild lost data.

2. **Costs to the Company in an Indirect Manner:**

1. **Interruptions in the Supply Chain:**
An interruption in the supply chain might have an effect on the manufacturing and distribution processes. It is possible for suppliers to miss their deadlines for delivering materials or products, which can cause manufacturing delays and result in lost sales.

2. **Harm Done to One's Reputation**

A considerable portion of an organization's indirect costs can be attributed to reputational harm. On social media and other channels, dissatisfied customers are ready to voice their opinions and vent their frustrations. A tarnished reputation can result in long-term income loss because clients will lose trust in the company and switch to other options in the market.

3. **The impact on operations:**

   1. **Decrease in Productivity:**
      The ability of personnel to carry out their duties is negatively impacted by downtime. It may result in lost work hours, decreased production, and dissatisfied staff members. Productivity declines can have a domino effect in certain fields, including healthcare, manufacturing, and logistics, for example.
   2. **Lost Opportunities in the Business World:**

A lull in activity can result in the loss of potential new business or partnership possibilities. Deals and market share can be lost if a company takes too long to react to consumer questions or engage in conversation with prospective customers.

4. **The Impact on the Customer:**

   1. **Dissatisfaction of the Customers:**
      Customers who are unable to access products or services as a result of downtime are likely to become frustrated. It has the potential to result in customer churn as people seek alternatives that are more trustworthy.
   2. **The Cost of Providing Support to Customers:**

During the delay, there was an increase in the number of consumer queries, support calls, and complaints, which required additional employees to manage. These expenses might quickly add up to a large amount.

Impact Particular to the Industry

1. **Online shopping and traditional retail:**
   Downtime in the e-commerce industry directly correlates to lost

sales. Customers are eager to move to different online merchants if they run into problems while the process of making a purchase due to the intense level of competition in the industry. In addition, the harm to one's reputation might have a lasting effect on the level of trust held by customers.

2. **Businesses Relating to Finance:**
In the world of finance, a period of downtime can result in considerable financial losses due to the missed opportunities to trade and the stalled processing of transactions. In addition, it may result in penalties imposed by regulatory agencies as well as ruined relationships with customers.

3. **Healthcare in general:**
Downtime in the healthcare industry can impede both the provision of patient treatment and access to medical records. Not only does this have an effect on the outcomes for patients, but it also creates major compliance and legal issues.

4. **Production and manufacture:**
During the manufacturing process, downtime can result in production delays, increased expenses, and interruptions to the supply chain. These disruptions might lead to the cancellation of orders and cause harm to the relationships with the customers.

5. **The importance of technology and SaaS:**

System availability is extremely important to organizations in the technology industry and suppliers of software as a service (SaaS). An interruption in service can result in a loss of income, penalties from the SLA, and customer attrition as customers look for alternatives.

Downtime Avoidance and Reduction Strategies

1. **Redundancy and Failover: What Are They?**
The implementation of failover methods and redundancy in essential systems assures that operations will continue normally

IT RESILIENCE

even in the event that a failure occurs. This is an essential step that can significantly cut down on downtime.

2. **Backup and recovery that is completely comprehensive:**
Data and system configurations should be backed up on a regular basis, both on-site and off-site. It is important to evaluate the efficiency of the backup and recovery operations to verify that they function as intended.

3. **The ability to scale and distribute the load:**
Build in scalability to manage rising demand and ensure that network traffic is evenly distributed
throughout the system. The balancing of loads helps to keep a system from being overloaded.

4. **Safety and Identification of Potential Dangers:**
Strong cybersecurity precautions can be of great assistance in warding off cyberattacks and data breaches. Install systems that can detect intrusions, and make it a habit to regularly update security policies.

5. **Diverse Territorial Composition:**
Spread out your information technology resources over a number of different geographic regions to guarantee their availability even in the event of disruptions at the regional level. Cloud-based solutions frequently give diversity in terms of location.

6. **Preventative Monitoring and Rapid Response to Incidents:**
Monitoring the health and performance of the system should be done proactively so that problems can be found and fixed before they cause severe failures. Create explicit incident response plans in order to reduce the amount of downtime experienced when problems occur.

7. **Training and Awareness for Staff Members:**
Employees should be educated about best practices, security awareness, and the roles they play in preserving the resilience of IT systems. The effects of incidents can be lessened if workers are given adequate information.

8. Testing and simulation on a regular basis:

It is important to evaluate the efficacy of various IT resilience strategies on a regular basis by testing and simulating a variety of different scenarios. Determine where you are lacking and work to strengthen those areas.

The impact of downtime on a company's operations is enormous and multi-faceted, having an effect not only on the financial but also on the non-financial components of the firm. Significant losses can be incurred as a result of factors such as lost revenue, damaged reputation, and disrupted operations. The specific impact differs from business to industry, with certain fields, such as online shopping and financial services, being especially susceptible.

Resilience in information technology should be a top priority for businesses in order to reduce

the impact of system outages. This entails the development of policies and technology that guarantee continuous availability of IT services, minimize disruptions, and speed up recovery. A comprehensive strategy for IT resilience must incorporate critical elements like as redundancy, backup and recovery, security measures, and proactive monitoring.

The capacity to prevent and limit downtime in today's increasingly competitive corporate landscape is not only an issue of financial survival; it is an essential component in preserving customer trust, sustaining growth, and achieving long-term success. The expense of unplanned downtime serves as a potent reminder of the significance of taking preventative actions to guard against it.

1.3 Key Components of IT Resilience

To be successful in today's globally interconnected and technologically advanced world, organizations must place a significant amount of reliance on their respective information technology (IT) infrastructure. Critical activities are supported by information technology systems, and any downtime in such systems can have a substantial impact on the bottom line, reputation, and trust that customers have in a business.

IT RESILIENCE

Resilience in information technology should be a top priority for businesses in order to reduce the risks associated with interruptions in information technology.

The ability of a company to sustain vital services and quickly recover from failures or disruptions in information technology is referred to as "IT resilience." In order to make sure that information technology systems are resilient and able to deal with unforeseen obstacles, it is necessary to use a combination of different technologies, procedures, and planning. In this piece, we will look into the most important aspects of IT resilience and highlight their significance in terms of ensuring the continuity of corporate operations.

Evaluation of Dangers and Taking Precautions:

Understanding the potential risks involved is one of the fundamental components of resilient information technology. It is critical for organizations to carry out exhaustive risk assessments in order to detect weak spots and potential dangers. This includes analyzing potential sources of interruption such as natural disasters, cyberattacks, failed hardware, and human error in the operation of the system. After these dangers have been recognized, it will be possible to devise a strategy that has been given careful consideration in order to eliminate them. The following should be outlined in this plan: prevention, response, and recovery strategies.

Both redundant and backup versions:

The robustness of an organization's information technology relies heavily on redundancy. It entails making copies of essential computer systems and data in order to guarantee that there will be a suitable replacement available in the event that one of the components fails. Data replication, server clustering, and separate locations for disaster recovery are all methods that can be used to provide redundancy. It is critical to maintain backups of critical data in order to facilitate a speedy recovery in the event that data is accidentally deleted or corrupted. Backups that are checked on a regular basis can assist reduce the amount of data that is lost in the event of a catastrophe.

Protection from Online Threats and Detection of Dangers:

Cybersecurity is a big area of worry in a world that is becoming increasingly digital. An efficient plan for maintaining IT resilience should incorporate stringent cybersecurity precautions to protect against dangers such as malware, ransomware, and data breaches. A robust cybersecurity infrastructure should consist of important components such as intrusion detection systems, firewalls, and continuous monitoring.

Business Continuity and Disaster Recovery, abbreviated as "BCDR," entails the following:

Planning for both the continuation of business operations and the recovery from any kind of disaster is vital for IT resilience. These plans detail how a company will continue to perform essential business operations during and after a catastrophic event or other form of disruption. BCDR strategies should include specific plans for communication, recovery procedures, and the identification of key employees accountable for carrying out the strategy.

Monitoring and Analytical Practices:

The detection of early warning indicators of prospective IT disruptions is made significantly easier with the help of real-time monitoring and analytics. Organizations are in a better position to proactively fix issues before they become catastrophic if they closely monitor the operation of their systems. In addition to this, advanced analytics can assist in the forecasting of possible issues and the enhancement of system performance.

Administration of Change:

In the world of information technology, change is always present, whether it takes the form of software updates, hardware replacements, or configuration adjustments. The ability to successfully manage these changes is a critical component of IT resilience. In order to prevent unanticipated interruptions, companies should implement well-structured change management processes. These processes should guarantee that all modifications made to information technology systems are exhaustively tested, documented, and recorded.

Training and Awareness for Staff Members:

People are typically the weakest link in the chain when it comes to the resilience of IT. Employees are required to have adequate training in security best practices and be aware of any potential dangers that may exist. Attacks based on social engineering, such as phishing, can represent a substantial risk. Human errors that could lead to interruptions can be helped to be avoided by participating in regular training and awareness programs.

Services provided using the cloud and virtualization:

Because of their adaptability and scalability, cloud services and virtualization technologies are extremely valuable components of resilient information technology. They make it possible for companies to rapidly react to shifting conditions, increase or decrease the amount of resources they need, and make use of redundancy in their data centers.

Compliance with Regulations:

There are legislative regulations in place for many different industries addressing the robustness of IT and the protection of data. It is essential to behave in accordance with these regulations. Companies have a responsibility to be knowledgeable of, and compliant with, the legal requirements that are associated with maintaining data security and business continuity.

Experimentation and Modeling:

The success of a plan to ensure the continuity of IT services is dependent on how well it is tested and simulated. Regular testing of the plan and the performance of disaster recovery drills are critical to ensuring that the plan functions as intended and can reduce the amount of downtime experienced in the event that a disruption occurs in the real world.

1.4 Resilience vs. Redundancy

In the ever-changing landscape of information technology, the phrases "resilience" and "redundancy" have become crucial to talks about preserving vital information technology systems and guaranteeing business continuity. This is because these terms refer to the ability of a system to recover quickly after a disruption or failure. Both of these ideas seek to solve the same overarching objective, which is the reducing the impact of IT failures or interruptions, but they go about doing so in very different ways and have very different repercussions. In this essay, the nuances of resilience and redundancy are discussed, and both of their strengths and shortcomings, as well as the need of striking the correct balance between the two when designing IT infrastructure, are brought to light.

Comprehending the Concept of Resilience:

When discussing an organization's information technology infrastructure, the term "resilience" refers to the capacity of that infrastructure to adjust to and recover from disturbances or breakdowns without having a significant effect on the organization's primary operations. In the field of information technology (IT), resilience refers to the ability to endure shocks, continue vital operations, and quickly return to normalcy in the face of unforeseen problems.

Important Constituents of Resilience:

Diversity and Flexibility: Resilient information technology systems are constructed with diversity in mind, encompassing a mix of technologies, vendors, and components. In addition, these systems are also designed to be as flexible as possible. Because of this diversity, businesses are able to become more flexible and adaptable, which in turn enables them to pivot and reconfigure their systems as necessary.

Response that is Dynamic: Resilience is dependent on a response that is dynamic to disruptions. This indicates that the information technology infrastructure is geared to identify problems, adjust to changes, and quickly recover. It might involve load balancing, intelligent resource allocation, and automatic failover procedures.

Risk Assessment and Mitigation: The first step in developing resilience is to conduct a comprehensive risk assessment in order to identify weak spots and potential dangers.

After that, organizations put into action ways to reduce the impact of certain risks. By taking such preventative measures, the likelihood of disruptions is decreased.

The Strategic Application of Redundancy Although redundancy is considered to be a component of resilience, its strategic application is carried out in order to guarantee the availability of essential resources. It is common practice to have redundant systems in place to deal with failover circumstances; nevertheless, these systems are not the primary emphasis of the resilience plan.

The Value of Being Able to Bounce Back

Ability to Adapt: Resilient systems have the ability to adjust to changing conditions, whether those situations are the result of hardware failures, software errors, or threats from the outside. They are able to keep operations going even when individual components fail.

Cost-Effective: There is a possibility that maintaining resilience will be less expensive than maintaining full redundancy. It enables firms to strategically spend resources rather than repeating everything, which is a huge time saver.

Enhanced Risk Management: Taking a proactive approach to risk assessment and mitigation helps organizations lower the possibility of interruptions and better prepare for unanticipated obstacles.

Recognizing the Role of Redundancy:

On the other side, redundancy is the practice of duplicating important components of an IT system or infrastructure. This can be done for redundancy purposes. The goal of incorporating redundancy into a system is to guarantee that, in the event that one of its components fails, there is a standby ready to take over and ensure that business as usual is not disrupted. The goal of redundancy is to build backup systems, which might take the form of individual pieces of hardware, individual pieces of data, or even complete IT environments.

Principal Constituents of Redundancy:

Replication: Data replication is a common component of redundancy. This refers to the process by which data is copied in real-time or near-real-time on secondary storage systems. This guarantees that data will be accessible at all times, even in the event that the primary store fails.

Redundant hardware or systems are maintained in a state known as "hot standby," in which they are prepared to take over for the primary system in the event that it fails. This reduces the amount of downtime as well as interruption.

Data Centers: A large number of companies practice data redundancy by keeping up with alternative data centers or disaster recovery locations. These locations have multiple copies of all critical data and systems in place to ensure that business operations can continue normally in the event of a disaster.

Load balancing is another method that may be used to provide redundancy. This method involves distributing the amount of traffic that is received across a number of servers. Traffic is immediately transferred to other servers in the event that one of the servers fails, which ensures that services are always available.

The Positive Aspects of Being Fired

High Availability The presence of redundancy ensures that the system will have a high level of availability. Even if the major components fail, redundant systems can take over without a hitch, reducing the amount of time the system is offline.

Data Protection: Redundancy is an important tool in preventing the loss of data. In the event that either the hardware or the software a business uses fails, they will be able to retrieve their data if they have data replication and backup solutions in place.

Enhancement of Resilience Even if redundancy by itself is not the same thing as resilience, it is an essential component in the process of improving the overall resilience of information technology systems. A more comprehensive resilience strategy may incorporate redundant components as one of its building blocks.

Finding a Satisfying Middle Ground:

Risk Tolerance: In order to establish how much downtime and data loss an organization can withstand, it is imperative that businesses analyze their risk tolerance. A high risk tolerance may need the implementation of additional redundancy, while a lower risk tolerance may call for the implementation of increased resilience measures.

When allocating resources, take into account any applicable spending restrictions in addition to the quantity of available resources.

Because redundancy can drive up costs, companies need to carefully utilize their resources if they want to maintain the cost-effectiveness of their infrastructure.

Criticality of Systems: The degree of criticality that a system possesses might vary depending on the system. It is essential to conduct an analysis to determine which systems are crucial to the operation of the organization and require a higher level of resilience or redundancy.

Ability to Adapt to Change: The field of information technology is always progressing. It is important for systems to be able to adjust to their environment, whether this is accomplished through redundancy, resilience, or a combination of the two.

Compliance and regulation: Certain industries have particularly stringent compliance obligations with relation to the safeguarding of customer data and the continuation of business operations. It is required of organizations that they comply with these requirements and build in redundancy and resilience when appropriate.

Examples from Everyday Life:

Due to the mission-critical nature of their business, companies in the financial services sector are required to have a high level of redundancy in their systems. The use of failover systems, redundant data centers, and real-time replication are all standard business procedures.

E-commerce: Resilience is a priority for e-commerce enterprises so that they can handle abrupt increases in traffic and maintain efficient operations during times of high demand for their products. The utilization of cloud-based solutions, load balancing, and auto-scaling are important components.

Healthcare: In order to provide quality care to patients and maintain the confidentiality of patient data, healthcare companies need to have both redundancy and resilience. It is essential to have redundancy in order to secure one's data, while resilience is necessary to ensure the safety of patients and the availability of systems.

The decision between redundancy and resilience in terms of information technology infrastructure is not an either/or proposition. Instead, the key is to strike the appropriate equilibrium. It is important for organizations to tailor their strategies according to their unique requirements, level of comfort with risk, and available resources.

When applied strategically, resilience and redundancy may protect information technology systems in tandem, ensuring that the systems continue to operate as intended, recover from any unanticipated problems, and adapt to new circumstances. When deciding between resilience and redundancy for your business, you should base your decision on a comprehensive understanding of your company's goals and your dedication to ensuring the smooth running of mission-critical processes.

Chapter 2

The Evolution of Cloud Technology

The storage, administration, and accessibility of data and applications have all been revolutionized as a result of cloud technology's widespread use in private and public sectors alike. Since its humble origins as a revolutionary idea, cloud computing has undergone substantial development over the course of its existence, eventually becoming an essential component of the technological landscape of the modern era. This evolution has been driven by breakthroughs in hardware, software, and networking as well as by a changing business landscape that requires solutions that are more adaptable and scalable. In the following paragraphs, we will investigate the history of cloud computing, beginning with its inception and following its progression all the way up to the present day.

1. **The Beginnings of Cloud Computing and Technology**
   1.1. The Technologies That Came Before Cloud Computing
   The origins of the idea behind cloud computing may be followed all the way back to the beginning of the personal computer era. One may argue that the mainframe and time-sharing systems,

both of which allowed several people to access a single computer, were antecedents of the cloud. These systems demonstrated some of the possible advantages that could be gained from centralizing computing resources.

1.2. The First Steps Toward Virtualization

The advent of cloud computing was significantly aided by the virtualization technology that was available at the time. Running several instances of an operating system on a single physical server was made possible by the use of virtual machines, which allowed for more effective use of the underlying physical hardware. The notions of resource pooling and dynamic allocation are at the core of cloud computing. This technology laid the groundwork for those ideas to become a reality.

1.3. The Beginnings of Cloud Services

The term "cloud computing" didn't come into widespread use until the late 1990s and early 2000s, when a number of new businesses started providing hosted services. Customers were granted remote access to programs and storage through the use of these services; nevertheless, in comparison to more contemporary cloud options, the services' reach was somewhat restricted.

2. The Ascent of Computing on the Cloud

2.1. Amazon Web Services (also known as AWS)

The introduction of Amazon Web Services (AWS) in 2006 was a significant step forward in the development of cloud computing technology and is considered to be one of the most important milestones. AWS was a game-changer because it supplied a wide variety of cloud services to businesses as well as developers. These services included storage, processing, and database management. It did this by introducing a pricing mechanism known as pay-as-you-go, which allowed customers to pay only for the resources that they really utilized.

2.2. The Origins and Growth of Virtualization

The technologies behind virtualization continued to advance, which simplified the process of managing and provisioning resources in the cloud. Virtual machine management has become more flexible and effective because to the development of technologies such as VMware and Microsoft Hyper-V.

2.3. The Growing Number of Cloud Service Providers

The accomplishments of Amazon Web Services (AWS) sparked the development of numerous additional cloud providers, such as Microsoft Azure and Google Cloud Platform. These cloud service providers made available to their clients a wider variety of cloud-based services and features, so contributing to the creation of a competitive market that stimulated innovation.

3. The Completion of the Development of Cloud Technology

3.1. Infrastructure as a Service (also written as IaaS)

As cloud computing became more advanced, the Infrastructure as a Service (IaaS) paradigm became increasingly prevalent. IaaS providers delivered virtualized hardware resources to their customers, which made it possible for enterprises to deploy and operate virtual machines, storage, and networking. Because of this flexibility, it became much simpler for businesses to expand or contract the size of their infrastructure in response to changing demands.

3.2. Platform as a Service (also known as PaaS)

Platforms as a Service (PaaS), which include Google App Engine, Heroku, and Microsoft Azure App Service, have made the process of developing and deploying applications more simpler. PaaS offered developers a greater degree of abstraction, which freed them to concentrate on developing code rather than worrying about infrastructure or scalability issues. PaaS also took care of those concerns for them.

3.3. Software as a Service (also known as SaaS)

Applications that provide software as a service (SaaS), such as Salesforce, Microsoft 365, and Dropbox, have gained a significant amount of popularity. Users are able to access software programs over the internet through the usage of SaaS, which eliminates the requirement for users to install or maintain the software. The way in which consumers and corporations utilized and paid for software was revolutionized by this paradigm.

4. Utilizing Cloud Technology in Commercial Settings

4.1. Savings on Costs and Efficient Use of Resources

The possibility of lower operating expenses while simultaneously achieving higher levels of productivity was one of the factors that encouraged businesses to embrace cloud computing. While still reaping the benefits of having resources available on demand from the cloud, organizations might lower their capital expenditures on hardware and data centers.

4.2. The Capacity for Scale and Flexibility

The cloud computing platform provided unparalleled scalability and adaptability. It would be simple for businesses to change their computer resources to match shifting demand, which would make it feasible for them to deal with surges in traffic or workload without having to make significant financial expenditures in infrastructure.

4.3. Contingency Planning, Business Continuity, and Disaster Recovery

Cloud computing made it possible to implement comprehensive disaster recovery and business continuity strategies. It is possible for data to be replicated across numerous data centers, which would reduce the likelihood of losing data in the case of a hardware failure or a natural disaster.

4.4. International Impact

Cloud service providers have extended their data center presence around the world, making it simpler for enterprises to access markets in other countries. This worldwide reach made previously unattainable chances for international expansion and cooperation available.

5. Concerns Regarding Both Security and Privacy

5.1. The Safety of the Data

Concerns regarding the safety of data increased as more and more companies moved their operations into the cloud. Cloud service providers were quick to react by making significant investments in various security features such as authentication, encryption, and access controls.

5.2. Obligations to Comply with Regulations

firms that use cloud technology have been presented with additional hurdles as a result of regulations such as GDPR and HIPAA. These firms are required to maintain compliance with laws pertaining to data protection and privacy. Cloud service providers made available various tools and services to assist enterprises in fulfilling these prerequisites.

5.3. Responsibility That Is Shared

The idea of shared responsibility was made popular by cloud security, according to which both the cloud provider and the customer share equal responsibility for the safety of the data and resources stored in the cloud. Because of the nature of this concept, a cooperative approach to security was required.

6. The Prospects of Cloud Computing Moving Forward

6.1. Computing at the Edge

The rise of edge computing, which brings compute and data processing closer to the site where it is needed, is one of the things that is planned for the future of cloud technology. This strategy is essential for applications that have a low-latency need, such as self-driving cars and Internet of Things devices.

6.2. Computing on the Quantum Level

The advent of quantum computing is on the horizon, and it has the potential to transform cloud technology by providing solutions to difficult problems at speeds never before seen. Cloud service providers are already investigating the viability of offering quantum computing.

6.3. Hybrid Architectures and Multiple Clouds

Hybrid and multi-cloud methods are gaining popularity as an increasing number of businesses are looking to optimize their information technology (IT) infrastructures by combining their existing on-premises infrastructure with cloud resources. This strategy provides both flexibility and redundancy in its execution.

6.4. Artificial intelligence and machine learning come in at number

Cloud services are currently undergoing the process of incorporating artificial intelligence and machine learning in order to give more advanced analytics, automation, and intelligent insights. These technologies are assisting organizations in optimizing the utilization of their data as well as the resources at their disposal.

From its early beginnings as an idea to its current position as a core aspect of contemporary computing, the development of cloud technology has been a remarkable journey. In its early days, cloud computing was merely a concept. The introduction of cloud computing has revolutionized the way in which organizations run their operations, handle customer data, and provide service to their clientele. It is critical for companies and individuals to keep abreast of the most recent innovations and fashions in the cloud computing area as the underlying technology continues to advance at a rapid pace.

Computing on the edge of networks, quantum computing, and the incorporation of artificial intelligence are just some of the promising developments that the future of cloud technology holds in store. As a result of these advances, the capabilities of cloud technology will be further enhanced, transforming it into a vital instrument that is capable of addressing difficult challenges and fostering innovation across a variety of industries.

As we look to the future, it is abundantly obvious that the development of cloud technology will continue to influence the face of the digital world, presenting new opportunities as well as new challenges for enterprises and individuals. In the years to come, realizing the full potential of cloud technology will require maintaining a flexible and open attitude toward the changes that will take place.

2.1 Historical Context of Cloud Computing

Cloud computing has quickly become an essential component of contemporary life, ushering in a sea change in the manner in which we store, analyze, and gain access to data and services. However, in order for us to have a complete comprehension of this technological marvel, it is necessary for us to delve into its historical context and trace its origins back to the early days of computers and information technology. This trip back in time will provide insightful information about the development and significance of cloud computing as you go through history.

The First Steps Toward Computerization:

To have a grasp on the historical background of cloud computing, we need to start with the evolution of computing itself. The first mainframe computers were developed in the middle of the 20th century, which is considered to be the beginning of the computing industry. These machines were enormous and very expensive, and they frequently required a full room to themselves. Dumb terminals were the entry point for users to access these computers, and this method may be interpreted as an early kind of remote computing.

In the 1960s, the idea of "time-sharing" was first introduced, which made it possible for numerous users to share a single mainframe at the same time. The concept of utilizing computing resources in a collaborative manner served as the groundwork for what would eventually be known as cloud computing.

The Beginnings of the World Wide Web:

The next important step in the development of cloud computing occurred in the backdrop of history when the internet was first created. ARPANET, which stood for the Advanced Research Projects Agency Network, was the forerunner of the contemporary internet. It was created in the late 1960s. ARPANET was first developed for use in the military and academic institutions, but it ultimately ushered in a revolutionary change in the manner in which information could be remotely accessed and disseminated.

The expansion of the internet's user base and accessibility made it possible to store and retrieve data remotely as the internet became more widely used. The progression of the internet was absolutely necessary for the advent of cloud computing in its modern form as we know it today.

Initial Thoughts about Clouds:

Although the concept of "cloud computing" had not yet been conceptualized, remote data processing was already a well-established practice at the time. The 1970s and 1980s saw the beginning of businesses beginning to provide timesharing services as well as distant data storage. This made it possible for companies to delegate their computing tasks to third-party service providers, a model that bears a strong resemblance to the cloud computing model used today.

The beginning of the 21st century witnessed the rise of Application Service Providers, sometimes known as ASPs. These companies offered their customers hosted software applications. These application service providers set the groundwork for the development of Software as a Service (SaaS) services, an essential element of cloud computing.

The Beginning of Computing on the Cloud:

Compaq Computer's CEO George Favaloro is credited as being the first person to use the term "cloud computing" in 1996. However, the concept did not start to gain significant traction until the 21st century. The introduction of Amazon Web Services (AWS) in 2002 was a significant step toward the widespread use of cloud computing. A wide variety of cloud services, such as processing power, storage space, and database management, were made available by AWS. This made the service available to companies of varying sizes.

The success that Amazon had with cloud computing encouraged other major technology companies, such as Google and Microsoft, to enter the market. This resulted in the rapid expansion of the cloud business. The emergence of cloud computing was made possible in large

IT RESILIENCE

part by the widespread availability of high-speed internet connections and the development of technologies that enable virtualization.

Technologies Relating to Virtualization

The advent of cloud computing was greatly aided by the development of virtualization technologies, which make it possible for several virtual servers to coexist and operate on a single physical server. This technology made it possible to save money, allocate resources effectively, and scale up without sacrificing flexibility. The advancement of these skills was significantly aided by VMware, one of the first companies to work in the field of virtualization.

The concept of Infrastructure as a Service (commonly known as IaaS), which is one of the three basic service models of cloud computing along with Software as a Service (SaaS) and Platform as a Service (PaaS), was made possible by virtualization as well.

The Revolution of Mobile:

In the middle of the 2000s, there was a mobile revolution that led to the proliferation of smartphones, which further increased the need for cloud services. Cloud computing has made it feasible for mobile devices to effortlessly access and retain data, overcoming the limits that were previously imposed by device storage. This change in user behavior led to a boom in the usage of cloud-based applications and services, including email and photo storage, which led to a rise in the total number of users.

The Surging Popularity of Big Data:

The emergence of big data and analytics provides cloud computing with yet another business possibility. The administration and processing of enormous databases became an increasingly difficult and pricey endeavor. Cloud service providers made available solutions that were both scalable and cost-effective, and they were able to meet the processing and storage demands of big data applications.

This event represented the convergence of cloud computing and data science, which led to the rise of both cloud-based analytics platforms and Data as a Service (DaaS).

Threats to Information Security and Compliance:

Concerns regarding data privacy and security surfaced at the same time that cloud computing began to gain popularity. It was necessary for suppliers of these services to address these concerns in order to win back the trust of businesses and consumers. In response, the industry developed comprehensive security protocols, compliance certifications, and technologies for data encryption in order to guarantee the safety of data stored in the cloud.

Strategies for Hybrid Clouds and Multiple Clouds:

The landscape of cloud computing is always shifting, and hybrid and multi-cloud techniques are becoming increasingly popular. The flexibility and control over one's data that are provided by hybrid cloud computing come from the combination of on-premises infrastructure with public and private cloud services. Multi-cloud techniques entail utilizing numerous cloud providers in order to prevent vendor lock-in and make the most of the unique capabilities and advantages offered by a variety of distinct platforms.

These tactics have evolved to become indispensable for businesses that want to make the most of their cloud resources and guarantee the continuation of their operations.

The Effects That Computing in the Cloud Has on Businesses:

Cloud computing has fundamentally altered the way in which businesses operate. It is no longer necessary for businesses to make significant preliminary expenditures in the IT infrastructure. They are able to adjust the level of their resources in response to changes in demand, which helps to lower their operational expenses. This flexibility has facilitated the growth of both small businesses and major corporations.

Cloud computing has also helped to democratize technology by making previously inaccessible high-end tools and computing power available to users all over the world. Because cloud services are readily available, even the playing field for competition between smaller companies and their larger counterparts has been leveled.

Computing in the cloud and the digital transformation:

IT RESILIENCE

The adoption of digital transformation initiatives, fueled by cloud computing, has emerged as one of the most pressing concerns for businesses in all sectors. Cloud computing makes it easier to be innovative and agile, as well as to provide better experiences for customers. Businesses are increasingly turning to apps and services hosted in the cloud in order to modernize their operations, enhance their capacity for decision-making, and maintain their level of competitiveness in the digital age.

The Prospects for Computing on the Cloud:

In the years to come, cloud computing will undergo continuous development. Computing at the edge of networks, quantum computing, and serverless computing are examples of up-and-coming technologies that have the potential to radically alter the landscape of cloud computing. These developments will solve difficulties relating to processing power, latency, and security.

Cloud service providers will place a primary emphasis on developing their skills in the areas of artificial intelligence and machine learning in order to offer intelligent automation and data-driven insights. When it comes to the collection, processing, and evaluation of data from connected devices, cloud computing will become increasingly important as the Internet of Things (IoT) continues to expand.

2.2 Types of Cloud Services (IaaS, PaaS, SaaS)

Cloud computing has completely altered the manner in which individuals and corporations gain access to, manage, and utilize various technological resources. These services, which may be broken down into Infrastructure as a Service (IaaS), Platform as a Service (PaaS), and Software as a Service (SaaS), offer varying degrees of capability and abstraction to cater to a wide range of information technology needs. In this piece, we will examine each of these cloud service models in depth, focusing on their characteristics, advantages, and various applications.

IaaS, or "Infrastructure as a Service," refers to the following:

IaaS stands for infrastructure as a service and is the first layer of cloud computing. It offers virtualized computing resources via the internet.

Traditional on-premises infrastructure, such as servers, storage, and networking equipment, can be replaced with this more flexible and cost-effective option provided by the cloud. Users don't have to make an investment in real hardware in order to provision and manage virtual computers, storage, and network resources when they use infrastructure as a service (IaaS).

IaaS Has the Following Key Features:

Virtualization: Infrastructure as a service (IaaS) is highly dependent on the technology of virtualization, which enables the development of several virtual instances (also known as virtual machines or VMs) on a single physical server. These virtual machines are capable of running a wide variety of operating systems and applications.

Scalability: Infrastructure as a service platforms provide scalability on demand, which enables users to raise or reduce the amount of resources as required. It is absolutely necessary to have this degree of adaptability in order to successfully manage shifting work loads and to maintain cost-effectiveness.

Self-Service: Users can provision and manage resources through a web-based control panel or

API, giving them authority over their computing environment. This type of service is known as self-service provisioning.

Pricing on a Pay-as-You-Go Basis: IaaS providers often adopt a pay-as-you-go or pay-per-use pricing model, which means that users only pay for the resources that they actually use. Because of this, there is no longer a requirement for significant initial expenditures of capital.

Advantages of Using IaaS Are:

IaaS reduces the need for maintaining and upgrading physical gear, which results in a reduction in both capital and operational expenses. This results in cost savings.

Scalability means that companies may simply expand or reduce the size of their infrastructure in response to changes in customer requirements.

IT RESILIENCE

Users have complete control over the software stack, which enables customization and the ability to run a broad variety of programs. Flexibility is achieved as a result of this control.

In the event of a crisis, many IaaS providers offer built-in backup and disaster recovery solutions, which boosts data redundancy and ensures the continuity of corporate operations.

Examples of IaaS in Action:

IaaS is a great option for hosting websites, web apps, and e-commerce platforms. If you are looking for web hosting, look no further.

The provisioning of virtual environments allows developers to test new applications or software updates without having an influence on production systems. This allows for more efficient development and testing.

Backup and Recovery of Data: IaaS Platforms Offer Reliable Backup and Disaster Recovery Solutions to Ensure Data Safety IaaS platforms offer dependable backup and disaster recovery solutions to ensure data safety.

High-Performance Computing: IaaS can be used for computationally intensive operations such as scientific simulations, rendering, and data analysis. These kinds of jobs require a lot of memory and processing power.

2. Platform as a Service (often referred to as PaaS)

When compared to IaaS, the amount of abstraction offered by PaaS, the subsequent tier in the hierarchy of cloud services, is significantly higher. PaaS platforms provide a completely managed environment for application development. This allows developers to focus on writing code and constructing apps while the cloud provider controls the underlying infrastructure, operating systems, and runtime environments. PaaS platforms are also referred to as platform as a service (PaaS).

Principal Attributes of PaaS:

PaaS platforms provide hosting services for web applications, databases, and middleware. This service is referred to as application hosting.

The code that developers have created can be deployed without the developers having to worry about the server's configuration or upkeep.

Tools for Application Development: PaaS providers typically include a collection of application development tools, libraries, and frameworks to help developers create their software more efficiently.

Scalability is a feature offered by PaaS systems, which enables applications to scale up and down automatically, making it simpler to meet the needs of a growing number of users.

PaaS platforms are designed to accommodate several users and applications while maintaining a high level of isolation between them. This feature is known as multi-tenancy.

Advantages of Using PaaS Are As Follows:

The ability of developers to concentrate on coding and innovation rather than infrastructure administration results in faster development.

PaaS eliminates the requirement for businesses to build and maintain their own infrastructure, which results in significant cost savings.

Scalability refers to the capability of PaaS platforms to manage increasing workloads while maintaining a high level of availability and performance.

PaaS settings encourage team cooperation and make it possible for developers to work on shared projects at the same time.

Examples of Uses for PaaS:

PaaS is an excellent option for developing web apps, regardless of whether the applications will interact directly with end users or will be used internally as business tools.

Database Management: PaaS platforms typically offer database services, which make data storage and management more easier to perform.

The creation and hosting of back-end services for mobile applications can be accomplished with the help of PaaS when developing mobile applications.

IoT Development: The applications and services that make up the Internet of Things (IoT) can reap the benefits of PaaS for managing their data and connections.

3. "Software as a Service" (often referred to as "SaaS"):

The Software as a Service model is the top layer of the cloud computing architecture, and it refers to the delivery of an entire software program via the internet. Users are able to gain access to and utilize software programs directly from within their web browsers while utilizing SaaS, which eliminates the requirement for users to install, maintain, or administer software on their local computers.

Accessibility: Software as a service (SaaS) apps may be accessed from any device as long as it has an internet connection, which gives them a high degree of adaptability and accessibility.

Automatic upgrades Because SaaS providers manage software upgrades and maintenance, users are guaranteed continuous access to the most recent features and security fixes at all times.

Multi-Tenancy: Software as a Service (SaaS) solutions are built to accommodate numerous tenants while preserving the confidentiality and integrity of their users' data.

Pricing that is determined by the length of a user's membership is called subscription-based pricing. Users of SaaS applications often pay a monthly subscription price, which can be more cost-effective for enterprises.

Advantages of using SaaS are as follows:

SaaS apps are simple to deploy and use, requiring only a minimal amount of support or resources from internal IT departments.

The necessity for software installation and maintenance is removed when using SaaS, which results in a reduction in the overall cost of using software.

Scalability refers to the ease with which SaaS programs can be modified to accommodate expanding user bases.

Collaboration: Many software as a service (SaaS) products are designed to make it easier for teams to work together remotely.

Examples of How SaaS Can Be Used:
Productivity Software SaaS provides access to a variety of helpful applications, like Microsoft 365, Google Workspace, and software for managing projects, all of which are designed to boost productivity and encourage cooperation.

Customer Relationship Management (CRM): CRM systems such as Salesforce and HubSpot offer platforms based on SaaS for managing customer interactions and sales processes. CRM stands for "customer relationship management."

Accounting and Finance Cloud-based accounting software, such as QuickBooks and Xero, helps organizations run their financial management operations more efficiently.

Email and Communication: Reliable email communication and collaboration tools can be obtained via SaaS email services like as Gmail and Outlook, for example.

2.3 Cloud Deployment Models (Public, Private, Hybrid)

Cloud computing has developed into a vital technology in the quickly advancing digital world of today, as it enables businesses to scale, innovate, and minimize the expenses associated with their infrastructure. The use of cloud computing is not a one-size-fits-all solution; rather, businesses have a variety of deployment options from which to select in order to satisfy their own requirements. There are three basic deployment types for the cloud: public, private, and hybrid. Each of these platforms offers a unique set of benefits and problems.

Open Cloud Storage

The public cloud is by far the most well-known and extensively used deployment strategy for cloud computing. In this paradigm, cloud service providers use a shared infrastructure to give numerous clients with access to various computing resources. These resources may include virtual machines, storage, and networking. These resources are provided to users via the internet, which makes it simple for individuals and companies alike to get their hands on them. The fact that public clouds share their resources with various users results in significant cost savings.

Because customers only pay for the services they actually employ, this model is ideal for enterprises of all sizes, especially those with limited budgets. Businesses are able to more easily respond to shifting customer requirements because to the nearly unlimited scalability offered by public clouds. Because resources can be provided or deprovisioned according to need, there is less of a chance of either over- or under-provisioning occurring. clients are spared of the duty of purchasing and managing hardware because the cloud provider owns and maintains the infrastructure. This benefits clients tremendously. Data centers are operated by public cloud providers all around the world to ensure low-latency access to their services in various geographic locations.

A deployment in the public cloud is appropriate for start-ups and smaller organizations who are looking for more affordable IT solutions. It is also appropriate for businesses that have fluctuating workloads and require the capability to instantly scale up or down their resource allocation. The use of public clouds is beneficial for projects with a global reach because these clouds typically contain data centers located in multiple areas. Applications that do well in this deployment model include web hosting, email services, and development environments. These are all examples of software that could benefit from shared resources and cost-effective solutions. However, there are a few obstacles that come with using public clouds. It is possible that sharing resources with others will raise security issues, particularly for companies that deal with sensitive data or operate in industries that are regulated. In addition, the availability of customization choices may be restricted in public clouds, making it more difficult to cater to specific needs. Last but not least, the expenses of bandwidth can quickly build up, which is especially the case when moving huge amounts of data into and out of the public cloud.

Personal Cloud Storage

The private cloud deployment model is diametrically opposed to the public cloud deployment model. It entails the establishment of a cloud infrastructure that is used just by one company, providing that company with full control over its resources, as well as its management and its level of security. This model can either be hosted internally or by a third-party source. Both options are available. Private clouds provide dedicated resources, which ensure that the data and applications used by an enterprise are kept separate from those used by other customers. Due to the fact that this isolation improves both security and privacy, it is a good option for companies that deal with sensitive data or organizations that must strictly adhere to compliance regulations.

Private clouds offer a higher level of control than public clouds, which enables businesses to better design their cloud infrastructure to match their unique requirements, whether those requirements pertain to industry-specific compliance standards or specialized application requirements. Private clouds can be hosted on-premises, providing full control and flexibility, or they can be hosted by third-party providers, providing a compromise between control and offloading the obligations of infrastructure maintenance. Both hosting options allow the flexibility to adapt to changing business needs. These deployment strategies are especially interesting to businesses who already have considerable IT investments and wish to utilize those assets within their cloud infrastructure. In particular, this is the case for corporations that use public clouds.

Private cloud deployment is highly recommended for businesses that must adhere to severe security and regulatory standards, such as those in the healthcare, finance, or government industries. Private clouds are beneficial to businesses who require complete control over their infrastructure and data, whether for reasons of customization or data sovereignty. Hosted private clouds offer businesses with significant investments in on-premises infrastructure a way to ease the transition into a cloud environment by combining the advantages of cloud computing with the control offered by on-premises systems. These businesses can take use of hosted private clouds. Private clouds, despite the fact that they offer superior control and protection, are not without their share of difficulties. The process of establishing and operating a private cloud infrastructure can be difficult, time-consuming, and resource-intensive, and it frequently calls for the employment of a specialized IT team. Because enterprises using private clouds are responsible for the construction expenditures as well as the continuing maintenance of the infrastructure, the related costs may be higher than those involved with using public clouds. In private clouds, achieving the same level of scalability as in public clouds can be difficult. As a result, businesses may need to overprovision resources in order to accommodate the peaks in their workloads.

Mixed or Hybrid Cloud

The implementation of a hybrid cloud brings together characteristics of both public clouds and private clouds to produce a cloud environment that is adaptable and versatile. This deployment approach enables businesses to combine the resources of both their private and public clouds, making it possible for data and applications to move fluidly between the two types of clouds. It strikes a balance between the control and security offered by a private cloud and the scalability and cost-effectiveness offered by a public cloud, making it possible to reap the benefits of both.

The ability of hybrid cloud environments to shift workloads between private and public clouds provides companies with the freedom to choose where to run individual applications based on the requirements of the application. This versatility is what gives hybrid cloud environments their name.

For instance, companies can employ a private cloud for workloads that are vital to the company's operations and sensitive in nature, while simultaneously accessing the public cloud for burst workloads at times of peak demand. The ability to perform "cloud-bursting" is one of the defining characteristics of hybrid cloud deployment.

Organizations who want to keep control over sensitive data or applications in a private cloud while benefiting from the scalability and cost-efficiency of public clouds for non-sensitive workloads are the ideal candidates for hybrid cloud deployment. This type of deployment is suitable for organizations that want to preserve control over sensitive data or applications in a private cloud. It is especially beneficial for companies that have changing workloads and need to scale their resources as the demand for their products or services changes. Hybrid clouds are ideal for businesses that want to extend their on-premises data centers into the cloud in a seamless manner so that they may maximize the return on their existing infrastructure investments.

However, hybrid clouds do not come without their own unique set of difficulties. The coordination and integration of services between public and private clouds can be difficult for businesses to do when they are attempting to manage the complexities of a hybrid environment. In addition, the portability of data and applications between different cloud environments might give rise to worries regarding the data's compliance and security. It is absolutely necessary to properly configure and protect a hybrid cloud environment in order to reduce these dangers.

2.4 Benefits and Challenges of Cloud Adoption

Cloud computing has completely altered the ways in which firms run their operations and manage their information technology infrastructure. The transition from traditional on-premises systems to cloud-based solutions has offered businesses with a wide range of benefits. These benefits have enabled businesses to streamline operations, save costs, and innovate more quickly. Having said that, this change does come with its own unique set of problems and things to think about. In this piece, we'll take a look at some of the most important advantages and difficulties associated with using cloud computing.

Advantages of Utilizing Cloud Computing

Savings on Costs: The ability to save money is one of the most significant benefits of using cloud computing. Through the use of cloud computing, organizations are able to avoid the initial capital costs that are connected with the purchase and maintenance of hardware and software. They instead pay for cloud services using a subscription model or a pay-as-you-go model, which lowers their operational costs and enables them to better control their budgets. In addition, cloud solutions

IT RESILIENCE

frequently make it possible to make better use of available resources, which helps reduce both waste and excess spending.

Scalability: Cloud systems are highly scalable, which enables businesses to rapidly adapt their resources to meet the ever-evolving demands of their customers. The flexibility to adjust resources in accordance with actual requirements is made possible by using the cloud. This applies whether one is scaling up to accommodate an unexpected spike in website traffic or scaling back during times of lesser activity. This scalability is especially important for organizations that experience fluctuating demands.

Cloud computing provides enterprises the ability to be more flexible and responsive to shifting

market conditions through the adoption of this technology. Cloud computing allows for the rapid deployment of new apps and functionalities, which in turn reduces the amount of time needed to bring a product or service to market. Because of their agility, organizations are able to maintain their competitive edge in industries that move quickly.

Accessibility: Because cloud services may be accessed from any location with an internet connection, they offer greater flexibility for working remotely and collaborating with others. This accessibility has taken on an increased level of significance over the past few years as remote work and hybrid work models have grown increasingly common.

Security and Disaster Recovery: Many cloud service companies make significant financial investments in data redundancy and security measures. They safeguard the data and applications by employing security professionals, providing solutions for data encryption, backup, and disaster recovery, and offering options for data encryption. In many cases, this can provide a level of protection that is superior to the security measures that can be implemented by individual enterprises.

Automatic Updates and Maintenance Cloud service providers take care of software updates, system maintenance, and patch management, hence decreasing the workload of in-house IT departments. This guarantees that businesses are constantly operating the most recent software and security updates without requiring them to commit additional resources.

Reach Across the Globe Cloud service providers often operate data centers in different regions, which enables them to have a worldwide reach and provide services with low latency. This is advantageous for companies who have customers located all over the world.

Predictability of Costs: Organizations only pay for the resources that they use, making it possible for cloud services to give cost predictability. The unexpected costs related with hardware breakdowns, maintenance, and capacity planning are eliminated as a result of this change.

Collaboration and Communication: In today's work environment, the use of tools for both collaboration and communication that are hosted in the cloud has become indispensable. They make it possible for teams to collaborate effectively, regardless of where they are located —in the same office or on different continents, for example.

Environmental Benefits: Cloud data centers frequently utilize energy-efficient technologies and are intended for high-density computing, both of which can result in a smaller carbon footprint when compared to conventional data centers.

The Obstacles in the Way of Cloud Adoption

Concerns Regarding Security Despite the fact that cloud service providers invest much in sophisticated security measures, it is the responsibility of enterprises to guarantee that critical data is effectively protected. Data breaches and security vulnerabilities are potential dangers, and organizations should establish strong access restrictions, encryption, and security best practices to mitigate these risks.

Compliance and Data Privacy: Many firms are subject to legislation and procedures for data privacy compliance, such as the General Data Protection Regulation (GDPR) or HIPAA. It might be difficult to ensure that cloud services are in compliance with the regulations that apply. Cloud providers must be carefully selected by organizations,

IT RESILIENCE

and then those providers' adherence to data protection and compliance standards must be evaluated.

Costs Involved in Data Transfer and Bandwidth The transfer of huge amounts of data to and from the cloud can result in high costs Involved in Bandwidth This is especially true for enterprises that have substantial data requirements. In order to keep these costs under control, meticulous planning and management are required.

Downtime and Reliability: Although cloud service providers strive for extremely high uptimes, there is still the possibility of downtime occurring due to power outages or routine maintenance. The possible effects of probable downtime on an organization's activities are something that must be considered, and the organization must also have backup plans in place.

Locking Oneself Into a Single Cloud Provider Can Lead to Vendor Lock-In Relying excessively on a single cloud provider can result in vendor lock-in. Moving from one cloud provider to another may be a difficult, time-consuming, and financially burdensome process.

It is essential to do an analysis of the long-term repercussions that will result from the selection of a cloud provider and to think about tactics that will prevent vendor lock-in.

The use of cloud services necessitates giving up some degree of control over the underlying infrastructure and the resources at your disposal. There is a possibility that businesses would lack visibility into the underlying infrastructure, which will make troubleshooting and performance improvement more difficult.

Data stored in the cloud may be subject to the rules and regulations of the nation in which the data center belonging to the cloud provider is situated. This raises the issue of data sovereignty. This can be problematic for companies that need to have control over the actual location of their data and faces hurdles for those companies.

Management of Costs Cloud services have the potential to cut costs, but they also have the potential to lead to unforeseen costs if they are not managed efficiently. It is critical to use effective cost management and optimization measures in order to keep cloud spending under control.

Complexity and a Lack of Skills: Managing cloud infrastructure may be difficult and requires knowledge of cloud services, architecture, and best practices. However, there is a skills gap in the industry. Many companies are struggling with a lack of skilled workers and need to either invest in training or acquire specialists who have experience working in the cloud.

Migration of Existing Systems and apps to the Cloud Can Present Integration Challenges Moving your existing systems and apps to the cloud can be a challenging process, especially when integration with on-premises or other cloud-based systems is required. During the changeover, there is a possibility that problems with compatibility and data synchronization will occur.

Chapter 3

Cloud's Role in IT Resilience

In today's hyper-connected world, the idea of resilience in information technology is more important than ever. The term "IT resilience" refers to an organization's capacity to continue providing critical services and running operations despite the presence of unanticipated disruptions or natural disasters. Hardware failures, cyberattacks, natural catastrophes, and any other incident that poses a risk to an organization's capacity to carry out its functions normally are all examples of the types of disruptions that can occur. The cloud has played a transformative role in improving the resiliency of IT, by providing businesses with new and inventive options for maintaining continuity, eliminating downtime, and protecting vital data. During this in-depth investigation, we are going to look into the multidimensional role that the cloud plays in IT resilience. Specifically, we are going to investigate its benefits, difficulties, best practices, and real-world applications.

Acquiring Knowledge on IT Resilience

The Importance of Maintaining IT Resilience

In the increasingly digital world of today, businesses and other organizations are dependent on the infrastructure and systems of information technology to perform effectively. Any kind of disturbance to these systems can result in severe financial losses, damage to reputation, and in some situations, the complete failure of an organization. The idea of IT resilience accepts the inevitability of disruptions and places the emphasis on an organization's capacity to endure them and quickly recover from any effects they may have. Resilience in information technology involves more than just backup and recovery; rather, it covers an all-encompassing strategy for preserving operational continuity in the face of a variety of obstacles.

Resilience in information technology is especially important in this day and age, as businesses are becoming more reliant on digital technologies and the scope and complexity of information technology systems are continually growing. A strong plan for IT resilience can assist firms in remaining flexible and adaptive to ever-changing conditions, so guaranteeing that key services continue to be accessible even in the event of disruptions.

IT Resilience Components and Mechanisms

Business Continuity Planning entails the creation of plans, as well as their ongoing maintenance and revision, which explain how a business will continue to do its critical tasks and provide necessary services in the event of a disruption.

Recovery from Disaster: Recovery from disaster refers to the process of restoring information technology systems and data following an interruption. This comprises procedures for data backup and recovery, as well as redundancy and failover systems for data centers.

High Availability: High availability solutions work to reduce the amount of time that information technology systems are offline by guaranteeing that they are always functioning. In order to accomplish this, redundancy, load balancing, and automatic failover techniques are required.

Data protection and security are both essential components of an effective information technology infrastructure. This involves encrypting

IT RESILIENCE

the data, controlling who can access it, and taking other precautions to prevent unwanted access or the corruption of the data.

Evaluation of Risk: In order to properly identify potential dangers and weak spots, it is critical to carry out exhaustive risk evaluations. Continuous risk assessments should be performed to determine how resistant an organization's IT infrastructure is to new threats.

Common Obstacles in the Way of IT Resilience

Complexity: The ability to manage resilience gets more difficult as IT environments become more complicated. It can be challenging to coordinate the many different components and make sure they all function together smoothly.

Developing and keeping resilient information technology systems can be an expensive endeavor. This covers costs associated with hardware, software, staff, and testing and maintenance that is performed on an ongoing basis.

The ever-increasing volume of data presents a formidable obstacle to the processes of data backup and restoration, as well as data protection. The effective management of significant amounts of data is a prerequisite for resilience.

Diverse Components of the Threat Landscape The diverse components of the threat landscape include natural catastrophes, cyberattacks, hardware failures, and other types of events that are disruptive. It is a significant challenge to get ready for as many different kinds of potential dangers as possible.

II. The Crucial Function of the Cloud in Maintaining IT Continuity

Recovery from Catastrophe Utilizing the Cloud

Traditional disaster recovery solutions frequently needed considerable capital investments in secondary data centers, which led to inefficiencies in terms of cost efficiency. Due to the fact that enterprises pay for cloud services on a subscription basis, cloud-based disaster recovery reduces the requirement for these upfront fees.

Scalability: Cloud-based disaster recovery solutions are highly scalable, which enables businesses to modify their DR resources to better meet their requirements as those requirements change over time. Businesses that experience shifts in their workload will find this scalability to be very beneficial.

On the event of a catastrophe, rapid recovery is made possible by disaster recovery solutions hosted on the cloud. Because the data is stored in the cloud, businesses are able to swiftly recover both their systems and their data, thereby reducing the amount of downtime they experience.

Reduced Management Expenses Managing traditional disaster recovery solutions can be a difficult and resource-intensive task at times. Cloud-based disaster recovery solutions shift a significant portion of the administration responsibility onto the cloud provider, allowing IT staff more time to concentrate on other important responsibilities.

Cloud-based data backup and restoration services

Automated Backup: Cloud-based backup solutions typically offer automated and regularly scheduled backups. This ensures that data is backed up on a consistent basis and in a reliable manner.

Redundancy in Geographic Locations Top cloud service providers distribute copies of their customers' data across numerous data centers located in a variety of geographic areas. This geographical redundancy makes data more resilient by insulating it from the effects of calamities in certain regions.

Versioning of Data: Cloud storage often allows data versioning, which enables businesses to restore earlier versions of files or data in the event that the data becomes corrupted or is accidentally deleted. This feature can be of great value in either of these scenarios.

Cloud-based data backup is both cost-effective and scalable because to the fact that organizations only pay for the amount of storage capacity that they really require.

Solutions for High Availability Hosted in the Cloud

Load balancing is a service that cloud providers offer to their customers that distributes incoming network traffic across numerous servers or instances of a given application. This ensures that the traffic will be automatically redirected to healthy instances in the event that one of the servers dies.

Auto-Scaling: Auto-scaling, which is based in the cloud, gives businesses the ability to dynamically adapt their resources in response to changes in demand. When there is a sudden increase in traffic, additional resources are made available in order to maintain continuous availability.

Failover Mechanisms: Cloud service providers offer failover capabilities, which make it possible for businesses to produce redundant instances of applications or services. In the event that one of the instances cannot service requests, traffic will be diverted to the failover instance.

Approaches Based on Multiple Clouds and Hybrid Clouds

In order to be resilient, solutions typically need to include both redundancy and diversity. Approaches based on multiple clouds and hybrid clouds give companies the opportunity to further improve the resiliency of their information technology.

Multi-Cloud: Using numerous cloud providers for various components of an IT infrastructure might help reduce the likelihood of vendor-specific problems and outages occurring. This strategy entails replicating mission-critical services across several different cloud service providers.

The flexibility and redundancy benefits of hybrid cloud computing come from the hybrid cloud's combination of on-premises infrastructure and cloud services. Scalability can be achieved by organizations by leveraging the cloud, yet essential components can be stored locally in their own data centers.

III. Taking Advantage of the Cloud's Benefits for Maintaining IT Availability

Economies of scale

The cost-effectiveness of cloud-based information technology resilience is one of its key advantages. The traditional approaches to disaster recovery and data backup typically involved substantial up-front financial investments in technology, data center space, and manpower. On the other hand, cloud-based solutions utilize a pay-as-you-go pricing approach, which does away with the requirement for significant initial investments. Organizations are able to subscribe to the cloud services they require, and they can increase or decrease their resource utilization as required. This model decreases the amount spent on capital expenditures and moves costs to a model that is more focused on operating expenses; as a result, it makes IT resilience more accessible to businesses of all sizes.

Scalability and adaptability go hand in together

Cloud computing solutions are extremely scalable, giving businesses the ability to modify their use of resources in response to shifting requirements. Because of the cloud's scalability, businesses are able to respond to seasonal changes in workloads and adapt their resource allocations to match growing business needs, both of which help them to maintain their agility and lower their operating costs. This scalability is especially beneficial for businesses that handle variable workloads since it allows those businesses to increase or contract their resource allocation in real time without the requirement for the provisioning of additional physical hardware.

Enhanced Safety and Protection of Personal Information

The most reputable cloud service providers make significant financial investments in various security measures, such as the staffing of specialized security teams, the use of robust encryption technology, and the use of access control methods. The utilization of cloud computing enables businesses to take advantage of the aforementioned security measures, which secure both their data and their infrastructure. Cloud service providers also provide choices for encrypting data while it is both in transit and while it is stored, making it possible to safeguard critical information. An additional layer of data security from the effects of localized catastrophes is provided by the geographical redundancy of data centers that span multiple regions.

Redundancy in Geographic Location

IT RESILIENCE

One of the intrinsic benefits of cloud computing is the geographical redundancy that major cloud service providers give their customers. The physical locations of cloud data centers are often spread out across a number of different regions. Because of this geographic diversity, the chance of losing data as a result of regional catastrophes like earthquakes, hurricanes, or floods is significantly reduced. The presence of redundancy means that data and services may be quickly restored from another location in the event that one of the data centers becomes inaccessible. This geographical resilience is especially beneficial for businesses that operate on a global scale or are based in regions that are prone to natural disasters.

Management and monitoring that is done automatically

Cloud-based IT resilience solutions typically provide automated management and monitoring capabilities as standard. These solutions offer businesses assistance in operating their systems in an effective manner, hence easing the burden of operational responsibilities placed on internal IT personnel. For example, automated backup and recovery procedures can have their scheduling and management handled without the need for manual intervention. In a similar vein, high availability and failover systems that are hosted in the cloud have the capacity to automatically respond to interruptions, hence decreasing the need for human intervention. Not only does this automation make operations more efficient, but it also shortens the amount of time needed to respond to urgent matters.

Concerns and Things to Take Into Account

Although there are many advantages to be gained from using the cloud in terms of IT resilience, businesses still need to be aware of certain issues and factors before they can implement cloud-based strategies.

Data Confidentiality and Regulatory Compliance

The legislation governing data privacy and the standards for compliance vary depending on the industry and the region. The degree to which cloud solutions adhere to these standards should be carefully considered by organizations. For instance, industries like healthcare and finance are subject to special data protection rules, such as those outlined in HIPAA and GDPR. These regulations are in place to safeguard patients' personal information. It is essential to make certain that cloud service providers adhere to all of the appropriate compliance standards and provide all of the necessary data protection precautions. It is imperative that businesses are open and honest about the location of their data, the individuals who have access to it, and the level of control they exercise over it.

Bandwidth, as well as the Costs of Data Transfer

When moving huge amounts of data to and from the cloud, especially for businesses that have big data requirements, might result in hefty bandwidth expenditures. In order to keep these costs under control, meticulous planning and management are required. It is essential to have a thorough understanding of the cost structure of data transfer inside the ecosystems of cloud providers in order to avoid any unexpected expenses. In addition, companies may need to take into consideration the amount of time necessary to transfer massive datasets to and from the cloud.

Locking in of a Vendor

A situation known as vendor lock-in can occur when there is an unhealthy reliance on a single cloud provider. Moving from one cloud provider to another may be a difficult, time-consuming, and financially burdensome process. It is absolutely necessary to conduct a thorough analysis of the long-term repercussions that will result from the selection of a cloud provider and to think about tactics that will prevent vendor lock-in. This involves employing tools and technologies as well as adhering to open standards in order to promote data portability between various cloud providers. When an organization adopts cloud-based IT resilience solutions, vendor lock-in should be a primary worry since it has the potential to limit the business's flexibility and negotiating power.

Competencies Needed and Necessary Instructions

IT RESILIENCE

There may be a need for specialized knowledge and abilities in order to manage cloud-based IT resilience solutions. The technologies that make up the cloud are always undergoing new iterations, therefore the IT departments of companies need to ensure that they are always up to date. Cloud service providers frequently make available training and certification programs to assist businesses in the process of developing the appropriate skill sets. Organizations also have the option of recruiting cloud specialists full-time or working with them on a contract basis to assist with the installation and administration of their IT resilience strategy.

Integration Obstacles and Difficulties

It might be difficult to integrate cloud-based IT resilience solutions with on-premises systems that are already in place. To ensure that there is no disruption in communication between on-premises resources and cloud-based ones, thorough planning and maybe tailored integration solutions are required. During the installation process, enterprises have to face obstacles such as compatibility concerns, data synchronization, and the movement of data between environments hosted in the cloud and those hosted on-premises.

Best Practices for the Resilience of Cloud-Based Information Technology

Detailed Analysis of the Risks Involved

A comprehensive risk assessment should serve as the basis for any IT plan that is resilient. It is important for organizations to recognize potential dangers and evaluate the possibility of those dangers as well as their impact. This evaluation needs to take into account a diverse set of potential outcomes, such as those resulting from natural disasters, hardware failures, cyberattacks, and human error. It is vital to update risk assessments on a consistent basis in order to take into account growing threats and changes in IT infrastructure.

Regular Practices and Examinations

It is absolutely necessary to conduct testing as well as drills in order to guarantee that IT resilience measures perform as intended. Regular disaster recovery drills and practice scenarios should be carried out by organizations in order to validate their procedures and infrastructure. This includes putting high availability configurations, failover mechanisms, and backup and recovery methods through their paces of testing. Performing drills on a regular basis helps ensure that the organization can efficiently respond to disturbances.

Encryption of Data and Other Safety Precautions

The safety and protection of data have to be given top priority in cloud-based information technology resilience initiatives. This involves encrypting data while it is both in transit and while it is stored. Access controls, multi-factor authentication, and encryption keys are some of the data protection measures that businesses should put into place. Audits and evaluations of vulnerability in information security can be helpful in locating potential flaws and devising solutions to fix them.

Management of the Data Lifecycle

It is absolutely necessary to have effective data lifecycle management in order to maximize savings and data availability. The archiving, storage, and deletion of data should all be governed by policies and processes that should be established by organizations. This guarantees that data is saved and retained appropriately for legal and operational requirements, so minimizing excessive costs and data clutter, while also ensuring that data is stored and retained appropriately.

Selection of Vendors and Negotiation of Service Level Agreements

Choosing the best cloud provider to work with is a crucial decision for maintaining IT resiliency. Potential vendors should be evaluated by organizations based on criteria such as compliance certifications, security measures, redundancy in data centers, and past uptime performance. In addition, businesses need to make sure they sign transparent service level agreements (SLAs) that spell out uptime guarantees, response times, and data recovery goals. Standardized Language Agreements (SLAs) play the role of legal contracts that obligate the provider to deliver the level of service that was promised.

3.1 Cloud as a Scalability Solution

In the continuously transforming digital landscape of today, the ability of an organization to quickly adapt and expand is often a critical factor in determining its level of commercial success. Scalability is an essential characteristic because it frees a business from the constraints imposed by its infrastructure, allowing it to expand its operations, meet rising levels of customer demand, and continue expanding. Computing in the cloud has quickly emerged as a game-changing solution for scalability, as it provides unrivaled flexibility and resources that can be deployed on-demand. In the course of this in-depth investigation, we will investigate how the cloud might serve as a scaling solution. Specifically, we will investigate its primary advantages, implementation methodologies, and real-world applications.

Acquiring Knowledge about Scalability
The Significance of Being Able to Scale

In the realms of both technology and business, scalability is an essential idea to understand. It is the ability of an organization to manage rising workloads and accept growth without experiencing a substantial reduction in performance or requiring a total rebuild of its infrastructure. This ability is referred to as "workload scalability." Scalability is frequently one of the most important determinants of a company's level of success in today's fast-paced and volatile marketplaces.

Scalability is necessary for a number of reasons, including the following:

As a result of factors such as seasonality, marketing campaigns, or unforeseen market events, businesses frequently face changes in customer demand that must be satisfied. Scalability gives an organization the flexibility to accommodate growing demand without causing any disruptions.

Scaling up or down resources according to requirements can help improve cost efficiency. When it comes to infrastructure, over-provisioning can result in excessive costs, while under-provisioning might cause problems with the system's performance. The ability to scale ensures that there is an adequate number of resources available at all times.

Advantage Competitif: Companies and businesses have a competitive advantage if they are able to quickly adjust to shifting market conditions and evolving client expectations. The ability to scale allows for quicker responses and more creativity.

Resilience Scalable systems are more resilient in the face of unforeseen occurrences, such as failures in the underlying hardware or spikes in the volume of traffic. Scalable systems can be designed with redundancy and failover measures included into them.

Scalability in Various Forms

Vertical Scalability, also known as scaling up, is the process of adding resources to an existing server or system. These resources can include the central processing unit (CPU), memory, or storage. It is possible to increase capacity, however there are practical restrictions and there may be downtime during the expansion if it is implemented.

Horizontal Scalability: This method, which is often referred to as scaling out, involves adding additional machines or servers to an existing network. The ability to accommodate nearly unlimited expansion with no interruptions in service makes this approach the method of choice for the majority of today's applications.

Scalability that is Elastic: Scalability that is elastic contains aspects of both horizontal and vertical scalability. It makes it possible to dynamically allocate resources according to the demand in the here and now. Cloud services are well-known for their flexibility to scale up or down with ease.

Scalability in Relation to the Cloud's Importance
Computing in the cloud refers to what?

Cloud computing is a paradigm in information technology that refers to the act of providing computing services through the use of the internet. Servers, storage, databases, networking, and software are just some of the components that make up these services. Cloud computing gives consumers the flexibility to access and use resources whenever they need to, while only having to pay for the services they really use.

IT RESILIENCE

IaaS stands for "infrastructure as a service," and it refers to a model of cloud computing that delivers virtualized computing resources via the internet. Users have the option to rent virtual computers, storage space, and networking components, all of which may be configured and managed according to their specific requirements.

Providers of "Platform as a Service" (PaaS) is an acronym that stands for platform as a service. PaaS offers developers a platform on which they can construct, deploy, and manage applications without having to worry about the underlying infrastructure. This makes the development process easier and speeds up the time it takes to get the product to market.

Software as a Service, sometimes known as SaaS, is a model for delivering software applications to customers on a subscription basis over the internet. These apps are hosted by the service provider, and users access them through web browsers. The service provider is also responsible for maintaining the program.

Scalability in the Cloud: Important Components to Consider

On-Demand Resources: Cloud service providers make on-demand resources like virtual servers, storage space, and database access available to their customers. Users are able to provide or de-provision resources in real time, which guarantees that they will have the capacity they require at the exact time they require it.

Auto-Scaling is a function that is offered by cloud platforms and it enables apps to automatically modify the number of resources that they utilize based on the demand that is occurring in real time. This guarantees the highest possible performance and efficiency at the lowest possible cost.

Load balancing refers to the process in which incoming network traffic is split up and distributed among many instances of an application using load balancers. This prevents any one instance from becoming overloaded, and it also has the ability to automatically redirect traffic away from instances that are failing.

Scalability advantages of the cloud

Economies of scale

Utilizing the cloud for scalability purposes results in significant cost savings, making it one of the cloud's most important advantages. Traditional methods of scaling frequently necessitated considerable initial capital expenditures for the purchase of new hardware and infrastructure. The cloud, on the other hand, operates on a pay-as-you-go model, which means that customers only pay for the resources that they really utilize. Because of this, there is no longer a requirement for making significant initial investments, and the costs can instead be modeled as an operational expense. In addition to this, it enables businesses to readily adjust their resource levels in response to shifting customer requirements, which lowers the likelihood of over-provisioning and overpaying.

Rapid expansion and innovativeness

The scalability offered by cloud computing makes it possible for businesses to experience quick expansion while also fostering rapid innovation. In conventional settings, getting new gear and setting it up can be a time-consuming procedure because of the way it is set up. On the other hand, the cloud provides access to additional resources in a manner that is nearly instant. This agility is invaluable in dynamic marketplaces, where the capacity to respond swiftly to new opportunities or unanticipated challenges can make the difference between success and failure for a business.

Superiority in Both Performance and Dependability

Cloud designs that can scale are meant to have high levels of performance and dependability. The use of load balancers helps to guarantee that traffic is dispersed uniformly and prevents certain components from becoming overloaded. The potential for downtime can be minimized by utilizing auto-scaling and redundancy methods, which give failover and backup options. These characteristics contribute to improved system performance and uptime, both of which are essential for ensuring continued customer happiness and the viability of the organization.

IT RESILIENCE

Expanding Across Geographies

Cloud service providers typically have data centers situated in multiple geographic locations across the globe. Because of this geographical diversity, firms are able to grow their operations into new areas without having to make investments in the physical infrastructure of those new countries. It makes it easier to rapidly deploy applications and services across many regions, while simultaneously meeting the criteria for local compliance and reducing the amount of latency experienced by users.

Recovery from Crises and Maintaining Resilience

Scalability solutions that are hosted in the cloud are naturally resilient. Increased disaster recovery capabilities can be achieved through the utilization of geographic redundancy, data replication, and backup solutions. Cloud-based disaster recovery solutions allow enterprises to swiftly restore services and data in the case of a data center failure or other disruptive occurrences, thereby reducing the amount of time that the services are unavailable and the amount of data that is lost.

Concerns and Things to Take Into Account
Protection of Personal Information and Safety

When utilizing the cloud for scalability, one of the primary concerns to have is regarding data security. Even if cloud service providers put a lot of money into security measures, it is ultimately the responsibility of the company to safeguard its own data and applications. This includes putting in place access controls, encrypting data, and taking other precautions to protect it. Compliance with industry-specific legislation, such as GDPR or HIPAA, is also essential, and businesses have a responsibility to ensure that cloud providers satisfy the relevant criteria.

Locking in of a Vendor

When utilizing cloud services for scalability, companies should exercise caution to avoid becoming locked in with a single vendor. If you are overly dependent on a single cloud service provider, it may be difficult to switch to another platform in the near or distant future. Organizations can reduce their exposure to this risk by adhering to open standards, making use of technologies that are cloud-agnostic, and contemplating multi-cloud plans that offer flexibility.

Monitoring as well as Expense Management

If the expenses are not carefully monitored and controlled, the variable and adaptable nature of cloud scaling can result in unpleasant surprises. Monitoring and cost management solutions that are resilient should be implemented by companies in order for them to monitor resource use, keep expenses under control, and continuously improve their cloud environments.

Incorporation as well as Compatibility

It might be difficult to integrate cloud-based scaling solutions with other cloud services or with on-premises systems that are already in use. It is possible that problems with compatibility and data synchronization will develop; therefore, companies should anticipate for the possibility of encountering integration hurdles throughout the phase of implementation.

Implementing Cloud Scalability with the Most Effective Best Practices

Comprehensive Arranging and Evaluation of Resources

Before beginning work on a cloud scalability project, businesses should first carry out a thorough analysis of the infrastructure, workloads, and scalability needs that currently exist inside their enterprises. This study needs to incorporate a comprehensive analysis of the compatibility of the apps that are currently in use with cloud services.

Architecture that is both Modular and Based on Microservices

Scalability can be improved by developing programs with a focus on modularity and microservices architecture during development. This strategy entails partitioning applications into a number of smaller, self-contained services that can be independently deployed and scaled. The result is an increase in both agility and resource usage.

Controls for Safety and Regulation Compliance

When preparing for the scalability of a cloud environment, security and compliance should be a primary priority. Install steps for the safety of data, including encryption and access controls. Regular security audits and vulnerability assessments should be carried out in order to locate and remedy any potential vulnerabilities.

Continuous Observation and Adjustments to Settings

Tracking both resource consumption and expenditures requires the implementation of effective monitoring and cost management technologies. Cloud settings should be continuously optimized to ensure that they are cost-effective as well as performance-efficient.

Preparedness and Response Efforts

Include planning for disaster recovery as part of your strategy for scaling in the cloud. Make sure that there are procedures for data replication and backup in place so that any disruptive situations will result in the least amount of data loss and downtime possible.

3.2 Cloud for Disaster Recovery and Backup

In this day and age of increased reliance on digital technology, businesses and organizations are confronted with an ever-increasing requirement to safeguard their essential data and secure the continuity of their operations in the event of unanticipated calamities and disruptions. Cloud computing has evolved as a strong solution for disaster recovery (DR) and data backup, offering a flexible, cost-effective, and dependable approach to secure data and applications. DR stands for disaster recovery, and it refers to the process of recovering data and applications after a catastrophic event.

In the course of this in-depth investigation, we will investigate how cloud computing can be utilized for disaster recovery and backup purposes. Specifically, we will investigate its benefits, implementation methodologies, best practices, and real-world applications.

Before we begin:

It is impossible to stress the significance of having a backup of your data and a plan in place in case of a calamity. Data loss, system downtime, and operational disruptions caused by natural disasters, technology catastrophes, or accidents caused by humans can have a disastrous effect on businesses and other organizations. For the purpose of limiting these risks and making certain that key data and services can be rapidly restored, it is essential to have a solid disaster recovery and backup strategy in place.

The Crucial Part That the Cloud Plays in Both Backup and Disaster Recovery

1. Data Storage and Redundancy Cloud service providers offer enormous, geographically dispersed data centers that have redundancy capabilities built right in. This redundancy means that data is copied across several locations, hence lowering the risk of data loss as a result of localized calamities or failures in the underlying technology.
2. **The capacity to scale:** Because cloud resources can be deployed on demand, businesses have the opportunity to rapidly grow their backup and disaster recovery solutions to match their unique requirements. Scalability is a key benefit of cloud computing. This flexibility is especially helpful during catastrophe recovery scenarios, since it may be necessary to utilize additional resources in order to restore operations.
3. Efficient Use of Resources Conventional methods of disaster recovery and data backup frequently called for considerable initial investments in physical infrastructure and off-site storage facilities. Cloud-based solutions use a paradigm known as pay-as-you-go, which does away with the requirement for significant upfront capital expenditures. The fact that companies only pay for the resources they consume makes disaster recovery and data backup significantly more cost-efficient.
4. **Accessibility:** Cloud-based disaster recovery and backup solutions can be accessible from any location provided that the location has access to the internet. Because of this accessibility, remote administration and monitoring are possible, which makes it much simpler to ensure that business as usual is maintained in situations in which employees are geographically dispersed.

5. **Automation:** Cloud systems have the ability to automate processes, which can help to streamline disaster recovery and backup procedures. Automating backups at regular intervals, failover methods, and the auto-scaling of resources during recovery efforts are all examples of what may be done using automation.

Advantages of Using the Cloud for Both Backup and Disaster Recovery

1. **Efficient Use of Resources:**
   The cost-effectiveness of cloud-based disaster recovery and backup is one of the most significant advantages of using this approach. Investing a large amount of capital in secondary data centers, hardware, and infrastructure was typically necessary for traditional disaster recovery solutions. As a result of the fact that businesses pay for cloud services on a subscription basis, cloud-based solutions eradicate these initial expenditures. As a result of the trend away from capital expenditures toward operating expenses, disaster recovery and data backup are now within reach of a greater variety of enterprises.
2. **Quick Return to Normal:**
   In the event of a catastrophe, businesses may recover quickly with the help of cloud-based disaster recovery technologies. Because their data and apps are stored in the cloud, businesses are able to swiftly recover their systems and data, hence reducing the amount of downtime they experience. Cloud systems provide a variety of features, including auto-scaling, failover methods, and data replication, which all help to a more expedient recovery procedure.
3. **Redundancy in Geographic Location:**
   The most successful cloud service providers typically operate data centers in a number of different geographic regions. This geographical redundancy helps to strengthen the data's resilience, which in turn protects it from regional calamities like as

earthquakes, hurricanes, and floods. Data and services can be promptly restored from another geographical area, ensuring that business operations will continue even in the case of a disaster confined to a specific location.

4. **Management That Is Made Much Easier:**
The management of traditional systems for disaster recovery can be difficult and resource-intensive at times. Cloud-based solutions shift a significant portion of the management responsibility onto the shoulders of the cloud provider. By taking care of responsibilities such as data replication, automated backups, and failover procedures, the cloud platform lessens the amount of work that needs to be done by the IT teams located on-premises.

5. **Capacity for Growth and Adaptability:**
When it comes to backup and disaster recovery, the scale and flexibility offered by the cloud are vital. Real-time resource alterations give organizations the ability to respond effectively to shifting customer requirements. This scalability is especially useful for businesses that experience quick growth or fluctuating workloads because it allows for more room for expansion.

6. **Availability of Access and Management from a Distance:**

Cloud-based solutions provide remote accessibility and management, which enables businesses to monitor and control their backup and disaster recovery methods from any location provided they have an internet connection. Accessibility like this is absolutely necessary for companies who run their operations in multiple locations or employ workers in different locations.

Examples of How Cloud-Based Backup and Disaster Recovery Can Be Used in the Real World

1. **Medical treatment:**
When it comes to protecting patient data and ensuring the availability of essential medical systems, the healthcare industry

relies largely on disaster recovery and backup solutions that are hosted on the cloud. Data redundancy, data storage in a secure environment, and disaster recovery capabilities are all supported by cloud solutions. In the event that a calamity strikes a specific area or there is a problem with the system, medical professionals can easily access patient records and continue to give necessary medical care.

2. **Businesses Relating to Finance**

   In order to guarantee uninterrupted access to their customers' financial information and transactions, financial institutions like banks and insurance companies rely on solutions for disaster recovery and data backup. Cloud-based solutions provide a high level of availability, a safe location for the storage of data, and the capability to recover quickly. These qualities are critical for ensuring that banking services continue to function normally even in the event that they are subjected to cyberattacks, failures in hardware, or disruptions at the regional level.

3. **Transactions conducted online:**

   Web traffic can be unpredictable for online shops, particularly during the shopping seasons leading up to major holidays and during times of special promotion. Cloud-based solutions make it possible for e-commerce enterprises to keep crucial sales data and guarantee that customers have uninterrupted access to their websites.

   Cloud-based resources are able to automatically scale to meet increased demand in the event of a sudden spike in traffic or a distributed denial of service attack (DDoS).

4. **Establishments of Higher Learning:**

The protection of student and administrative data at educational institutions, from elementary schools to universities, is mostly handled via cloud-based backup and disaster recovery systems. Even in the event that an information technology system experiences a failure or disruption, these solutions guarantee that important applications, student records, and learning management systems will continue to be available.

Concerns and Things to Take Into Account

1. **Safety and the protection of personal information:**
   When utilizing the cloud for disaster recovery and backup, the protection of data and the upkeep of security are two of the most important concerns. Even while cloud service providers put a lot of money into security measures, it is ultimately the responsibility of the company to protect the data it stores. Controls on data access, data encryption, and other data protection measures are crucial components of any effective security strategy.

2. **Locking in a Vendor:**
   An unhealthy dependence on a single cloud provider might result in a situation known as vendor lock-in. Switching from one service provider to another can be a challenging, time-consuming, and expensive endeavor. In order to reduce the impact of this risk, businesses should adhere to open standards, make use of technologies that are cloud-agnostic, and contemplate multi-cloud plans that provide flexibility.

3. **Supervision and Management of Expenditures**
   If cloud-based solutions are not effectively monitored and controlled, the solutions' inherently dynamic nature can result in expenditures that were not anticipated. Monitoring and cost management solutions that are resilient should be implemented by companies in order for them to monitor resource use, keep expenses under control, and continuously improve their cloud environments.

4. **Compatibility and Integrity of Integration:**

It might be difficult to integrate cloud-based disaster recovery and backup solutions with pre-existing on-premises systems or with other cloud services. It is possible that problems with compatibility and data synchronization will develop; therefore, companies should anticipate for the possibility of encountering integration hurdles throughout the phase of implementation.

Guidelines for the Successful Deployment of Cloud-Based Backup and Disaster Recovery Systems

1. **Integrated and All-encompassing Planning and Evaluation:**
   Before beginning a cloud-based disaster recovery and backup project, businesses should first do a thorough analysis of their existing IT infrastructure, data assets, and requirements for disaster recovery. This evaluation needs to take into consideration the prioritizing of data, as well as recovery time objectives (RTOs), recovery point objectives (RPOs), and compliance requirements.
2. **Architecture that is Modular and Comprised of Microservices:**
   The incorporation of modularity and microservices architecture into the development of apps can make backup and disaster recovery more easier. This strategy entails partitioning applications into a number of smaller, self-contained services that can be independently deployed and scaled. The result is an increase in both agility and resource usage.
3. **Safety and Regulatory Compliance Precautions:**
   When it comes to disaster recovery and backup preparation, security and compliance ought to take precedence. Install steps for the safety of data, including encryption and access controls. Regular security audits and vulnerability assessments should be carried out in order to locate and remedy any potential vulnerabilities.
4. **Continued Observation and Improvement:**
   Tracking both resource consumption and expenditures requires the implementation of effective monitoring and cost management technologies. Cloud settings should be continuously optimized to ensure that they are cost-effective as well as performance-efficient.

5. Planning for the Recovery from a Disaster:

You should incorporate disaster recovery planning into your cloud-based backup and disaster recovery strategy. Make sure that there are procedures for data replication and backup in place so that any disruptive situations will result in the least amount of data loss and downtime possible.

Cloud-based disaster recovery and backup solutions have fundamentally changed the way in which businesses protect vital data and guarantee their operations will continue uninterrupted. These solutions include cost-effectiveness, speedy recovery, regional redundancy, streamlined management, scalability, accessibility, and the ability to perform remote management. Applications of cloud-based disaster recovery and backup in the real world encompass a wide range of industries, including healthcare, finance, e-commerce, and education, among others.

When implementing cloud-based methods, however, businesses really need to be on the lookout for potential threats in the areas of security, vendor lock-in, monitoring, and integration. By adhering to best practices and remaining educated about future trends and advances in disaster recovery and backup, businesses may better exploit the full potential of cloud-based solutions, increasing the likelihood that they will be well-prepared to take advantage of the opportunities presented by the digital age. Cloud-based disaster recovery and backup not only protect data and systems, but they also provide the confidence and peace of mind that come from knowing that business continuity is assured, even in the face of the unexpected. Cloud-based disaster recovery and backup not only protect data and systems, but they also provide the peace of mind that comes from knowing that business continuity is assured.

3.3 Cloud for Data Redundancy and Replication

In this day and age, data is the most vital resource for any firm. The need to keep, access, and safeguard one's data has emerged as one of the most important requirements for every organization, be it a multinational enterprise, a government body, or an individual. In this setting, data redundancy and replication are two essential methods that have risen to prominence, and the cloud has emerged as an essential enabler for putting these strategies into action.

A Comprehension of the Redundancy and Replication of Data

Both data redundancy and data replication are strategies that are utilized in order to guarantee the availability and integrity of data. They provide an effective technique of preventing data from becoming inaccessible or lost by addressing the issues of data loss, hardware failures, and data corruption. They also handle the challenges of data loss.

Redundancy in the Data:

The process of producing several copies of the same data is known as data redundancy. It is common practice to keep these copies in distinct locations or on distinct media storage devices. The purpose of redundancy is to protect against the loss of data caused by the breakdown of hardware. For instance, in the event that one of your hard drives dies, you should still have a redundant copy of your data stored on another one of your drives.

The Replication of Data:

The concept of data replication is an extension of the concept of redundancy. It does not simply create numerous copies of data; rather, it actively synchronizes data across several systems or locations in real time or in a manner that is almost as fast as real time. This makes sure that the most recent and up-to-date version of the data is always accessible, even in the event that something goes wrong. In high-availability circumstances, when continuous data access is essential, replication is frequently employed as a data management strategy.

The Importance of the Cloud in the Process of Data Duplication and Replication

1. **Capacity to Grow:**
   Cloud platforms provide access to storage capacities that are almost unimaginably large. The amount of data that an

organization generates can very readily be used to either increase or decrease the capacity of its storage needs. This scalability is a crucial advantage for adopting redundancy and replication strategies since it reduces the need to manage and maintain complex on-premises infrastructure. This scalability is a key advantage for implementing redundancy and replication strategies.

2. **Geographical Scope and Coverage:**
Cloud service providers typically have data centers spread out in various parts of the globe. This geographical diversity makes it simpler to implement data replication across several regions, which in turn reduces the likelihood that data will be lost as a result of disasters confined to certain locations. It also helps users in different parts of the world enhance the speed at which they can access the service.

3. **Computerized Instruments:**
Cloud service providers make available a wide variety of programs and services that are designed to automate the process of data replication and redundancy. These technologies can be set up in a variety of configurations that allow for the creation of numerous copies of data, the management of replication, and the monitoring of data integrity. This makes it easier for IT personnel to do their jobs and increases the likelihood that data redundancy and replication will be carried out correctly.

4. **Efficient Use of Resources:**
It may be more cost-efficient to store data on the cloud, particularly when weighed against the expense of constructing and maintaining storage solutions on-premises. Pay-as-you-go pricing models are offered by cloud providers, which means that businesses only have to pay for the amount of storage that they really use. This cost-efficiency applies to data redundancy and replication, since businesses are able to modify their solutions according to their finances and the requirements of their operations.

5. **Availability to All:**

Cloud storage allows users to view their data from virtually any location provided they have an internet connection. This ensures that even in the event of a catastrophe taking place at one location, data may still be accessed from another location, making the availability of the data very high.

Concerns and Things to Take Into Account

Although there are many advantages to be gained from using the cloud for data redundancy and replication, there are also a number of problems and factors that companies need to take into mind.

1. **Safety first:**
   The storage of data in the cloud necessitates the implementation of stringent security measures to prevent data breaches and defend against unwanted access. The use of encryption, access controls, and the management of identities are three essential aspects of cloud security.
2. **Obeying the rules:**
   Specific regulations concerning data protection and compliance must be adhered to by various sectors of the economy and geographic areas. The compliance of an organization's data redundancy and replication solutions in the cloud with the aforementioned rules is an absolute necessity.
3. **The transfer of data and the latency of it:**
   Concerns regarding speed of data transfer and latency may arise throughout the process of duplicating data to the cloud. To ensure that data can be copied in a timely way, organizations need to consider both the capabilities of their own networks and the options made by the cloud provider.
4. **Management of the Data Lifecycle :**
   The flexibility of the cloud can cause data sprawl, which is when businesses store more information than they actually require. It is necessary to have efficient data lifecycle management in order

to keep costs under control, maintain data redundancy, and replicate data effectively.

5. **Planning for the Recovery from a Disaster:**

Even though the cloud is a great tool for data redundancy and replication, businesses still need to have comprehensive disaster recovery plans in place. These plans should detail the actions that should be taken in the event that the cloud provider is affected by a catastrophic event.

Examples Taken From the Real World

Netflix: Data redundancy and replication are handled by Amazon Web Services (AWS), which is used by Netflix. They assure that their streaming service will continue to be highly accessible and resistant to disruptions by replicating data across a number of different data centers hosted by AWS.

Cloud platforms are used by NASA's Jet Propulsion Laboratory to store and reproduce mission-critical data from a variety of space missions. Because of its capacity to accommodate a wide range of locations and its adaptability, the cloud is an excellent option for fulfilling this function.

Redundancy and replication performed on the cloud are two of the safeguards that Salesforce, a market leader in customer relationship management (CRM) software, employs to keep client data available while also ensuring its safety. They do this across a number of data centers to ensure that the data will always be accessible.

Data redundancy and replication are key tactics for assuring the integrity and availability of data in this day and age, when data is the money of the digital economy. The cloud has emerged as a major enabler of these initiatives, thanks to the advantages it offers in terms of scalability, geographic distribution, automation, cost-efficiency, and accessibility.

Even if the advantages of cloud-based redundancy and replication are substantial, businesses still need to handle issues such as data transfer, latency, compliance, data lifecycle management, and disaster recovery planning. By giving each of these aspects due consideration, businesses can maximize the benefits that the cloud has to offer in terms of data redundancy and replication. In doing so, they can ensure that their data will continue to be robust and accessible in the face of obstacles and catastrophes. The future of data redundancy and replication appears to be bright, with the prospect of solutions that are even more dependable and effective in the not-too-distant future. This is due to the continual development of technology as well as the efforts of cloud service providers.

3.4 Cloud-Based Monitoring and Automation

Real-time monitoring, proactive management, and seamless automation of IT infrastructure and services have become absolutely necessary in the fast-paced digital landscape of today. Cloud-based monitoring and automation are two technologies that are intricately tied to one another and have recently emerged as significant solutions for accomplishing these goals. This article examines the significance of cloud-based monitoring and automation in the digital age, as well as its benefits and applications for various fields.

Comprehending the Concept of Cloud-Based Monitoring and Automation

Monitoring Conducted Via the Cloud:

The technique of continuously viewing and assessing the performance and health of information technology resources, applications, and services that have been deployed in the cloud or on-premises is what is referred to as cloud-based monitoring. It entails collecting, aggregating, and visually representing data from multiple sources, like as servers, networks, databases, and applications, in order to provide insights into the state and performance of those components. Monitoring solutions provide IT departments with dashboards, alerts, and reports to assist them in making educated decisions and resolving issues as quickly as possible.

Automation that is Hosted on the Cloud:

The technique of managing and controlling information technology resources and services in the cloud using programming is referred to as cloud-based automation. It makes use of scripts, policies, and workflows to automatically carry out mundane tasks, maximize the utilization of available resources, and react appropriately to shifting environmental conditions. Automation lowers the amount of manual intervention that must be performed in order to manage infrastructure and services, which enables businesses to improve their levels of productivity, consistency, and scalability.

The Importance of Control and Monitoring Carried Out Via a Cloud-Based Platform

Real-Time Insights: Cloud-based monitoring offers real-time visibility into the performance and status of IT assets, which enables IT teams to identify and manage issues before they have an impact on users and operations. This preventative strategy improves service quality while also reducing the amount of downtime experienced.

Scalability refers to the cloud's ability to readily increase or decrease the amount of resources used in response to changes in demand. Cloud-based automation enables businesses to take advantage of this scalability by automatically providing, deprovisioning, and optimizing resources in response to changes in the amount of work being done, so guaranteeing that costs are minimized.

Automation minimizes the amount of manual labor needed to administer information technology infrastructure and services, hence improving efficiency. It is possible to automate routine and repetitive processes within information technology, such as software patching, backups, and resource provisioning. This will free up IT professionals to focus on more strategic work.

Automation helps to guarantee that duties are carried out in a manner that is consistent and in accordance with any predetermined policies. This decreases the likelihood of mistakes being made by humans and guarantees that configurations and procedures continue to conform to the highest possible levels of both best practices and security standards.

Cost Optimization: Organizations can better manage their expenditure on cloud services if they automate the process of resource allocation and scaling based on patterns of consumption. This helps to keep operational costs under control and minimizes unnecessary over-provisioning.

The Advantages of Using the Cloud for Monitoring and Automation

1. **An Increase in Both Reliability and Availability:**
   Monitoring that is performed in the cloud can assist businesses in preserving high levels of availability and reliability. It is able to detect problems in real time, which enables a rapid response to prevent disruptions in service. The failover techniques and redundancy configurations can be triggered automatically through the use of automation.
2. **Increased Safety Measures:**
   Monitoring systems can discover potential weaknesses and threats to security in a timely manner. The ability of organizations to respond to security incidents through the implementation of established security policies and isolation measures is made possible by automation. This allows enterprises to reduce the potential impact of security breaches.
3. **Operations That Are Simplified:**
   Automation makes difficult operational tasks easier to perform. It speeds up common procedures like as software upgrades and configuration changes, cutting down on the amount of manual labor required and reducing the likelihood that incorrect configurations would be used.
4. **Infrastructure that can be scaled up:**
   Automation performed in the cloud ensures that the scalability of the infrastructure can keep up with changing demand. It is

able to dynamically allocate resources when necessary and release them when they are no longer required, hence maximizing the utilization of resources and the costs associated with doing so.

5. **Optimization of Available Resources:**

Automation helps to maximize the use of available resources, which in turn can lead to significant cost reductions. It is possible to automate the shutoff of unused resources, and resource allocation can be based on the level of demand that is really being met. This ensures that resources are used effectively.

Various Applications for Monitoring and Automation Based on the Cloud

Monitoring Application Performance Cloud-based monitoring solutions are able to monitor the performance of web applications, application programming interfaces (APIs), and microservices. They give enterprises the ability to identify and address performance bottlenecks by providing insights on response times, error rates, and user experience.

Management of Infrastructure Cloud-based automation can provision, configure, and manage infrastructure resources in an agile and consistent manner. This enables better business agility. This is especially helpful for DevOps approaches, which make frequent use of an approach known as infrastructure as code (IaC).

Security and Compliance: Organizations can more easily remain in compliance with various security standards and requirements when continuous monitoring is implemented. Automation makes it possible to automatically undertake security audits, respond to potential attacks, and enforce security regulations.

Control of Costs Cloud-based automation enables cost control through the dynamic scaling of resources in response to changing demand. It also has the capability of scheduling the beginning and ending hours of non-production environments, which helps cut down on wasteful spending.

IT RESILIENCE

Data Backup and Disaster Recovery: Automation can be used to handle backup and recovery procedures, ensuring that data is routinely backed up and that it can be rapidly restored in the event that data is lost or the system fails.

Log Management and Analysis Cloud-based monitoring technologies have the ability to aggregate logs from a variety of sources and do log analysis on those logs. Log analysis standards can be specified, and then automation can be used to trigger alerts and actions based on those standards.

Concerns and Things to Take Into Account

Implementing monitoring and automation systems can be a challenging endeavor due to their inherent complexity. For an organization to successfully implement and maintain these systems, it needs both knowledgeable employees and careful planning.

Integration: It can be difficult to guarantee that monitoring and automation solutions will integrate seamlessly with the existing information technology infrastructure. It is necessary to have a well-defined plan as well as an architectural approach.

Data Privacy and Compliance: Organizations are required to comply to data privacy legislation and security standards while monitoring and automating operations that include sensitive data. This is necessary to ensure compliance.

Over-Automation: The automation of an excessive number of procedures without first giving each one significant consideration might result in mistakes and unforeseen consequences. It is important for businesses to find a happy medium between human control and automated processes.

Monitoring and automation that is performed in the cloud have rapidly become vital tools for managing digital ecosystems. Real-time insights, enhanced dependability, scalability, and cost optimization are some of the benefits that they provide. The use of these technologies is revolutionizing the way companies function, making it possible for them to more effectively and efficiently meet the expanding requirements of the digital age. In a business world that is becoming increasingly dynamic and competitive, businesses have the ability to guarantee that their information technology infrastructure and services will continue to have a high level of availability, security, and responsiveness if they use cloud-based monitoring and automation.

Chapter 4

Cloud Security and Compliance

The rapid advancement of technology has ushered in a new era of digital transformation, and cloud computing has been an essential component in the paradigm change that this ushers in. Cloud computing is becoming increasingly popular among businesses all over the world as a means of improving the scalability, cost-effectiveness, and operational efficiency of their operations. However, as businesses move their operations to the cloud, they will face significant issues with security and compliance. In this article, which is three thousand words long, the author goes deeply into the complex realm of cloud security and compliance in order to gain an understanding of the changing landscape, best practices, and the important nexus between security and regulatory compliance in the era of cloud computing.

The Internet of Things and the Cloud Computing Revolution

Cloud computing is a paradigm that involves the delivery of computing services, such as storage, databases, servers, networking, software, analytics, and intelligence, via the internet to offer speedier innovation, flexible resources, and economies of scale. At its core, cloud computing is a model that involves supplying computer services, such as storage, databases, servers, networking, software, and intelligence. Cloud computing allows businesses to make the transition from traditional on-premises infrastructure to services hosted in the cloud, which gives them the freedom to grow their information technology resources in accordance with their requirements while also minimizing the requirement for major upfront capital expenditures. This revolution has had a huge impact on the operations of firms as well as the strategies they employ. Nevertheless, this shift presents its own unique set of issues, notably in regards to maintaining compliance and ensuring security.

II. The Constantly Changing Terrain of Cloud Security

1. The Threat Landscape Facing Cloud Computing

Data Security Flaws

Breach of data security is an ongoing worry in cloud computing environments. In order to get unauthorized access to sensitive data, attackers may take advantage of flaws in cloud computing systems or compromise user credentials. Once they have gained access, they can steal data, interfere with services, or install malware in order to gain further access to the network.

Threats From Within

Cloud security is made more difficult by the presence of insider threats. Insiders who are malicious, such as workers or contractors who have access to cloud resources, have the potential to actively breach cloud security or mistakenly reveal critical data. It is a difficult endeavor that requires a combination of technical and organizational procedures in order to successfully detect and prevent threats from within a company.

Attacks on the DDoS Protocol

DDoS assaults, also known as distributed denial of service attacks, can cripple cloud services to the point where customers can no longer use them. Because of the potential for these attacks to interfere with corporate operations, it is absolutely necessary for companies to have comprehensive DDoS mitigation techniques

IT RESILIENCE

in place.

Model of Responsibility That Is Shared

In a setting that makes use of cloud computing, the shared responsibility model specifies how the cloud service provider and the customer should divide up the various security duties that must be met. Whether Infrastructure as a provider (IaaS), Platform as a Service (PaaS), or Software as a Service (SaaS) is utilized, the specific tasks may be different from one cloud provider to the next. Customers are need to be aware of their own security commitments in this paradigm, which can be a source of confusion as well as potential security flaws.

2. Recommendations for Cloud-Based Security Best Practices

Management of Identities and Access Requests (IAM)

The implementation of efficient IAM techniques is absolutely necessary for the upkeep of cloud security. Utilize robust authentication mechanisms, implement access with the least amount of privilege possible, and routinely audit and monitor user access in order to avoid unauthorized or excessive rights from being granted.

A code or cipher

Encrypt data both while it is at rest and while it is in transit to prevent unauthorized access to the data. To protect sensitive data from unauthorized access and disclosure, effective encryption measures should be utilized.

Monitoring for Safety and Reaction to Unexpected Events

In order to discover security breaches in a timely manner and provide appropriate responses, it is important to implement continuous security monitoring and create an incident response strategy. Make use of solutions for security information and event management (SIEM) in order to centralize and investigate security events.

Protection of Networks

Firewalls, intrusion detection and prevention systems, and other network security controls should be utilized to ensure the safety of the cloud network. Implement configurations for a Virtual Private Cloud (VPC) or a Virtual Private Network (VPN) in order to compartmentalize resources and secure network traffic.

The Classification and Management of Data

It is important to treat data in accordance with how sensitive it is, thus you should classify it first. Taking this approach helps ensure that sensitive data is protected in an appropriate manner and is kept apart from information of a lesser importance.

Management of Patches

Maintaining cloud services and systems with the latest updates and security fixes is essential. As a result of the frequency with which attackers aim their attention at software and hardware flaws, patch management is absolutely essential.

Awareness Training on Safety and Security

Investing in security awareness training for staff will educate them on the importance of

following security regulations, as well as best practices and prevalent risks.

3. Compliance in the Age of Cloud Computing

1. **Frameworks for the Regulation of**

   The General Regulation on the Protection of Data (GDPR)

   The General Data Protection policy (GDPR) is an all-encompassing data protection policy that applies to businesses that handle the personal data of people of the European Union (EU). It mandates stringent criteria for data protection, such as the reporting of data breaches, the preservation of the rights of data subjects, and the appointment of a Data Protection Officer (DPO).

   HIPAA is an acronym for the Health Insurance Portability and Accountability Act.

   HIPAA is the law that dictates how sensitive patient information is to be protected in the healthcare industry. Protected health information (PHI) must be kept private and secure at all times by

covered entities and their business associates, who are required to follow stringent standards and protections in this regard.

PCI DSS stands for the Payment Card Industry Data Security Standard.

PCI DSS is an absolutely necessary standard for businesses that deal with credit card transactions. It details the security requirements that must be met to protect the data of cardholders and prevent data breaches.

Act of Sarbanes and Oxley (SOX)

The Statement on Auditing Standards (SOX) is a set of recommendations for financial reporting and internal controls that is primarily aimed at publicly traded firms. For the purpose of preventing financial fraud and ensuring the integrity of financial statements, compliance is of the utmost importance.

2. Obstacles to Overcome When Trying to Achieve Cloud Compliance

Responsibility that is Shared

Compliance work is made more difficult by the shared responsibility approach that characterizes cloud computing, as was discussed earlier. It is essential, in order to minimize compliance lapses, to have a solid understanding of where the responsibilities of the cloud service provider end and those of the customer begin.

The concept of data sovereignty and data residency

It is possible for data to be kept in data centers that are located in many countries. This gives rise to concerns over the residence of data and the sovereignty of data, particularly in light of the GDPR and other data protection legislation.

The Encryption of Data

Encryption may present a difficulty to compliance even though it is a recommended best practice for data security. A number of legislation call for very certain encryption standards and key management procedures, both of which must be adhered to by businesses.

Audit Trails and Logging are Available Here

Keeping detailed audit trails and logs for cloud-based services can be difficult, particularly when dealing with setups that use multiple clouds. It can be difficult to fulfill all of the compliance criteria for auditability.

Monitoring for Compliance and Providing Reports

Due to the dynamic nature of cloud services, continual assessment is required to verify that they are in compliance with regulatory requirements. Ongoing compliance monitoring and reporting in the cloud can be a complex process due to this requirement.

IV. The Relationship Between Compliance and Cloud Security

1. **The Approach That Is Driven By Compliance**

   Finding the Regulations That Are Applicable

   The first step for organizations is to determine which regulations are pertinent to their business practices and the information they manage. This requires conducting a detailed regulatory examination in order to guarantee complete compliance.

   Establishing a Mapping Between Security Controls and Regulations

   When rules have been found, the next step for businesses is to map their security measures to the precise requirements of the regulations. This involves determining which kinds of safety precautions are essential in order to meet the requirements of the compliance program.

   Putting in Place Controls for Security

   After the mapping is complete, the business must then put into place the appropriate security measures in order to achieve compliance. This may include making improvements to the security measures that are already in place, as well as adopting new technologies and processes.

   Keeping an Eye on Things and Filing Reports

   It is vital to maintain continuous monitoring in order to assure ongoing compliance. Organizations should have robust reporting procedures in place so that they can show compliance when it is expected of them, and they should have security technologies and policies in place to detect any deviations from compliance requirements.

2. **An Approach Centered on Strengthening Security**
   Evaluation of Dangers
   Carry out an exhaustive risk assessment to determine the organization's unique weak spots and potential dangers, then document your findings. This assessment contributes to the organization's ability to adjust its security measures to the specific circumstances of the business.

   Structures of Protection
   As a foundation for rigorous security processes, implement well-known security frameworks like the NIST Cybersecurity Framework or ISO 27001. These frameworks provide a standard for security. The protection of digital assets is made easier with the help of these frameworks, which offer detailed instructions.

   Regular Advancement in Quality
   The process of ensuring security ought to be continual and iterative. It is important to evaluate and improve security measures on a regular basis in order to stay ahead of evolving threats and improvements in technology.

   Cooperative effort
   Create an environment in which all parties involved, from individual employees to third-party providers, have a culture of security awareness and collaborate. The maintenance of a risk-free atmosphere is everyone's responsibility.

   The Response to an Incident
   Create a comprehensive incident response plan in order to address any breaches of security in a timely and efficient manner. This is absolutely necessary in order to meet the standards for breach notification and reduce the severity of the impact that security incidents have.

3. A Combination of the Two Strategies

Start with ensuring your safety

To begin, you should put in place robust security procedures that are based on well-known frameworks and industry standards. This establishes a rock-solid base upon which protection can be built.

Coordinate with the Compliance

After the security framework has been implemented, the next step is to synchronize it with the applicable compliance standards. This may involve adapting the currently in place security measures in order to satisfy particular regulatory requirements.

Monitoring and auditing on a regular basis

Maintaining a continuous monitoring and auditing program for security measures is essential to ensuring continuing compliance as well as adapting to ever-changing rules and threats.

The Response to an Incident

In order to address security events while still complying to regulatory regulations, incident response capabilities should be included into the hybrid strategy.

5. The Function of Internet Service Providers in the Cloud

1. **Public Offerings of Securities**

   Customers can improve their security posture by making use of the CSP's tools and services, which are often offered as part of a comprehensive package. The administration of identities and access, encryption services, firewalls, and intrusion detection systems are all examples of this category. Customers have the option of utilizing these services to strengthen their existing security protocols.

2. **Compliance Accreditations and Certifications**

   CSPs will usually seek a variety of compliance certifications and attestations to demonstrate their dedication to both compliance and security. These certifications can lessen the compliance burden placed on consumers by demonstrating that the CSP's infrastructure and services are in line with the requirements of a particular set of regulations.

3. **Communication Regarding the Division of Responsibilities**
CSPs are obligated to articulate in an understandable manner the duties that are shared between themselves and their respective customers. They have a responsibility to make sure that their consumers are aware of the security responsibilities that are uniquely theirs under the shared responsibility model.

4. **Data Center Security**
CSPs put a significant amount of money on the data center's physical protection. This is an extremely important part of data residency and sovereignty, as it ensures that data is stored in a secure manner that is in accordance with the applicable legislation.

5. **Cloud Computing Security Association (CSA)**

The Cloud Security Alliance is a well-known group that advocates for the utilization of tried-and-true procedures to ensure the safety of cloud computing. A significant number of CSPs are members of the CSA and take part in the process of developing cloud security best practices and standards.

4.1 Addressing Security Concerns in the Cloud

Computing in the cloud has completely revolutionized the way in which businesses function by providing scalability, flexibility, and cost-effectiveness. Cloud services bring with them a myriad of benefits; yet, along with those benefits come a host of issues and concerns regarding data security. It is essential to address these concerns in order to guarantee the safety of sensitive data and essential systems while they are stored on the cloud.

In this article, which is one thousand words long and is intended to provide a full overview of this essential component of contemporary technology, we will investigate the key security risks that are associated with the cloud as well as solutions to alleviate those concerns.

1. **An Understanding of the Concerns Regarding Cloud Security**

It is crucial to understand the most frequent issues that businesses experience when adopting cloud services before going into specific strategies to handle cloud security concerns. This should be done before diving into specific methods to address cloud security concerns.

1. **Violations of Data:**
   There is a huge fear around data breaches on the cloud. Vulnerabilities in cloud systems, compromised user passwords, or unsecured configurations can all cause these problems. The unauthorized access to sensitive data, theft of data, or alteration of data are all potential outcomes of breaches.
2. **Dangers that Come from Within:**
   Insiders who have malevolent intent or employees who make mistakes unintentionally can both be a significant threat to the company's security. They may purposefully breach security, or their activities, such as misconfigurations, may accidentally expose sensitive data. Both scenarios are equally possible.
3. **The loss of data:**
   Accidental deletion of data, malfunctioning hardware, or software defects are all potential causes of data loss. Even while providers of cloud services have included data redundancy mechanisms, there is still a risk of data loss if the settings are not optimized.
4. **DDoS Attacks, Also Known As**
   DDoS assaults, also known as distributed denial of service attacks, can cripple cloud services to the point where customers can no longer use them. These attacks have the potential to impede business operations as well as access to services for customers.
5. **A Model of Responsibility That Is Shared**

IT RESILIENCE

In a cloud context, there is something called a shared responsibility model, which outlines the responsibilities that are shared between the customer and the cloud service provider. It is essential for effective security to have a thorough understanding of these duties; nevertheless, this can also be a source of confusion and potential security holes.

II. Approaches to Addressing Concerns Regarding Cloud Security

Now that we've established the nature of these cloud security challenges, let's investigate potential solutions that would improve overall security posture.

1. **Management of Identities and Access Requests (IAM):**
   The importance of strong IAM in cloud security cannot be overstated. To ensure that only authorized users are able to gain access to resources, strong authentication methods, such as multi-factor authentication (MFA), should be implemented. Use the concept of least privilege, which states that users should only be granted the rights that are required for the roles they play. Review and audit user access on a regular basis to prevent users from gaining unlawful or excessive privileges.
2. **The use of encryption:**
   Encrypt the data both while it's moving and while it's sitting. For the purpose of preventing unwanted access to sensitive information, robust encryption measures should be utilized. The vast majority of cloud service providers offer encryption services that are very simple to incorporate into cloud-based resources.
3. **Monitoring of the security system and response to incidents:**
   Establish a system of constant security monitoring to identify unusual occurrences, activities that raise suspicion, and potential security holes. SIEM tools, which stand for security information and event management, can be used to both consolidate and analyze security occurrences. Create a well-defined incident response

strategy that includes explicit methods for identifying security issues, minimizing their effects, and reporting them.

4. **Protecting Your Network:**
Protect the cloud network by implementing network security controls such as firewalls, intrusion detection and prevention systems (IDPS), and others. Isolate resources by using various technological configurations, such as a Virtual Private Cloud (VPC) or a Virtual Private Network (VPN). These precautions assist in securing network communications and preventing unauthorized access.

5. **The Classification and Management of Data:**
It is important to treat data in accordance with how sensitive it is, thus you should classify it first. Taking this approach helps ensure that sensitive data is protected in an appropriate manner and is kept apart from information of a lesser importance. Tools for data loss prevention, also known as DLP, can assist in monitoring and protecting data in accordance with its classification.

6. **Maintenance of Patches:**
Maintaining cloud services and systems with the latest updates and security fixes is essential. Attackers usually focus their attention on weak spots in both the software and the hardware of a system. An efficient procedure for managing patches guarantees that computer systems are kept safe from exploiting previously identified flaws.

7. **Training in the Awareness of Security Risks:**

Invest in security awareness training for your staff as well as your end users. It is important to
educate them on the importance of following security standards, best practices, and the common hazards they may face. Employees who are adequately informed are a crucial line of defense against potential security risks.

III. A Model of Joint and Shared Responsibility

It is absolutely essential to have a good understanding of the shared responsibility model. It makes the distinction between the consumer and the cloud service provider regarding who is responsible for what in terms of security. The particulars could be different depending on the kind of cloud service that is being utilized, such as Infrastructure as a Service (IaaS), Platform as a Service (PaaS), or Software as a Service (SaaS).

In Infrastructure as a Service (IaaS), the cloud provider is responsible for the security of the underlying infrastructure, whereas the client is responsible for the security of the applications, data, and operating systems that they put on that infrastructure.

When using PaaS, the security of the platform is handled by the provider, while the customer is responsible for protecting their data and applications.

When an application is hosted in the cloud using the SaaS model, the security of the application as a whole, including the infrastructure, data, and access, is the responsibility of the cloud provider.

The shared responsibility model requires both clients and cloud providers to perform their respective roles in securing the underlying infrastructure. clients must be aware of their own security requirements, and cloud providers must carry out their duties.

IV. Compliance and the Security of the Cloud

Organizations are frequently required to demonstrate that they are in compliance with industry-specific legislation and standards. These regulations may include the Health Insurance Portability and Accountability Act (HIPAA), the Payment Card Industry Data Security Standard (PCI DSS), and many others besides. The General Data Protection Regulation (GDPR) is one example of one of these regulations. Due to the shared responsibility model and the ever-changing nature of cloud services, achieving compliance in the cloud is a difficult and time-consuming endeavor to undertake.

1. **Obstacles to Compliance When Working in the Cloud**
   Shared accountability: As was discussed previously, the shared accountability approach makes it more difficult to comply with regulations. In order to prevent compliance lapses, customers need to have a clear understanding of the scope of their responsibilities.
   Data stored in the cloud may be located in data centers that are physically located in a variety of nations. This raises the questions of data residency and data sovereignty. This gives rise to concerns over the residence of data and the sovereignty of data, particularly in light of the GDPR and other data protection legislation.
   Encrypting Data While it is generally accepted that encryption is a good practice for information security, compliance issues might occur when some legislation demand a particular encryption standard and certain key management procedures.
   Audit Trails and Logging: It can be difficult to keep full audit trails and logs for cloud-based services, particularly in setups that use more than one cloud service. It can be difficult to fulfill all of the compliance criteria for auditability.
   Ongoing compliance monitoring and reporting in the cloud might be challenging due to the complexity of the environment. Due to the dynamic nature of cloud services, continuous evaluation is required to guarantee that they are in compliance with regulatory standards.
2. **Methods to Meet Compliance Requirements While Working in the Cloud**

Determine whether Regulations Apply: The first thing that organizations need to do is determine whether regulations apply to the activities they run and the data they manage. This requires conducting a detailed regulatory examination in order to guarantee complete compliance.

IT RESILIENCE

Identifying Regulations and Mapping Security Controls to Them
Once regulations have been discovered, companies are required to match security controls to specific regulatory needs. This involves determining which kinds of safety precautions are essential in order to meet the requirements of the compliance program.

Following the mapping process, enterprises are obligated to put into place the required security controls in order to achieve compliance. This may include making improvements to the security measures that are already in place, as well as adopting new technologies and processes.

Monitoring and reporting on compliance is vital to ensuring continued compliance, hence

continuous monitoring is required. Organizations should have robust reporting procedures in place so that they can show compliance when it is expected of them, and they should have security technologies and policies in place to detect any deviations from compliance requirements.

The Function of Cloud Service Providers (also Known as CSPs)

1. **Public Offerings of Securities**
   Customers can improve their security posture by making use of the CSP's tools and services, which are often offered as part of a comprehensive package. The administration of identities and access, encryption services, firewalls, and intrusion detection systems are all examples of this category. Customers have the option of utilizing these services to strengthen their existing security protocols.
2. **Conformity Assessments and Certifications:**
   CSPs will usually seek a variety of compliance certifications and attestations to demonstrate their dedication to both compliance and security. These certifications can lessen the compliance burden placed on consumers by demonstrating that the CSP's infrastructure and services are in line with the requirements of a particular set of regulations.

3. **Communication Regarding the Division of Responsibilities**
CSPs are obligated to articulate in an understandable manner the duties that are shared between themselves and their respective customers. They have a responsibility to make sure that their consumers are aware of the security responsibilities that are uniquely theirs under the shared responsibility model.

4. **Security in the Data Center:**
CSPs put a significant amount of money on the data center's physical protection. This is an extremely important part of data residency and sovereignty, as it ensures that data is stored in a secure manner that is in accordance with the applicable legislation.

5. **Cloud Security Alliance (CSA), also known as:**

The Cloud Security Alliance is a well-known group that advocates for the utilization of tried-and-true procedures to ensure the safety of cloud computing. A significant number of CSPs are members of the CSA and take part in the process of developing cloud security best practices and standards.

4.2 Regulatory Compliance and Data Governance

Data is an extremely significant asset in the digital environment of today since it is the catalyst for corporate operations, decision-making, and innovation. As organizations become more dependent on data, they are faced with the challenge of navigating a complicated web of regulations and legislation that are designed to safeguard the privacy of persons, maintain the security of data, and ensure transparency. It has become a vital part of company strategy to ensure regulatory compliance and data governance, which assists businesses in the management and protection of their data assets. Within the scope of this 1000-word investigation, we will investigate the symbiotic relationship that exists between regulatory compliance and data governance, as well as their significance and the impact that they have on modern day corporate operations.

Comprehending the Necessity of Compliance with Regulations:

The term "regulatory compliance" refers to the process of adhering to the rules, regulations, standards, and guidelines that have been established by various regulatory authorities, including governing organizations, industry groups, and other regulatory authorities. These regulations cover a wide range of topics, such as the financial sector, healthcare, the protection of the environment, and, most importantly, the protection of personal information. The fundamental objective of regulatory compliance is to guarantee that corporations behave in an ethical, transparent, and responsible manner, with the secondary goal of minimizing the risks that are associated with non-compliance.

Within the field of data governance, regulatory compliance is an extremely important factor in protecting individuals' right to privacy and maintaining the safety of sensitive data. Regulations governing data privacy, such as the General Data Protection Regulation (GDPR) of the European Union and the California Consumer Privacy Act (CCPA), set stringent rules on the manner in which enterprises must acquire, keep, handle, and exchange personal data. Failure to comply with regulations can result in substantial fines, repercussions from the law, and harm

to one's reputation. Because of this, it is absolutely necessary for companies that collect or handle personal data to have an awareness of these standards and to comply with them.

Data Governance Reduced to Its Bare Essentials:

On the other side, data governance is a comprehensive discipline that comprises rules, procedures, and practices for managing and preserving an organization's data assets. This is done in order to ensure that the data assets of the business are safeguarded. It does so by putting in place a structure that guarantees the data's quality, consistency, and safety throughout its entire lifecycle, beginning with its acquisition and storage and continuing through its processing and eventual disposal. Data governance that is effective requires a methodical approach to data management, the promotion of trust in the quality of data, and the facilitation of decision-making that is informed.

The formation of data stewardship responsibilities, data cataloging, data classification, and access controls are all components of the various tasks related to data governance. These measurements give enterprises the ability to develop a coherent structure for data management and match it with their strategic goals, allowing them to better serve their customers. In the quest of data integrity and compliance, data governance is not limited to the implementation of technical solutions; rather, it is an all-encompassing strategy that takes into account people, processes, and technology.

The Point Where Compliance and Data Governance Meet:

The relationship between regulatory compliance and data governance is described as symbiotic due to the fact that each contributes to the other's growth and development. In many cases, the imposition of compliance requirements serves as the impetus for the development of effective data governance systems. In order for businesses to demonstrate that they are in compliance with legislation governing data protection, they need to know what data they own, where it is held, who has access to it, and how it is utilized. Data governance provides the tools and methods necessary to answer these questions and take action when appropriate.

For instance, the General Data Protection Regulation (GDPR) requires all enterprises to establish a Data Protection Officer (DPO) who is accountable for ensuring compliance. This function is highly aligned with the tasks associated with data governance, since DPOs oversee data processing activities, evaluate data risks, and devise ways to protect individuals' data rights. In a similar vein, data governance policies assist firms in meeting a fundamental need of the GDPR—the maintenance of accurate records of processing activities.

In addition, data governance makes a contribution toward the construction of a transparent data environment, which is an essential component of compliance. Regulatory agencies frequently demand that enterprises produce transparent documentation of their data handling procedures, data flows, and subjects' rights to their data. The documentation process can be made easier for enterprises with a well-structured data governance program, which assists these firms in meeting these standards and demonstrates their commitment to data protection.

Regulatory Compliance and Data Governance Have the Following Benefits:

Risk Mitigation: Regulatory compliance and data governance work together to identify risks connected with data breaches, data loss, and non-compliance and to develop strategies to reduce such risks. In today's data-driven environment, proactive risk management is more important than ever.

Quality of the Data The principles of data governance improve the quality of the data by defining the definitions of the data, ensuring that the data are accurate, and preserving consistency. For the purposes of decision-making and reporting, accurate data is absolutely necessary.

Operational Efficiency: The streamlining of data management procedures through the implementation of governance principles leads to operational efficiency, which in turn reduces errors and duplications that are related to data.

Reputation and Trust: Customers, partners, and other stakeholders are more likely to have faith in compliant firms that place a priority on data governance. In the world of business, trust is an intangible asset that is extremely precious.

Advantage in the Market: Companies who excel in regulatory compliance and data governance are in a better position to adapt to changing rules, gain an advantage in the market, and attract clients that place a high value on data security and privacy.

Effective data governance enables organizations to derive useful insights from their data, which in turn fosters innovation and contributes to the expansion of businesses.

Concerns and Things to Take Into Account:

Compliance Can Be Complicated With Regulations Because regulations are always being updated, it can be difficult to stay in compliance with them, particularly for businesses that operate in various locations. Keeping up with the ever-evolving legal landscape is an ongoing challenge.

Allocation of Resources: Putting into practice data governance demands a major investment of resources, particularly in terms of staff, technology, and training. It's possible that more manageable for larger businesses, but not necessarily for smaller ones.

Training on data privacy is necessary for employees, as they need to be knowledgeable about data protection rules and the concepts of data governance. It is absolutely necessary to provide sufficient training.

Data silos: In larger businesses, data can be dispersed over a variety of departments and systems, which can lead to data silos, which impede effective data governance initiatives.

Solutions Relying on Technology It might be a challenging endeavor to choose and put into action the most appropriate technology solutions in order to assist data governance.

The Prospects for Regulatory Compliance and Data Governance in the Near Future:

The regulatory compliance and data governance needs of a company will continue to be at the forefront of that organization's concerns as the importance of data increases. The digital landscape is always shifting, and increasing numbers of people are becoming concerned about the privacy of their data. For this reason, it is absolutely necessary for organizations to take the initiative to adjust to ever-shifting legislation and to make use of data governance procedures.

It is possible that in the years ahead, businesses will be subject to legislation regarding data privacy that are more stringent, as well as an increase in the demand from customers for transparency and control over their personal information. As a consequence of this, regulatory compliance and data governance will become even more crucial in order to preserve the trust of customers and prevent the legal penalties that may result.

In addition, the development of technologies such as artificial intelligence (AI) and machine learning (ML) presents both new issues and opportunities in the realm of data governance. The processes of data governance can be automated with the assistance of these technologies, which can also increase data quality and data security. Nevertheless, they also bring forth new complications in relation to algorithmic bias, the ethical use of data, and the fulfillment of already established standards.

4.3 Best Practices for Securing Cloud-based Resilience

The adoption of cloud computing has revolutionized the method in which businesses manage their information technology (IT) infrastructure and maintain business continuity. Cloud-based resilience, which is also often known as disaster recovery as a service (DRaaS), enables businesses to secure the data and applications they rely on in the event of an interruption caused by a natural or man-made calamity. However, despite the fact that cloud-based resilience provides benefits such as simplicity and scalability, there are also new security problems that need to be addressed. In this investigation of a thousand words, we will delve into the best methods for protecting cloud-based resilience, which will ensure that your company can retain its operations and the integrity of its data even in the face of adversity.

1. **Encryption of Personal Information as the Primary Step Towards Safety**

    The use of encryption is essential to ensuring the safety of data stored in cloud-based environments. It is important to encrypt data at all times, whether it is at rest or in transit. Cloud providers of the modern day make available sophisticated encryption techniques, but it is up to enterprises to put these mechanisms into effective use. Use encryption not only for data that is being stored in the cloud but also for data that is being transmitted to and from the cloud as well as data that is moving around inside the cloud itself. The maintenance of encryption keys is an extremely important task because a failure to do so can result in a data breach.

2. **Multi-factor Authentication (also Known as MFA): Keeping Access Secure**

   It is of the utmost significance to protect the access you have to your cloud-based disaster recovery environment. The requirement of various kinds of verification prior to giving access is one of the primary benefits of multi-factor authentication (MFA). Even if an attacker gains access to your password, Multi-Factor Authentication (MFA) ensures that they won't be able to access your account without the second factor, which is typically a mobile device or biometric information.

3. **Use Identity and Access Management (IAM) to Regulate Which Users Have Which Privileges**

   IAM ensures that only those who are permitted to do so have access to the resources and data contained within your cloud-based disaster recovery solution. Implementing role-based access control, also known as RBAC, allows you to define the capabilities of each user or group. Permissions should be reviewed and updated on a regular basis in order to reduce the risk of privilege escalation or unlawful access.

4. **Ongoing vulnerability scanning and security audits at regular intervals: Continue to be proactive.**

   Regular security audits and vulnerability scans should be carried out in order to locate and address any security flaws that may have been discovered. Manual audits offer a more in-depth analysis of security policies and configurations than their automated counterparts do. Automated scanning technologies can help detect potential vulnerabilities in a system.

5. **Testing of Data Backup and Recovery Procedures: Experience Is the Key to Success**

   It is essential to routinely test your backups and recovery strategies, despite the fact that cloud-based resilience frequently focuses on disaster recovery as its primary concern. In the event that a catastrophe occurs, this assures that all of your data and applications may be completely recovered. Testing not only checks your disaster recovery plan, but it also assists you in identifying and mitigating possible problems before they escalate into catastrophes.

6. **Diverse Locations of Data Centers for Geographical Redundancy**

   Think about having geographical redundancy so you can be more resilient. Distributing data across many data centers or regions assures that your data and applications will continue to be accessible even in the event that a single site is rendered inaccessible as a result of a natural disaster or an electrical outage. A significant number of cloud service companies incorporate data center redundancy into their offerings.

7. **Protect Private Information Through Proper Data Segmentation and Classification**

   There is not a uniform standard for all data. Implementing data categorization and segmentation is an effective method for separating sensitive or vital data from information of a lesser significance. This strategy guarantees that the most sensitive data is protected by the greatest level of security, hence decreasing the potential damage that could be caused in the event of a breach.

8. **Monitoring and Logging: Identifying Potential Dangers and Taking Corrective Actions**

   Continuous monitoring and logging are absolutely necessary in order to recognize and respond to any threats. Utilize powerful monitoring tools to keep track of the activity on the system and to set up alerts for potentially malicious conduct. The provision of a comprehensive history of events by logs is of incalculable value when it comes to the investigation of occurrences and the comprehension of the magnitude of any breach.

9. **Make Sure Your Team Is Well-Informed About Security Policies and Training**

    It is not sufficient to simply have security measures in place; your staff must also be aware of and adhere to any security regulations that are in place. Employees are better able to identify potential security risks and understand their part in securing your cloud-based resilience system when they participate in ongoing training and awareness campaigns.

10. **Have a contingency plan in place and be ready for the worst.**

    Incidents are still capable of taking place despite the use of all preventative measures. It is essential to have a well-defined incident response plan in order to reduce the amount of damage caused and the amount of downtime experienced. This plan must to include procedures for locating, containing, eradicating, and recovering from any security incidents that may occur.

11. **Service-Level Agreements (SLAs) and Vendor Security: Determine Which Providers Can Be Trusted**

    Consider the service level agreements (SLAs) and security standards of potential cloud-based resilience providers before making a choice. Make sure that they have the proper certifications and that they comply with the industry requirements for security. Determine how quickly they can respond to a crisis and how seriously they take the protection of sensitive data.

12. **Legal Obligations Regarding Compliance with Data Protection Regulations [12]**

    You might be required to comply with various data protection standards, such as GDPR, HIPAA, or CCPA, depending on the nature of your business and where you are located. To protect yourself from potential legal ramifications, check to see that your cloud-based resilience policies are in line with the standards of these rules.

13. **Evaluation of Third-Party Vendors and Risks Associated with Them**

If the robustness of your cloud-based operations depends on the services or vendors of third parties, you should conduct in-depth risk assessments of those partners. Make that they have strong security measures in place, such as encryption, access controls, and the ability to respond to incidents.

14. **Secure Development Methods and Procedures: The Importance of Code Security**

    Put secure coding methods at the top of your organization's to-do list if it builds custom applications for cloud-based resiliency. In order to locate and fix any vulnerabilities that may exist in your apps, you should conduct security audits and penetration tests.

15. **Planning for the Continuity of Business Operations: Going Beyond Data**

It is important to keep in mind that maintaining business operations is equally as important as data recovery when it comes to cloud-based resilience. Develop a business continuity strategy for your corporation that addresses all parts of the company, including communication, staff, and infrastructure, and ensure that it is routinely updated.

Chapter 5

Cloud Migration Strategies

The movement of modern firms' operations to the cloud has emerged as a critical step on the path to digital transformation for those businesses. In order for businesses to fully reap the benefits of cloud computing, they need to formulate and carry out migration strategies that are both efficient and successful. This thorough book will delve into the many different facets of cloud migration, detailing methods, obstacles, and best practices to assist businesses in making the successful transfer to the cloud.

Acquiring Knowledge on Cloud Migration

The process of moving an organization's data, apps, and other business pieces from servers that are located on-premises to servers that are located in the cloud is referred to as cloud migration. This change requires a sequence of decisions and steps to be taken, and it has the potential to have a substantial effect on the organization's day-to-day operations.

Why Should You Move to the Cloud?

IT RESILIENCE

1. **Efficient Use of Resources**
   The pay-as-you-go model that is offered by cloud services eliminates the requirement for making significant preliminary expenditures in infrastructure and hardware. Because of its adaptability, this solution can result in significant cost reductions.

2. **Capacity to Grow**
   Cloud service providers make their resources available on demand, which enables organizations to adjust the size of their IT infrastructure to meet their evolving requirements in real time. This adaptability is especially beneficial for companies that experience a fluctuating amount of work.

3. **Availability of Access**
   The cloud offers remote access to data and apps, making it simpler for employees to operate from anywhere. This ability to work remotely is becoming increasingly vital in a society that is becoming increasingly digital.

4. **Safekeeping**
   There are several cloud providers, and many of them make substantial investments in security measures, which frequently allow them to outperform the capabilities of on-premises data centers. Data encryption, data backup, and disaster recovery are all included as standard features in cloud computing.

5. **Creative Achievement**

Cloud services typically incorporate cutting-edge technology like machine learning, artificial intelligence, and integration of IoT devices into their offerings. This can provide firms with the ability to innovate and maintain their competitive edge.

Migration to the Cloud in Various Forms

1. **Rehosting, often known as "lift and shift"**
   In this strategy, companies simply transfer their already established data and apps to the cloud without making any other

substantial adjustments. This strategy is rapid and less disruptive, making it a fantastic alternative for firms that want to migrate quickly while minimizing the amount of change that occurs during the process.

2. **Changing the platform**

   Replatforming, sometimes referred to as lift, tinker, and shift, is the process of making very minimal modifications to apps or data in order to make them compatible with cloud storage. Because of this, performance, scalability, and cost-efficiency can all be improved, while downtime can be reduced.

3. **Rearchitecture, often known as refactoring**

   Refactoring entails making significant alterations to the architecture of the existing application in order to fully capitalize on the capabilities of the cloud. Although this strategy may be time-consuming and expensive, the end product may be applications that are more effective and scalable.

4. **Reconstructing**

   Rebuilding is effectively the same thing as starting the application development process from scratch in order to make full use of cloud-native capabilities. This strategy requires the most effort and resources to implement, but it also has the potential to produce the most productive and economical results.

5. **Calling it quits**

It's possible that some programs or data won't work with the transfer process. It's possible that some companies will opt to retire or decommission particular systems rather than migrate them to the cloud in certain circumstances.

Important Things to Think About Before Moving

1. **The Goals of the Organization**

   Clearly describe the business goals you want to accomplish with the migration. Know exactly what it is that you want to accomplish, whether it is lowering costs, increasing scalability, or enhancing performance.

2. **Observance of Regulations and Safety**

   Make sure that the cloud service provider you choose is in compliance with the mandatory regulatory criteria that are specific to your sector. Create a thorough data and application protection plan by developing a comprehensive security strategy.

3. **Analysis of the Data**

   Conduct an analysis of your data to establish which pieces need to be relocated, which ones may be archived, and which ones can be discarded. The process of migrating data is frequently one that is difficult and time consuming.

4. **Compatibility of the Applications**

   Conduct an analysis to determine whether or not your existing applications are compatible with the cloud environment. There may be certain legacy applications that call for considerable modifications.

5. **An Estimate of the Cost**

   Gain an understanding of the financial ramifications of moving to the cloud. Take into account not just the charges associated with the relocation but also the continuing operations costs in the cloud.

6. **Instruction of Staff**

Make sure that your IT team is knowledgeable on cloud technology as well as the best practices for using them. Training and ongoing education are necessary components of a successful move.

Strategies for Moving to the Cloud

Rehosting, often known as "Lift and Shift"

The most efficient and uncomplicated method of relocation is known as rehosting. It entails transferring apps and data from servers located on a company's premises to servers located in the cloud with little to no modification. The goal is to preserve the infrastructure that is already in place while minimizing the level of complexity and risk. This strategy, on the other hand, would not fully capitalize on the benefits of cloud-native computing and might lead to an underutilization of the cloud's resources.

Switching Platforms

In terms of the level of complexity involved, replatforming falls somewhere between rehosting and refactoring. It is also known as lift, tinker, and shift. During the migration process, companies that use this methodology may make some relatively minor alterations to the data or apps being moved into the cloud. This may involve improving the system's overall performance, scalability, or cost-effectiveness. It's a trade-off between quickness and optimization for the long run.

Refactoring, also known as rearchitecture

Refactoring is the process of making significant modifications to the architecture of an application in order to take full use of cloud-native capabilities. This strategy frequently calls for the alteration of the code, which can be time-consuming and expensive. On the other hand, this leads to applications that are more effective and scalable and that make full use of the possibilities of the cloud.

Reconstruction of

Rebuilding uses the most resources of all of the available options. It requires essentially starting from scratch and redeveloping the application so that it can run natively in the cloud. Although this strategy demands the most time and effort, it frequently results in the solutions that are both the most productive and the most economical.

Giving up their careers

There are situations in which staying put is the most prudent course of action regarding migration. Because of redundancy, obsolescence, or incompatibility with the cloud environment, organizations may decide to retire or decommission specific applications, data, or infrastructure. This decision may be made at the organizational level. This results in a reduction in complexity and a savings of resources.

Migration to the Cloud Presents Obstacles

1. **Compliance and the Protection of Data**
   A big worry during and after the transfer is making sure that data is both secure and compliant throughout the process. Organizations are required to maintain compliance with relevant industry rules and execute stringent security precautions.
2. **The Transmission of Data and Bandwidth**
   Transferring significant amounts of data to the cloud for the first time can be a time-consuming process and may put a strain on the bandwidth that is available. This may result in longer periods of downtime during the move.
3. **The compatibility of the applications**
   Not all apps are designed to run in a cloud environment, and those that do may need considerable adjustments or even redevelopment before they can perform their functions properly. This could be a process that uses a lot of resources.
4. **Management of Expenses**
   Migration to the cloud may result in cost savings; however, if it is not handled effectively, it may also result in expenses that were not anticipated. Spending on the cloud should be carefully monitored and optimized by organizations.
5. **Interruptions to Business and Periods of Downtime**
   Even when migration is meticulously planned, the process can still result in downtime and inconvenience to business. The level of interruption that can be tolerated should be kept to a minimum.
6. **Deficiencies in Competencies**

The information technology departments of many companies discover that they lack the expertise and skills necessary to effectively manage cloud resources. Eliminating this skills gap is absolutely necessary for a successful move.

Migrating Successfully to the Cloud: Proven Methods and Procedures

1. **Make Exhaustive Plans**
   Develop a comprehensive plan for the move, including its objectives, timetable, resources, and potential hazards. Think about the various possibilities, and prepare yourself for a range of outcomes.
2. **Analysis of the Data**
   Carry out a careful analysis of all of the data you have. It is important to have a clear understanding of what needs to be moved, what can be archived, and what can be decommissioned. The complexity of the migration procedure is simplified as a result of this.
3. **Put an Emphasis on Safety**
   Maintain a focus on security throughout the entirety of the relocation process. Encryption, access limits, and monitoring are all important data protection measures that should be implemented.
4. **Make Sure You Use the Appropriate Cloud Service Provider**
   Select a cloud service provider that meets all of your requirements, such as those for regulatory compliance and the limitations imposed by your budget.
5. **Put Automation to Use**
   Utilize automation tools and scripts so that the migration process may be streamlined, errors can be reduced, and time can be saved.
6. **Continue to Monitor and Improve**
   Maintain constant vigilance over the state of your cloud environment and look for ways to improve its performance. This involves both the management of costs and the enhancement of performance.
7. **Education and the Promotion of Competences**
   Ensure that your IT team is capable of handling cloud resources in an efficient manner by investing in training and upskilling opportunities for them.
8. **Examine Meticulously**

Test thoroughly both before and after the migration in order to identify and address any problems that may arise. Because of this, there is a lower chance of outages and disruptions.

5.1 Planning and Assessing Your IT Infrastructure

The foundation of any modern company is its information technology (IT) infrastructure, which must be meticulously laid out and expertly administered. It grants businesses the ability to continue to be competitive, adaptable, and sensitive to the ever-changing needs of the digital market. In this extensive guide, we will discuss the crucial steps of planning and evaluating your IT infrastructure. We will emphasize the significance of strategic thinking, best practices, and the tools that are required to build a solid technology foundation that is prepared for the future.

The Importance of Information Technology Infrastructure

1. **Continuity of Business Operations**
   Maintaining company continuity requires a dependable information technology infrastructure. It makes certain that essential computer systems and data are accessible at all times, especially in the face of unanticipated occurrences like as natural catastrophes or cyberattacks.

2. **Capacity to Grow**
   It is essential to have the capacity to adjust the level of IT resources used to meet changing business demands. An infrastructure that has been well developed can accommodate abrupt development, adjust to changes in the market, and sustain expansion.

3. **Efficient Use of Resources**
   The effective planning and administration of information technology infrastructure can result in cost reductions. Organizations are able to more effectively manage resources if they maximize the usage of available resources and reduce the amount of downtime experienced.

4. **Flexibility**
   Having an infrastructure that is flexible enables businesses to rapidly adjust to shifting market conditions and incorporate new technology. Maintaining one's agility is necessary in order to compete effectively.
5. **Safekeeping**

When it comes to defending against cyberattacks and preserving sensitive data, having a secure infrastructure is absolutely necessary. Vulnerabilities can be identified and addressed with the help of a comprehensive assessment.

Putting Together a Plan for Your IT Infrastructure

1. **Specify Your Organization's Goals and Aims**
   To get started, you should make sure that the plan for your IT infrastructure is aligned with the overarching business goals of your organization. It is important to have a good understanding of the technological capabilities that are required to support these aims.
2. **Conduct an Inventory of the Already Existing Infrastructure**
   Carry out a detailed analysis of the existing state of your information technology infrastructure. This covers resources for the data center as well as hardware, software, and networks. Take notes on everything you own, how it is put to use, and its current state.
3. **Identify Emerging Trends in Technology**
   Maintain a level of awareness on the latest technological trends and advancements in your

   sector. If you are aware of what is on the horizon, you will be better able to plan for the requirements and opportunities of the future.
4. **Evaluate Both Your Workload And Your Performance**
   Be aware of the strains that are being imposed on your infrastructure. Keep an eye on performance data, determine

where bottlenecks are occurring, and evaluate how scalable your systems are.

5. **The Financial Plan and the Distribution of Resources**
   Create a budget that is based on reality and takes into account both the initial setup costs and the continuing maintenance costs. Utilize a systematic allocation of your resources to guarantee that vital areas will receive sufficient investment.

6. **An Analysis of the Dangers**
   Determine the potential dangers and weak spots in your infrastructure. Take into account the risks posed by cybersecurity, any relevant regulatory issues, and any disaster recovery plans.

7. **Capacity to Grow**

Make preparations for future expansion by ensuring that your infrastructure can expand or contract proportionately to meet changing demands. This is of utmost significance for companies that see shifts in the volume of their activity.

Analyzing Your Information Technology Infrastructure

1. **Keeping an Eye on Performance**
   Maintain a regular monitoring schedule for the functioning of the various components of your infrastructure, such as servers, network devices, and storage systems. Determine any potential performance bottlenecks and locations that could use some tweaking.

2. **A Check of the Security**
   It is important to conduct frequent security audits in order to discover potential weaknesses and dangers. Make certain that your data is appropriately secured and that it can withstand any assaults that may be launched against your infrastructure.

3. **An examination of compliance**
   Conduct an audit of your compliance measures and check that they are up to date in order to guarantee that your infrastructure

complies with all applicable rules and industry standards. This is very important for fields such as the medical and financial industries.

4. **Planning for Capabilities**
Conduct an analysis of the capacity of your infrastructure to assess whether or not it can meet the demands of both the present and the future. Determine whether resources are being over- or under-utilized, and make adjustments as required.

5. **Optimization of Available Resources**
Reduce your environmental impact by maximizing the use of your resources. Consolidating servers, virtualizing infrastructure, or shifting to a model based on the cloud could all be necessary steps in this process.

6. **Contingency Planning and Data Backup**
Conduct a review and ensure that your backup and disaster recovery plans are up to date. In the event that data is lost or an outage occurs, it is imperative that data and essential systems be able to be rapidly restored.

7. **The Management of the Technology Lifecycle**
Keep an eye on the lifecycles of both the software and the hardware components. When it's getting close to the end of a system's useful life, it's time to start planning for improvements or replacements.

8. **Comments From Users**

Collect information about end-users' experiences with the infrastructure by asking for comments from such users. This input has the potential to discover difficulties with usability as well as performance challenges.

Planning and Evaluation of Information Technology Infrastructure Using Best Practices

1. **Predictability**
   Establish an ongoing routine for the evaluation of the IT infrastructure. Performing regular assessments enables you to detect problems at an earlier stage, recognize trends, and take preventative measures.
2. **Creating Documentation**
   Ensure that an exhaustive documentation of your infrastructure is kept. This comprises an inventory of the gear, diagrams of the network, licensing for the applications, and the configuration settings.
3. **Concentrate on Safety**
   When doing your assessments, make safety your top priority. Maintain an up-to-date awareness of the most recent security threats, and make it a priority to safeguard your infrastructure with the most recent security solutions.
4. **Capacity to Grow**
   From the beginning, you should have scalability in mind. Make certain that your infrastructure can adapt to the changing demands of your firm without causing substantial disruptions.
5. **Mechanized Processes**
   Make use of automated tools in order to monitor, collect data, and provision resources. Automation has the potential to both increase productivity and lower the likelihood of mistakes being made by humans.
6. **Integration of Cloud Services**
   Think about incorporating cloud services into the overall strategy for your infrastructure. Cloud computing systems have the potential to offer scalability, flexibility, and cost effectiveness.
7. **Knowledge and experience**

Engage with information technology professionals who have expertise in the planning and evaluation of infrastructure. Their expertise can provide direction for your decisions and assist you in avoiding mistakes that are all too typical.

Planning and Evaluation Tools for Information Technology Infrastructure

1. **Instruments for Surveillance**
   Monitoring software like as Nagios, Zabbix, and SolarWinds are examples of tools that are helpful in keeping track of the performance and health of infrastructure components.
2. **Detection and Monitoring Devices**
   Nessus and OpenVAS are two examples of useful security scanning technologies that can assist in locating vulnerabilities and weak points in your system.
3. **Administration of Configurations**
   Automating configuration management and ensuring consistency across infrastructure components can be accomplished with the assistance of tools such as Puppet, Ansible, and Chef.
4. **Platforms for the Management of Cloud Resources**
   Platforms such as AWS Management Console and Azure Portal offer enterprises that make use of cloud services both visibility and control over the cloud's underlying resources.
5. **Application Software for Documentation**

Creating and maintaining documentation of your infrastructure can be made easier with the assistance of applications like Microsoft Visio, Lucidchart, and draw.io.

Planning and assessing your organization's information technology infrastructure in an effective manner are absolutely necessary in order to guarantee that your company's technological base will continue to be solid, productive, and in line with business goals. The ability to modify and improve one's infrastructure quickly enough to keep up with the rapid pace of technological advancement is becoming an increasingly valuable competitive advantage. Organizations can put themselves in

IT RESILIENCE

a position to prosper in a digital landscape that is always shifting by adhering to best practices and making effective use of the appropriate technologies. In the fast-paced world of information technology infrastructure, staying ahead of the competition requires regular inspections and proactive planning.

5.2 Lift-and-Shift vs. Re-architecture

Moving data and applications to the cloud is a necessary step for businesses that want to reap the benefits of cloud computing. When setting out on this trip, selecting the most appropriate migration strategy is one of the most important considerations that must be made. The "Lift-and-Shift" method and the "Re-architecture" method are two key methods that are frequently discussed. In this extensive guide, we will delve into the complexities of these two approaches, highlighting their differences, advantages, and considerations, with the purpose of assisting you in making an informed selection that is congruent with the objectives and resources of your company.

Migration Using Lift and Shift Techniques
Gains to Obtain:

Lift-and-Shift is often the quickest approach to move to the cloud, and it is also one of the simplest methods. It entails packaging up already-existing apps and transferring them to a cloud infrastructure without making any significant modifications. This is an excellent option for businesses who are looking for a swift relocation procedure.

Organizations can typically reduce their migration expenses by retaining their existing settings and refraining from investing in major restructuring. This helps them achieve more cost efficiency. With this strategy, there is no need for considerable rebuilding to take place.

Reduced Disruption Because the application code will not be significantly altered, there will be very little interference with the way the business now functions. It's possible that end-users won't even notice the move.

This approach has a lower potential for error than others because it does not call for significant modifications to the source code. It is an option for companies that want to evaluate the benefits of working in the cloud but don't want to make significant alterations to their existing infrastructure.

Taking into account:

Lift-and-Shift may not be able to fully leverage the benefits of cloud-native capabilities such as auto-scaling, serverless computing, and advanced data services. Despite the fact that it can bring you to the cloud rapidly, Lift-and-Shift may not be able to get you there as quickly.

Efficiency and Scalability: It is possible that existing programs have not been optimized for cloud computing, which could result in inefficient utilization of available resources and a lack of scalability.

Technological Debt: If you operate applications in the cloud without making any changes to them, you may find that over time you build technological debt. This may result in greater operational expenditures as well as issues with maintenance.

Applications continue to function in the same manner as before, which reduces the number of opportunities to innovate and take advantage of new technologies that the cloud makes available.

Migration Re-architecture (Rearchitecting) Re-architecture (Rearchitecting)

Gains to Obtain:

Re-architecture helps businesses to properly optimize their programs for use in cloud environments, which is essential for cloud optimization. This typically results in enhanced performance as well as cost efficiency and scalability.

Scalability and Flexibility: Cloud-native capabilities such as auto-scaling and serverless computing become accessible, which enables businesses to respond flexibly to changes in customer demand.

Potential for Innovation: In order to foster innovation, businesses should rethink and restructure their applications before embracing new cloud services such as machine learning, big data analytics, and IoT integration.

Reduced Accumulation of Technical Debt Because re-architected applications are constructed to be more effective and maintainable in the cloud, the amount of technical debt that is accumulated over time is reduced.

Taking into account:

Re-architecting is a complicated and time-consuming procedure that has the potential to interfere with the normal operations of an organization while it is being migrated. It calls for a considerable investment of resources and a high level of competence.

Increased Expenses: Because of the necessity of rebuilding and possibly the incorporation of new cloud services, this strategy typically results in increased initial expenditures.

Impact on Users Retraining of end-users may be necessary if significant modifications are made to the apps. During the shift, organizations have a responsibility to manage the expectations and experiences of their users.

Expertise Is Required: Re-architecting calls for a comprehensive comprehension of cloud technology as well as the particular requirements of the enterprise. The need for skilled architects and developers cannot be overstated.

Figuring Out the Best Strategy to Use

1. **Aims of the Company:**
   Choose the Lift-and-Shift method if speed and minimizing disruption to operations are two of your top concerns, and if you want to test the waters of the cloud without making a substantial financial investment.
   Re-architecture is the strategy you should choose if your company's objectives involve maximizing performance while also maximizing scalability and innovation. Give it some thought if you're prepared to dive headfirst into cloud-native capabilities.
2. **Existing Facilities and Infrastructure:**
   This strategy may be appropriate for you if you have a legacy

infrastructure that is difficult to rework or if you require a swift migration. Lift-and-Shift describes such an infrastructure.

Re-architecture: If your current architecture is ineffective and you are seeking for ways to improve it in the cloud, this strategy is a better fit for what you are looking to accomplish.

3. **The Availability of Resources:**

   The Lift-and-Shift method is less resource-intensive, which is beneficial if you have a restricted amount of both resources and knowledge.

   Re-architecture: This strategy may be beneficial in the long run if you already possess the appropriate resources and knowledge or are prepared to make an investment in acquiring them.

4. **Your Comfort Level With Risk:**

   Lift-and-Shift is a strategy that is typically deemed to have a lower risk because it does not involve significant changes to the source code. The level of risk that a company is willing to take can benefit from using this option.

   Re-architecture is a strategy that entails a higher level of risk because it calls for large changes to be made to applications. It is appropriate for businesses that are willing to take on larger risks in exchange for greater returns.

5. **Perspective on the Long Term:**

This strategy may be adequate for your needs if you are primarily concerned with a migration that takes place over a relatively short period of time with a minimum amount of disruption.

Re-architecture: If you have a long-term goal for your cloud-based infrastructure and want to utilize the full potential of cloud services, this method coincides with that vision. If you are interested in learning more, check out this article.

5.3 Managing Data Migration

In the data-driven world we live in today, efficient data management is absolutely necessary for organizations to not only thrive but also

IT RESILIENCE

continue to be competitive. The migration of data is an essential aspect of this process, which is frequently called for as a result of technological advancements, system replacements, or the implementation of new software. When it comes to managing data migration, the goal is not only to move data from one location to another; rather, it is to ensure the data's integrity, minimize disruptions, and adhere to data compliance rules. This all-encompassing reference examines data migration, including its significance, various methodologies, potential problems, and recommended best practices for ensuring a smooth and effective move.

Acquiring Knowledge of Data Migration
Changing over to a newer operating system or piece of software
Changing out outdated computer systems
Making the move to the cloud
Bringing together information from a variety of sources
Introducing cutting-edge software programs for commercial use
Regardless of the reasons behind the migration, it is vital to effectively migrate data in order to keep the data's integrity, accessibility, and security intact throughout the process.

The Importance of Performing Data Migrations

1. **The Quality and Integrity of the Data :**
   The migration of data presents a chance to improve data quality by sorting, cleaning, and organizing the data while it is in transit. Because of this, the data contained within the new system are guaranteed to be dependable, accurate, and consistent.
2. **Continuity of Business Operations:**
   Downtime and service interruptions are minimized to a minimum by a data transfer plan that is well-executed. During the entirety of the relocation procedure, it guarantees that access to vital data will be maintained.
3. **Effectiveness in Business Operations:**
   Improving operational efficiency can be accomplished by

migrating to more efficient systems or cloud platforms, which can also reduce expenses and demands placed on resources.

4. **Obligation to comply:**
   legislation concerning data protection and compliance must be adhered to during data transfer. Examples of such legislation include the General Data Protection Regulation (GDPR) and industry-specific standards. Failure to comply may result in legal repercussions as well as damage to one's reputation.

5. **Accessibility of the Data:**

During and after the migration, users should still be able to access and make use of the data. It is necessary to ensure the availability of data in order to maintain business continuity and make decisions.

Planning for the Migration of Data

1. **Complete Information Dump and Load:**
   This technique entails exporting all of the data that is contained within the source system, most of the time into a standardized format, and then importing it into the destination system. It is uncomplicated and appropriate for less extensive data sets; nevertheless, when used to extensive amounts of data, it can be time-consuming.

2. **ETL, which stands for "extract, transform, and load":**
   ETL, or extract, transform, and load, is a data migration approach that is commonly used to extract data from the source system, modify that data so that it fits the structure of the destination system, and then load that data into the new environment. The use of ETL technologies helps to automate this process, which in turn makes it more effective for handling complex data migrations.

3. **The Migration of Streaming Data:**
   In streaming data migration, data is continually transported from the source system to the destination system in real-time or near

real-time. Streaming data migration is also known as continuous data migration. This strategy is appropriate for situations in which the data must be continually updated.
4. **Migration of Data in Parallel :**
The pace of the migration process can be increased by the use of a technique known as parallel

   data migration, which includes transmitting data in many parallel streams. It works very well with large datasets but requires precise coordination in order to preserve the integrity of the data.
5. **The synchronization of the data:**

Synchronizing data guarantees that information in both the source system and the target system is accurate and up to date. Any alterations that are made in one system will immediately be reflected in the other. Database migrations and migrations from one cloud environment to another are common applications for this method.

Problems Associated with Data Migration

1. **The deletion or corruption of data:**
When migrating huge amounts of data, there is an increased likelihood that some or all of the data will become corrupted or lost throughout the process. To avoid these kinds of problems, thorough planning and validation are absolutely essential.
2. **Interruptions and Periods of Downtime:**
The process of migrating data might cause downtime or disruptions to the operations of an organization. It is essential to effectively manage this downtime and reduce the effects it has.
3. **Mapping of Data and Data Transformation:**
It's possible that the data will need to be mapped and converted before it can be used in the destination system. This process can be difficult, especially when working with different forms of data.
4. **Protecting the Data:**
It is critical to protect the confidentiality and security of data

during the relocation process. Breach of data security might have very serious repercussions.

5. **Obligation to comply:**
The migration of data must be done in accordance with any applicable data protection legislation as well as any sector-specific requirements. The failure to comply may have serious repercussions, both legally and monetarily.

6. **The Distribution of Resources:**

The movement of data necessitates the commitment of a substantial amount of resources, such as time, skill, and infrastructure. Inadequate resources might result in delays and even the cancellation of a project.

Best Methods for Data Transferring Practices

1. **Integrated and All-encompassing Planning:**
Start with an exhaustive migration plan that outlines your goals, dates, resources, and any potential problems that may arise. Make a plan for addressing errors and validating the data.

2. **Analysis of the Data:**
Carry out an exhaustive analysis of the data that is going to be moved. Find data that is unnecessary, out of date, or irrelevant and that may be archived or deleted to cut down on the amount of data that needs to be moved.

3. **Cleaning up the Data:**
Perform data cleaning to guarantee that the information is correct, consistent, and free of errors. This process can be automated with the use of data cleansing tools and scripts.

4. **Data Must Be Backed Up:**
Make sure you have backups of the data in the source system before you migrate them. This makes it possible to restore data in the case that there are problems with the migration.

5. **Mapping and Transforming the Data:**
The data will be mapped from the source system to the target

system, and any transformations that are required will be applied. This process can be made easier with the help of data mapping tools and scripts.

6. **Evaluation and Authentication:**
Before the migration can be finished, the data in the destination system needs to be tested and validated in great detail. Checks to validate the data ought to pick up on any inconsistencies or mistakes.

7. **Protecting the Data:**
Protect the data that is being migrated by putting in place stringent security measures. This involves the use of encryption, access controls, and the transport of data in a secure manner.

8. **The documentation includes:**
Throughout the entirety of the migration process, ensure that thorough documentation is kept. This comprises migration plans, data mapping, validation results, and the resolution of any problems that may have arisen.

9. **Communication with Users:**
Maintain communication with end users regarding the migration process, any potential disruptions, and any necessary steps they must take. The ability to communicate effectively helps to alleviate anxiety and enables a seamless transition.

10. **The Monitoring of Data**

After the migration, the data in the target system should be continuously monitored so that any problems may be found and fixed as soon as possible.

Tools for the Migration of Data

1. **Tools for ETL:**
ETL tools, which stand for "Extract, Transform, and Load," automate data migration processes like as data extraction,

transformation, and loading. Examples of ETL solutions include Informatica, Talend, and Apache Nifi.

2. **Services for migrating data to the cloud:**
The process of migrating data to the cloud can be made much easier by using the migration services offered by cloud providers. Data Migration Service on Amazon Web Services (AWS) and Google Cloud Data Transfer Service are two examples.

3. **Tools for the Migration of Databases:**
For the purpose of moving databases to new platforms, database-specific solutions such as AWS Database Migration Service and Oracle Data Pump were developed.

4. **Platforms for the Integration of Data:**

Real-time data streaming and integration are both possible with the assistance of data integration platforms such as Apache Kafka, Apache Nifi, and Microsoft Azure Data Factory.

The migration of data is a complicated and essential activity that can have a considerable influence on the data integrity, security, and operations of an organization. Investing in detailed preparation, adhering to data compliance standards, following best practices, and making use of the necessary tools and technologies are required of enterprises in order to guarantee a seamless and effective data migration.

Not only does a well-executed data transfer reduce the likelihood of disruptions and the loss of data, but it also improves the quality of the data and opens the door to enhanced decision-making and increased operational efficiency. Data migration will continue to play an essential part in the process of keeping businesses competitive and adaptive in a digital landscape that is constantly shifting as new technologies emerge.

5.4 Cost Considerations in Cloud Migration

Migration to the cloud is a strategic step for many companies due to the cloud's promise of cost savings, scalability, and agility. To ensure a smooth and profitable transfer to the cloud, it is essential to have a thorough awareness of the complexities involved in cloud migration costs.

IT RESILIENCE

In this extensive guide, we will investigate the primary cost concerns associated with migrating to the cloud. These concerns will include a discussion of the elements that have an impact on expenses, as well as cost-cutting techniques and effective management procedures for cloud migration budgets.

The Financial Implications of Migrating to the Cloud

Moving to the cloud can result in significant cost savings, but doing so is not without its share of logistical challenges. It is essential to have a solid grasp of the dynamics of the costs before making any judgments.

Contrast Initial Expenses with Ongoing Expenses:

Initial Migration Expenses: These are the costs that are associated with planning, training, and the initial migration activities, such as re-hosting, re-platforming, or re-architecting applications. Upfront Costs: These are the expenses that are associated with first migration activities.

After the migration has been finished, ongoing costs will come into play. These ongoing costs include subscriptions to cloud services, data storage, network bandwidth, and operational fees.

Model Based on Paying as You Go:

Pay-as-you-go pricing is the standard mode of operation for cloud service providers. This means that businesses only pay for the resources and services that they actually use. When compared to typical on-premises data centers, which frequently fail to make optimal use of their capabilities, this can result in significant cost savings.

The ability to predict costs:

Cloud service providers often provide their customers with monitoring tools and cost calculators that assist businesses in estimating and keeping tabs on their expenditures, so making it simpler to plan for and control costs.

Ability to scale up:

Because of the scalability of the cloud, organizations are able to adapt their resource allocation in response to changes in demand. This allows them to avoid overprovisioning and the associated costs of paying for wasted capacity.

Possibilities for Creative Effort:

Cloud computing enables users to access cutting-edge services such as artificial intelligence, machine learning, and analytics for large amounts of data. Although these services have the potential to spur innovation, using them will result in higher expenses.

Cost Aspects That Should Be Considered When Moving to the Cloud

1. **A Strategy for Emigration**

   The migration strategy that is used has a considerable impact on the costs. The lift-and-shift method, also known as re-hosting, is typically the quickest and least expensive option, but re-architecting can be more resource intensive and expensive, but it can result in cost savings over the long term.

2. **The Cost of Data Transfer:**

   Data transfer fees may be incurred whenever data is moved from servers located on-premises to those located in the cloud. These expenses are determined by the volume of data transferred as well as the pricing scheme utilized by the supplier.

3. **Calculating the Resource Needs:**

   It is essential to ensure that the cloud resources, such as virtual machines and storage, are sized appropriately. When evaluating the needs, it is important not to overestimate them because this might result in higher expenses. However, underestimating can lead to problems with performance.

4. **Costs Related to Software and Licensing:**

   The budget for the migration should include for the fees associated with purchasing licenses for software, databases, and operating systems. Bring-your-own-license (BYOL) alternatives are provided by a number of cloud providers, whereas usage fees are collected by others.

5. **Education and the Acquiring of New Abilities:**

   For efficient cloud management, it is vital to make investments

in the training and upskilling of your information technology personnel. If you ignore this facet, it could lead to inefficiency as well as a rise in costs.
6. **The Cost of Storing Data:**
The cost of storing data in the cloud can vary widely due to the availability of multiple storage tiers at a variety of price points. It is absolutely crucial to handle data storage effectively in order to prevent spending money that is not necessary.
7. **The costs of the network and the bandwidth:**
Especially for applications that receive a lot of traffic, the transmission of data and utilization of bandwidth can result in additional costs. Controlling costs effectively requires first and foremost the optimization of network usage.
8. **Backing up and Recovering Your Data:**
The implementation of data backup and recovery solutions is necessary for maintaining business continuity; nevertheless, there are associated costs connected with this requirement. In order for organizations to have efficient expense management, they need to review their backup and recovery strategy.
9. **Tools for the Optimization of Costs:**

Numerous cloud providers make available cost optimization solutions that, in addition to delivering insights and recommendations, help to cut costs. When enterprises make use of these technologies, it can help them save money.

Strategies for Saving Money When Migrating to the Cloud

1. **Appropriate Sizing of Cloud Resources:**
Conduct resource utilization analysis on a regular basis to guarantee that your resources are the appropriate size. The process of rightsizing can result in significant cost savings.
2. **Instances that Have Been Reserved:**
When a business makes a commitment to use cloud resources

for an extended length of time through reserved instances, the cloud provider will frequently provide the organization a discount. These pledges have the potential to result in significant cost reductions.

3. **Observable Examples:**

   Spot instances are offered at a price that is significantly lower than the price of on-demand instances. Even though they can be stopped at any time, they are ideal for non-critical workloads that involve processing in batches.

4. **Computing Without Servers:**

   Serverless computing solutions, such as Amazon Web Services Lambda and Microsoft Azure Functions, dynamically scale resources to meet demand. This feature can result in significant cost reductions for applications whose workloads vary.

5. **The data tiering system:**

   Implement solutions for data tiering, which involve moving data that is accessed less frequently to storage tiers that have lower costs. This lowers the costs associated with data storage.

6. **Automatic Leveling:**

   Utilize auto-scaling features to modify resource capacity according to demand, and use these capabilities effectively. This guarantees that resources are utilized effectively while simultaneously lowering expenses during times of low demand.

7. **Maximize the Efficiency of Data Transfer:**

   Reduce the amount of data that needs to be transported in order to cut down on the associated expenses of data transfer. This can be accomplished by maximizing the efficiency of data transfer methods, such as by compressing the data or performing incremental data transfers.

8. **Conducting Frequent Cost Audits:**

   Maintain a constant vigil over cloud costs and make use of the cost management tools offered by cloud service providers in order to locate and address areas of wasteful spending.

IT RESILIENCE

9. **Turn Off Any Resources That Aren't Being Used:**
   Locate the resources that are not currently being utilized, and then turn them off. This covers both the development and testing environments, which, when they are not being used, should be powered off.
10. **the process of consolidation**

Wherever it is possible to do so, consolidate your workloads and apps. Saving money on costs associated with inefficient resource consumption can be accomplished by cutting down on the number of instances and services.

Guidelines for Efficiently Managing the Expenses Involved in Cloud Migration

1. **Establish a Transparent Budget:**
   Create a detailed budget that takes into account all of the costs associated with the relocation. Include a cushion to account for unforeseen expenses.
2. **Carry out a Cost Benefit Analysis:**
   Before beginning the relocation process, a complete cost analysis should be performed, taking
   into account all relevant elements. The entirety of the project lifecycle ought to be included in this study.
3. **Monitoring of Expenditures and Provision of Reports:**
   Put in place the necessary tools and procedures to enable real-time monitoring and reporting of costs. Because of this, proactive cost management is possible.
4. **Framework for the Governance of Costs**
   Create a framework for cost governance that outlines duties, policies, and procedures for managing cloud-based expenditures.
5. **Responsibility for Costs and Chargebacks:**
   Establish procedures for cost allocation and chargeback in order

to promote accountability for cloud computing expenditures by attributing them to certain departments or projects.

6. **Optimization in a Constant Way:**
   Maintain a routine for analyzing and improving cloud resources and services. Cloud environments are always changing, thus it is vital to continuously optimize in order to maintain cost management.

7. **Ongoing Inspections:**
   It is important to perform periodical audits in order to discover areas of cost inefficiency and to make any necessary improvements.

8. **Training that is Provided at a Low Cost:**
   Investing in efficient training for IT staff will help them acquire competence in cloud computing and maximize the use of available resources.

9. **Policy Regarding Right-Sizing:**
   Implementing a right-sizing policy will help guarantee that available resources are utilised effectively and that unnecessary expansion is avoided.

10. **Being Aware of the Cost:**

In order to raise awareness of costs throughout the organization and ensure that all stakeholders are aware of the financial implications of their activities, promote cost awareness.

Cost control during the migration to the cloud is one of the most essential components of a smooth cloud transfer. Cloud migration comes with a variety of financial advantages; nevertheless, it must be meticulously planned, followed by an in-depth cost analysis, and continuously monitored to ensure that expenses are kept under control.

Organizations are able to harness the cost effectiveness, scalability, and agility of the cloud while keeping a budget that is in alignment with their financial goals and resources if they examine the cost variables, apply initiatives for cost savings, and follow best practices. Effective cost management is a critical component of successful cloud migration in today's ever changing cloud computing environment.

Chapter 6

Building Resilient Applications

The need for apps that are resistant to failure has never been greater than it is in the frenetic digital landscape of today. A system's resilience measures its capacity to respond effectively to novel challenges while preserving its fundamental capabilities. Building apps that are resilient is vital if you want to provide a seamless experience for your customers, reduce the amount of downtime your business experiences, and safeguard your organization's reputation. This in-depth book will delve into the idea of application resilience, investigate the significance of it, and present actionable insights and best practices for constructing software that is fault-tolerant and robust.

Before we begin:
Acquiring Knowledge of the Applications of Resilience

Applications are considered resilient if they can continue to function well in spite of unforeseen obstacles, such as malfunctioning hardware or software, unexpected increases in user traffic, or attacks from the outside world. These problems might present themselves in a variety of ways, including as server failures, interruptions in network service, or abrupt spikes in the number of users. Failure is an inevitable part of life,

IT RESILIENCE

and building resilience is not about avoiding it but learning to deal with it and go on.

The Value of Being Able to Bounce Back

User Experience: Unplanned downtime or decreased performance can lead to disgruntled users, which in turn can result in a damaged reputation for the business. Applications that are resilient guarantee that users may access and use your services without experiencing any interruptions.

Maintaining business continuity is essential given the potential for application failures to cause large monetary losses. The effects of failures are lessened and corporate activities are kept running smoothly thanks to resilience.

Applications that are resilient typically have a higher capacity for scaling. As a result of their capacity to adjust to growing demand without succumbing to the pressure, they are ideally suited for expansion.

Resilience can also serve to improve one's level of security. Systems that are more resistant to the occurrence of failures are typically better able to endure assaults and intrusions.

Components Crucial to the Formation of Resilient Applications

Tolerance for Errors

The capacity of a system to continue operating normally despite the presence of errors or breakdowns is referred to as its fault tolerance. This entails designing your program to handle failures in a graceful manner, regardless of whether they are brought on by software flaws, hardware issues, or unanticipated events.

Duplication of effort

The concept of redundancy refers to the practice of producing duplicates of essential parts or services contained within an application. The use of redundancy can assist ensure that if one component of your system fails, another can take over without any disruption, so minimizing any downtime that may occur.

Adjusting the Loads

The incoming network traffic is split up and distributed over a number of servers or instances when load balancing is used. By doing so, we assure that not a single server will become overloaded, which improves both performance and dependability.

Keeping an Eye Out and Sounding the Alarm

It is absolutely necessary to monitor the health and performance of your application. You are able to respond proactively to problems by continuously monitoring important metrics and setting up alerts. This allows you to respond to problems before they have an effect on users.

Resilience Methods and Techniques

Breakers in the circuit

In a distributed system, circuit breakers are an example of a pattern that can be used to handle faults. They have the ability to stop a service from continually attempting to carry out an operation that has a high probability of failing, which helps conserve resources and prevents failures from snowballing.

Attempting Again Mechanisms

It is typical practice to try again to complete operations that have failed while dealing with temporary failures. In the event that an operation fails, the system has the ability to automatically restart the process, typically with increasing intervals of time between each attempt, until it either succeeds or exceeds a predetermined limit on the number of times it may try again.

Declination with Elegance and Charm

Building programs in such a way that they can continue to function, albeit with decreased capabilities, even when some components fail or when they are under a heavy strain is an example of graceful degradation. Users will still be able to access important functionality as a result of this, despite the fact that some non-essential functions may be inaccessible.

Microservices and the Ability to Adapt

Microservices architecture has the potential to improve system resilience by isolating individual components. This makes it simpler to recognize and address problems impacting a particular service without having an effect on the whole system. Nevertheless, it also presents obstacles, such as network connectivity and service discovery, which call for careful control on the part of the administrator.

Developing Applications for the Web That Are Resilient
Patterns of Design that Promote Resilience

A number of different design patterns, such as the Bulkhead pattern (which involves isolating elements of the system to prevent one failure from affecting others), the Timeout pattern (which involves imposing time limitations for operations), and the Retry pattern (which was described before), can be utilized to strengthen the resilience of a web application.

Problems with Web Services and How to Fix Them

The handling of failures in online services includes the employment of solutions such as request queuing to manage spikes in traffic, circuit breakers to protect services from high load, and rate limitation to avoid service abuse.

The Stability of Data

Data is a key part of online applications, and ensuring its durability is one of the most important things developers can do. This include performing regular backups, replicating data, and making procedures for data recovery in the event that data is lost.

Best Practices for Constructing Applications That Are Resilient

Put redundancy at the top of your list of priorities since it is your safety net. Always have a backup of your most important data and services, so that if one goes down, you can switch to the other.

Automate Recovery: When problems occur, manual intervention should be kept to a minimum as much as possible by using automated recovery techniques. Scaling and failover procedures that are automated are included in this.

Utilize a Load Balancing Strategy: Load balancing helps to distribute traffic equally and can avoid individual servers from becoming overburdened.

Establish a System of Comprehensive Monitoring: Make use of various monitoring tools in order to keep track of performance and health measures. Set up notifications so that your team is immediately informed of any problems.

Utilize Chaos Engineering: Chaos engineering entails introducing faults into your system on purpose in order to test its ability to withstand them. It can assist you in pinpointing areas of your application that need improvement.

Create a Plan for Disaster Recovery In order to recover from catastrophic setbacks or data breaches, you need to create a plan for disaster recovery that describes how to do so.

Training and Documentation: Make certain that your staff has received adequate training on resiliency techniques and that there is extensive documentation for recovery procedures.

Regular Testing: You should perform load testing, stress testing, and disaster recovery drills on a regular basis in order to test the resilience of your application.

Implement Security Measures To defend your application from risks that could threaten its resilience, such as distributed denial of service (DDoS) assaults or data breaches, you should implement security measures.

Continuously Improving Resilience: Resilience is a Process That Never Stops. Maintaining an ongoing assessment and improvement plan for your application's resiliency is critical as your software undergoes continual development and new difficulties emerge.

6.1 Developing Cloud-Native Applications

Applications that were built specifically for the cloud are currently at the forefront of modern software development. They are created with the intention of delivering services that are scalable, resilient, and highly available by capitalizing on the power and flexibility of cloud computing. In this extensive book, we will discuss what it means to develop cloud-native applications, the fundamental ideas and best practices involved, as well as how these applications are revolutionizing the

IT RESILIENCE

way that we construct and distribute software in an era dominated by the cloud.

What exactly are applications that are native to the cloud?

Microservices Architecture: Cloud-native applications are often constructed utilizing a microservices architecture, in which the application is broken down into small, independently deployable services that communicate with each other via application programming interfaces (APIs). The flexibility and scalability of this design are improved.

Containerization: Containerization tools like Docker play an important part in cloud-native application development. They encapsulate the application code as well as the runtime and any dependencies, which makes it much simpler to deploy and maintain applications in a variety of cloud settings.

Orchestration: Container orchestration platforms, such as Kubernetes, are frequently used by cloud-native applications. These platforms help to automate the deployment, scaling, and management of containerized services. The use of orchestration helps guarantee that applications have a high level of availability and are able to manage fluctuating workloads.

Scalability refers to the ability of cloud-native apps to grow horizontally, which means that new instances of a service can be added to accommodate greater traffic if necessary. This scalability is absolutely necessary in order to fulfill the requirements of modern, ever-changing workloads.

These applications are designed to be resistant to the effects of any failures that may occur. They are able to autonomously recover from errors in either the hardware or the software without significantly interrupting service.

Continuous Delivery and DevOps: Cloud-native development places an emphasis on collaboration between the teams responsible for development and operations. Automation, continuous integration, and continuous delivery (CI/CD) pipelines are utilized in order to rapidly and dependably supply updates.

Cloud-native applications are frequently built to be stateless, which indicates that they do not retain session data or user state on the server. This is because cloud-native applications are hosted on the cloud. Due to the fact that every instance may accept requests, this makes scaling and recovery much simpler.

The Fundamentals of Building Applications That Are Native to the Cloud

1. **Agnosticism Regarding Clouds**
   Cloud-native applications should be built with cloud-agnostic architecture in mind, which means they are compatible with a variety of cloud service providers. This strategy protects you from being locked into a single vendor and gives you the freedom to select the cloud services that are most suitable for your unique requirements. Utilizing standard application programming interfaces (APIs), containerization, and open-source technologies are the means through which cloud agnosticism can be accomplished.

2. **Application program interfaces (APIs) and microservices**
   The implementation of a cloud-native architecture must first begin with the use of microservices. Each microservice ought to have its own well-defined application programming interface (API), which makes it possible for the services to be developed, deployed, and scaled independently. This architecture also supports resilience, which means that the failure of a single microservice need not necessarily effect the application as a whole.

3. **Containers and Orchestration in Cloud Computing**
   The process of application packaging and deployment is made easier by containers, particularly Docker. You are possible to manage containers on a massive scale by utilizing container orchestration solutions such as Kubernetes. Your application will be highly available and resilient as a result of the automation of

IT RESILIENCE

deployment, scaling, load balancing, and self-healing that they provide.

4. **Computerization of infrastructure and the use of code for it**
Take advantage of automation in each and every stage of the lifecycle of your application. In order to define and provision resources, you should make use of infrastructure as code (IaC) tools such as Terraform or AWS CloudFormation.
Automate the processes of testing, deployment, and scaling to produce development and operations that are both faster and more dependable.

5. **Continuous Integration and Continuous Delivery (often abbreviated as CI/CD)**
Automating the testing, building, and deployment of your application can be accomplished by putting in place CI/CD pipelines. By ensuring that new features and bug fixes are sent to production in a timely and consistent manner, CI/CD helps to shorten the amount of time that passes between when changes are made to the code and when users can access the updated version.

6. **Services for Those Without a State**
Scaling stateless services and recovering from failures are far simpler endeavors. If you want your services to remain stateless, you should avoid storing user-specific data on the server and instead choose to manage sessions using stateless session management or external data storage.

7. **Observability and Methods of Monitoring**
Applications built specifically for the cloud must to be outfitted with monitoring and observability instruments. Utilize software applications like as Prometheus, Grafana, or AWS CloudWatch in order to gather, examine, and report on metrics, logs, and traces. This data assists in the diagnosis of problems, the enhancement of performance, and the guarantee of a great user experience.

8. **Safety Measures in Every Layer**
From the very beginning of the development process all the way

through, security should be a top focus. Implement industry-recognized best practices for application security at each level of the application, including the application code, container images, APIs, and infrastructure. Implement controls for identity and access management (IAM) to limit users' access, and encrypt data to keep sensitive information secure.

9. **Engineering of Chaotic Systems**

In the field of chaos engineering, failures are purposefully introduced on purpose in order to evaluate an application's resilience. You may make your system more robust and able to recover from unanticipated problems if you take the proactive step of recognizing the weaknesses that exist within it.

10. **Management of the Data**

Think about the data storage and management processes involved in your cloud-native application. Select the proper data storage options and put backup, replication, and data recovery plans into action in order to guarantee the availability and integrity of the data.

The Advantages of Developing Applications That Are Native to the Cloud

Scalability refers to the ability of cloud-native apps to easily scale up or down in response to changes in user demand. This scalability is absolutely necessary for today's ever-changing workloads.

Resilience refers to the ability of cloud-native applications to resist disruptions and swiftly get back up and running afterward. Because of this, there will be very little downtime, and the overall experience for users will be improved.

A Shorter Time to Market Automation, continuous integration and continuous delivery, as well as microservices, all make it possible to build and release new features and upgrades more quickly.

Cloud-native applications are more resource-efficient than traditional ones because they may employ their available resources in a dynamic manner and scale back their operations during times of low demand.

Cost Reductions: Cloud-native applications can lead to cost reductions by optimizing resource utilization and requiring users to pay only for the resources they actually use.

Increased Collaboration DevOps approaches encourage increased collaboration between development teams and operations teams, which ultimately results in more streamlined procedures for both development and operations.

Advantages in Flexibility and Selection: Because cloud-native apps are not bound to any one cloud service provider, you have the freedom to select the cloud services that are most suitable to your requirements.

Enhanced Security Every layer of the program has the potential to incorporate security best practices, such as encryption and automation, which will make the application more safe overall.

Concerns and Things to Take Into Account

There are a number of problems and factors to take into account while designing cloud-native applications, despite the fact that the benefits of doing so are enormous.

The adoption of cloud-native techniques and technologies can be accompanied by a steep learning curve, and this is true for both the operations teams and the developers.

The implementation of microservices, containerization, and orchestration all have the potential to make the development process more complicated.

Inadequate resource provisioning or a lack of cost management might lead to unanticipated charges, despite the fact that cloud-native applications can be very cost-effective.

There is a risk of being locked in with a single vendor while using some cloud services, despite ongoing attempts to promote cloud neutrality. When utilizing proprietary services, exercise extreme caution.

Concerns Regarding Security The cloud-native architecture brings up some new concerns regarding security. Make sure that you handle concerns about security at each successive level of your application.

Integration of Legacy Systems The process of integrating cloud-native applications with pre-existing legacy systems can be difficult. Think about how all of these different systems will work together.

Compliance and Regulations: Ensure that your cloud-native applications are compliant with the regulations that govern the industry as well as any data protection legislation that may apply.

Use Cases for Applications Built Natively for the Cloud

Web apps: Web apps take advantage of the scalability and robustness of cloud-native architecture, which ensures a seamless user experience even when there is a surge in the volume of website traffic.

API Services: Cloud-native microservices are perfect for establishing API services that are scalable and adaptable and can manage a high volume of queries. This is because cloud-native microservices are built to run on the cloud.

Applications for the Internet of Things (IoT) The ability to manage huge data streams and provide real-time processing and analysis are essential capabilities for applications for the Internet of Things (IoT), which rely on cloud-native technologies.

E-commerce Platforms: Since cloud-native applications are a natural fit for e-commerce sites, which require scalability to meet seasonal and promotional traffic increases, cloud-native applications are a good choice.

Cloud-native solutions are utilized in the process of delivering multimedia material to audiences all over the world in a dependable and time-efficient manner.

Data Analytics: Cloud-native apps are able to provide the necessary processing power and storage scalability for workloads that are heavily dependent on data.

In today's fast changing technological landscape, businesses who want to maintain their competitive edge should seriously consider the benefits of cloud-native application development. Businesses have the ability to develop software that is not only highly accessible, scalable, and resilient but also efficient and cost-effective if they adopt cloud-native principles such as microservices, containerization, orchestration, and automation. These principles are included in the cloud-native framework.

The benefits of designing cloud-native apps, such as faster time to market, increased collaboration, and flexibility, make it an appealing strategy for the development of modern software, despite the fact that there are hurdles to overcome and issues to address. Cloud-native applications will play a crucial part in determining the direction that software development and deployment will take in the future as cloud computing continues to make strides forward.

6.2 Microservices, Containers, and Serverless Computing

Microservices, Containers, and Serverless Computing are three important paradigms that have emerged as game-changers in the ever-evolving landscape of application development. Each of these paradigms has the potential to transform the way applications are developed. Each of these technologies carries with it a unique set of benefits and has exerted a significant influence on the manner in which modern applications are conceived, created, and put into use. In this in-depth tutorial, we will investigate the three mainstays of contemporary software architecture, discuss the relevance of each, and go through the major factors to take into account when making a decision between them.

The Microservices Provide the Building Blocks for Modular Systems

1. **Capacity to Grow**

   Granular scalability is made possible by using microservices. Instead of scaling the entire application, you might choose to increase the resources allocated to certain services that are experiencing high demand. This leads to the most efficient use of available resources.

2. **Adaptability**
   Each microservice can be built using the technology stack that is most appropriate for the specific purpose it will do. Because of this flexibility, developers are able to select the appropriate tools and frameworks for the task at hand, which results in services that are both effective and specialized.
3. **Improvements in the Localization of Defects**
   Microservices are neither connected to or dependent upon one another. Even if one of the services fails or runs into problems, this does not necessarily have an effect on the program as a whole. Because of its isolation, the system is more resilient and tolerant of errors.
4. **Development Using Agile Methods**
   Agile development approaches can benefit from using microservices. It is possible for teams to work on specific services independently, which enables development, testing, and deployment to occur more quickly.
5. **Delivering on a Continuous Basis**

Continuous delivery (CD) is simplified when microservices are used as the building blocks. It is possible to deploy updates and new features on a more frequent basis while causing only minor disturbances to the program as a whole.

Adopting microservices does, however, come with some obstacles, such as additional complexity in managing the inter-service communication, the need for consistent data, and the requirement for effective monitoring and governance. These challenges may be overcome, though.

Containers are the environments that are portable while remaining consistent.

1. **Stability of behavior**
   Containers guarantee that environments remain consistent

throughout the development and production processes. The issue of "it works on my machine" will no longer be an issue because the same thing that works on a developer's laptop will work the same way in a production environment.

2. **Transportability**

   Containers offer a high degree of portability. You can use the same container image to execute applications on a variety of platforms, such as on-premises servers, virtual machines, and the cloud services provided by a number of different companies.

3. **Efficient Use of Resources**

   Containers make better use of available resources than the more conventional virtual machines (VMs). They do this by sharing the kernel of the operating system that is running on the host machine, which minimizes overhead and makes it possible to run several containers on a single host.

4. **Instantaneous Deployment**

   Containers may be started and terminated in a short amount of time, making them an excellent choice for applications that call for rapid scalability or are components of continuous integration and continuous delivery (CI/CD) pipelines.

5. **Being on Your Own**

Applications are kept from interfering with one another by virtue of the level of isolation that is afforded by containers. This is essential for both the management of resources and the safety of the environment.

Docker is currently the most widely used containerization technology, and container orchestration solutions such as Kubernetes have seen considerable adoption for managing containers in production environments. Scaling, load balancing, and application changes can all be done automatically thanks to Kubernetes.

However, there are also drawbacks associated with containers, such as a higher learning curve for developers who are new to the technology and the potential for increased complexity when maintaining containerized applications at scale.

Computing without servers is a paradigm shift toward event-driven, cost-effective computing.

1. **Efficient Use of Resources**
   The requirement to provide and maintain servers is removed from the equation when you use serverless computing because you only have to pay for the computing resources that are utilized during the function's execution. When used to applications that experience varying workloads, this cost model may prove to be quite cost-effective.
2. **Capacity to Grow**
   Serverless solutions automatically scale functionality to manage multiple requests at the same time. Your application will be able to manage any load by automatically creating more instances of the function in proportion to the amount of traffic it receives.
3. **Decreased Costs Associated with Operation**
   The cloud provider is responsible for managing the server infrastructure, keeping the operating system up to date, and applying any necessary security patches. It is possible for developers to concentrate on developing code, which results in quicker development cycles.
4. **Architecture that is Driven by Events**
   Because serverless computing is fundamentally event-driven, it is ideally suited for use in applications that either require asynchronous processing or must react in real time to incoming events.
5. **Execution without a State**

It is the nature of functions to be stateless, which means that they do not store any information from one invocation to the next. The architecture encourages both ease of use and expansion of capacity.

IT RESILIENCE

When it comes to particular use cases, such as online APIs, real-time data processing, and automated processes, serverless computing is a fantastic option to consider. Due to the fact that most serverless systems impose constraints on the amount of time that a process may run, it is not a good fit for applications that need to run for an extended period of time.

Figuring Out the Best Strategy to Use

1. **The Complicated Nature of the Application**

   Microservices are an ideal solution for complex systems that require a wide range of technologies and contain several components.

   Containers are adaptable to a broad variety of applications, ranging from simple single-service designs to sophisticated multi-service architectures.

   Serverless computing is ideal for straightforward, stateless, event-driven programs that are amenable to being partitioned into a number of smaller services.

2. **Administration of Resources**

   It is necessary to actively manage the resources of the infrastructure in order to scale microservices.

   Containers provide a balance between manual control and automated processes, which enables efficient management of available resources.

   Serverless computing eliminates the requirement to supply and maintain servers through the use of an abstract resource management system.

3. **The sensitivity to latency**

   Because microservices offer greater control over latency, applications that must adhere to stringent latency constraints can utilize them successfully.

   Containers offer good control but may have somewhat higher latency than microservices due to the overhead of the container

runtime. Microservices have been shown to be more efficient.

Serverless: Suitable for applications that require just moderate amounts of latency, while it is possible that it is not the optimal choice for applications that require extremely low amounts of latency.

4. **The Difference Between Event-Driven and Always-On**

   Microservices are always-on and continuously running services that are well-suited for software applications that demand high levels of availability.

   Containers are useful because they offer flexibility for event-driven as well as always-on applications.

   Serverless computing is perfect for event-driven applications, which run their code only in reaction to the occurrence of certain events.

5. **Considerations Regarding the Budget and the Costs**

   When using microservices, you will need to manage the underlying infrastructure, which, when optimized, might result in cost reductions but may also demand greater administration effort from you.

   Containers offer flexibility in resource distribution, which has the ability to optimize costs. Despite this, infrastructure management is still required for containers.

   Because you only pay for the resources that are needed during the function's execution, serverless computing is typically more cost-effective for applications that have variable workloads.

6. **Knowledge Already Acquired**

Microservices call for specialized knowledge in the administration of infrastructure and services.

To work with containers, you need to be conversant with the technologies of containerization and orchestration.

Developers that have prior expertise working with serverless platforms and programming can access serverless environments.

6.3 Designing for Failure and Recovery

In the modern digital landscape, where high availability and smooth user experiences are of the utmost importance, designing for failure and recovery has emerged as an essential component of application development. It is necessary to construct systems that are resilient, meaning they can endure, adapt to, and recover from failures. This in-depth guide examines the significance of "designing for failure," as well as the fundamental concepts and industry standards that should be followed when developing resilient applications that can recover normally from unforeseen problems.

The Necessity of Being Able to Bounce Back

Complexity is something that is built into modern programs, particularly ones that run in the cloud. They are dependent on a wide variety of interrelated components, ranging from infrastructure and networking to databases and services provided by third parties. Failures are not an issue of if, but rather when, they will occur within this complex web of dependencies. The smooth running of your application may be jeopardized by unforeseen occurrences such as malfunctioning hardware or software, problems with the network, or abrupt increases in the volume of traffic.

1. **The Experience of the User**
   Users may become frustrated as a result of the application being unavailable or performing poorly. Users will continue to have a favorable experience overall if your services are resilient enough to withstand disruptions and allow them to keep using them.
2. **Continuity of business operations**
   There is a potential for severe financial loss as well as damage to your organization's brand when an outage occurs. The effects of failures are lessened and corporate activities are kept running smoothly thanks to resilience.
3. **Capacity to Grow**
   Applications that are resilient are typically more scalable. As a

result of their capacity to adjust to growing demand without succumbing to the pressure, they are ideally suited for expansion.

4. **Safekeeping**

   It is possible for resilience to improve security. Systems that are more resistant to the occurrence of failures are typically better able to endure assaults and intrusions.

5. **Obligation to comply**

Regulatory requirements for business continuity and catastrophe recovery can be found across many different industries. It is very necessary to design for failure and recovery in order to satisfy these compliance standards.

Principles to Consider When Designing for Both Success and Failure

1. **Embrace the Concept of Redundancy**

   The concept of redundancy refers to the practice of producing duplicates of essential parts or services contained within an application. Because of this redundancy, even if one component of your system fails, another may take over without any disruption, which will cut down on any downtime. You might, for instance, have numerous database servers that are able to handle read and write requests, or load balancers that spread traffic over multiple application instances. Both of these are examples of common architectures.

2. **Make sure you have fault tolerance in place.**

   The ability of a system to continue running, albeit with diminished capability, despite the presence of faults or failures is what is meant by the term "fault tolerance." Your program should be designed so that it can gracefully handle errors. In order to ensure that the system can endure failures without causing catastrophic results, it is important to implement failover techniques as well as measures such as retries and circuit breakers.

IT RESILIENCE

3. **Recuperation Through Automation**

   Automate recovery procedures as much as possible to reduce the amount of time spent manually responding to errors. Your application can automatically adapt to changing conditions and recover from problems with the help of automated scaling and failover mechanisms. This eliminates the need for human intervention.

4. **Observe and Sound the Alarm**

   It is absolutely necessary to do in-depth monitoring of the health and performance of your application. Maintain a consistent monitoring schedule for critical indicators such as resource utilization, response times, and error rates. In order to facilitate prompt action in response to problems, you should configure alerts that will notify your team whenever the aforementioned metrics vary from permissible ranges.

5. **Take Exams and Get Ready**

   Load testing, stress testing, and disaster recovery drills should be performed on your application on a regular basis to ensure its resilience. The results of these tests will assist you determine where your system is lacking and whether or not it is able to recover properly from errors.

6. **Planning for a Graceful Decay in Appearance**

   The process of designing your application to continue running with reduced capabilities in the event that certain components fail or when it is under to excessive demand is referred to as graceful degradation. It makes sure that users can still access crucial functionality even if some other features that aren't as important aren't available.

7. **Make a Plan for Responding to Emergencies**

Create an all-encompassing disaster recovery plan that details how to get back up and running after severe setbacks, data breaches, or other types of catastrophic events. Conduct regular checks to ensure that this plan is carrying out as intended.

Best Practices for Constructing Applications That Are Resilient

1. **Give Redundancy Highest Priority**
   Your fallback plan is called redundancy. It is essential to create multiple copies of vital services and data so that, in the event that one fails, the other can take over effortlessly. Redundancy can be accomplished in a number of ways, such as through the use of database replication, server clusters, or failover techniques.

2. **Implement Robotic Process Automation for Recovery**
   You can reduce the amount of time your application is down by automating its recovery. Implement auto-scaling so that resources are adjusted based on demand, and set up automated failover procedures so that backup systems are switched over in the event that the primary systems fail.

3. **Ensure that the load is evenly distributed.**
   The incoming network traffic is split up and distributed over a number of servers or instances when load balancing is used. By doing so, we assure that not a single server will become overloaded, which improves both performance and dependability. Load balancers also have the ability to automatically redirect traffic away from instances that have failed.

4. **Establish All-Encompassing Observational Measures**
   Make use of monitoring tools in order to keep a constant eye on the performance as well as the health of your application. Set up alerts that will warn your team of issues in a proactive manner so that you may address them before they have an effect on users.

5. **Employ methods of chaos engineering**
   In the field of chaos engineering, failures are purposefully introduced on purpose so that your system's resilience may be evaluated. It can assist you in locating areas of your application that

require improvement, allowing you to take preventative measures in this regard.

6. **Precautions to Take for Safety**

    Put in place security precautions to shield your application from dangers that could weaken its resistance. This includes protections against assaults known as distributed denial of service (DDoS), as well as data encryption and detection of intrusions.

7. **Undergo Routine Examinations**

    Load testing, stress testing, and disaster recovery drills should be performed on your application on a regular basis to ensure its resilience. The results of these tests will assist determine whether or not your system is able to recover properly from errors and operate effectively under a variety of different circumstances.

8. **Instructional Materials and Documentation**

    Make certain that your team has received adequate training in resiliency methods and that there is thorough documentation of recovery procedures. In times of crisis, having protocols that have been thoroughly documented is absolutely necessary.

9. **Ongoing and Constant Improvement**

Building resilience is a process that never ends. Maintaining an ongoing assessment and improvement plan for your application's resiliency is critical as your software undergoes continual development and new difficulties emerge.

The Obstacles Faced When Designing for Both Success and Failure

Implementing resilience measures can add complexity to your program, which in turn makes it more difficult to administer and maintain.

Cost: Redundancy and fault-tolerant systems frequently call for additional resources, which can lead to an increase in the expenses of running the system.

Testing: Validating the resilience of your application can be a time- and resource-intensive process that requires testing as well as chaotic engineering.

Over-Engineering: It is possible to over-engineer for resilience, investing in redundancy or fault tolerance that may not be justified by the actual hazards of the situation. Over-engineering can be avoided by avoiding some common pitfalls.

Managing an application that is highly accessible and robust calls for continual operational efforts, such as monitoring, updating, and planning for disaster recovery. These costs are referred to as "operational overhead."

When working with highly accessible systems, implementing security measures and maintaining compliance with industry laws can be a difficult and time-consuming process.

It is not just a practical requirement, but also an absolute must for success in business to plan for failure and rehabilitation. Failures are unavoidable in today's world of highly sophisticated, networked apps and cloud-based infrastructure. A robust application is not only able to resist these errors, but it is also able to recover rapidly from them, which ensures a great user experience and minimizes the impact on the business.

Build applications that are not just highly available but also able to adapt and thrive in the face of adversity by adhering to best practices such as prioritizing redundancy, automating recovery processes, and implementing robust monitoring and security measures. This may be accomplished by building applications that are not only capable of thriving in the face of adversity but also prioritizing redundancy. To ensure that your applications are able to survive the ever-evolving difficulties posed by the digital ecosystem, resilience is not a one-time effort but rather one that demands constant attention and continual improvement.

Chapter 7

Monitoring and Testing

Monitoring and testing are two of the most important aspects of developing modern software applications. Strong monitoring and testing procedures are an absolute necessity in this day and age, when apps are expected to have a high level of availability, to perform well, and to be responsive to the requirements of their users. In this extensive guide, we will discuss the significance of monitoring and testing, as well as their respective roles in guaranteeing the dependability of applications, fundamental principles, and best practices, as well as the tools and strategies that may be used to efficiently execute these concepts.

The Necessity of Keeping an Eye on Things

1. **The Quick Identification of Problems**
   Monitoring enables the early identification of a variety of issues, including performance concerns, security breaches, and others. Intervention at an early stage can prevent these issues from having an impact on the user experience or the operations of the organization.

2. **An enhanced overall user experience**

   Monitoring plays an important role in ensuring that apps are both available and responsive. This is absolutely necessary in order to provide a pleasant experience for users and to keep existing users.

3. **Making decisions based on the analysis of data**

   Monitoring yields important data as well as new and useful insights. It provides visibility into how applications are working in real time and pinpoints areas in which improvements are required, which enables data-driven decision making.

4. **Capacity for Growth and Optimization of Resources**

   Monitoring is helpful in gaining an idea of how resources are being used. It enables proactive scalability and resource optimization, which guarantees that applications can effectively manage rising workloads.

5. **Safety and Regulatory Compliance**

Monitoring is an essential element in both security and regulatory compliance. It helps uncover potential vulnerabilities, unauthorized access, and irregularities in the system.

Principles Crucial to an Efficient System of Monitoring

1. **Outline your goals in crystal-clear terms**

   Establish your goals explicitly before beginning to set up monitoring. Determine what it is you wish to keep track of, the exact measurements you will require, and the objectives you wish to accomplish.

2. **Select the Appropriate Performance Indicators**

   Choose metrics that are pertinent to both the performance of your application and the application itself. Response time, error rates, resource utilization, and user involvement are some common measures.

3. **Visibility in Real Time (RTV)**

   Visibility in real time is an essential component of monitoring. Make sure that you have the capability to view and evaluate the behavior of your application and infrastructure as it is taking place.

4. **Making aware**

   When certain predetermined thresholds are exceeded, your team should be notified through the alerting methods you have up. You'll be able to respond more promptly to problems and avoid disruptions in service with the help of alerts.

5. **The Detection of Anomalies**

   Utilize anomaly detection in order to locate patterns or behaviors that are not typical or that deviate significantly from what is anticipated. This is especially helpful for discovering performance concerns as well as breaches in security.

6. **The Storage and Examination of Data**

   Keep track of historical monitoring data so that you can analyze and identify trends later. Analysis of data over a prolonged period of time can help uncover patterns and is helpful in capacity planning.

7. **Cooperative effort**

   Working together is essential. Make sure that the appropriate groups and individuals have access to the monitoring data and alarms, and that they are able to collaborate on the problem-solving process.

8. **The Loop of Feedback**

Create a feedback loop for continual improvement using the data from your monitoring efforts. Review the monitoring data on a regular basis so that you may make educated decisions that will improve the performance and dependability of your application.

Methods Most Appropriate for Efficient Supervision

1. **The Use of Instruments**
   Your code and infrastructure should be instrumented so that they can generate the appropriate metrics for monitoring. Instrumentation tools like as Prometheus and StatsD, as well as application performance monitoring (APM) solutions, are quite popular.
2. **Tracking in a Distributed Manner**
   When working with complicated applications that are distributed, using distributed tracing to track requests as they move through the various components is recommended. Distributed tracing is a capability that can be provided by tools such as Zipkin and Jaeger.
3. **The Practice of Centralized Logging**
   Logs from your application's many components can be collected and analyzed more easily with the help of centralized logging. You may improve the efficiency of your log management by utilizing software like the ELK stack (Elasticsearch, Logstash, and Kibana) or Splunk.
4. **Keeping an Eye on the Infrastructure**
   Keep an eye on the state of your infrastructure, including the servers, containers, and cloud services, and make sure everything is working properly. Monitoring tools for infrastructure such as Nagios, Zabbix, and Datadog provide insights into the consumption of system resources and the overall health of the system.
5. **Monitoring of Application Performance (also known as APM)**
   Consider using application performance management (APM) solutions such as New Relic, AppDynamics, or Dynatrace to obtain in-depth insights into the performance of your application. These solutions can provide diagnostics at the code level and trace transactions from beginning to end.
6. **Observation of the User Experience**
   In order to have an understanding of how people interact with your application, user experience monitoring should be implemented. Applications such as Google Analytics, New Relic

Browser, and Applitools are examples of software that can offer insights on user behavior and performance.

7. **Artificial Observational Methods**

   Utilize synthetic monitoring tools to evaluate the operation of your application from a variety of locations and devices. This will allow you to imitate how users interact with the application. This assists in identifying performance issues before they become noticeable to actual users.

8. **Security and Surveillance**

Include security monitoring as part of your strategy so that you may identify and respond to potential security weaknesses and threats. When it comes to security monitoring, tools and systems such as SIEM (Security Information and Event Management) can be quite helpful.

The Necessity of Performing Tests

1. **The Assurance of Quality**

   Testing guarantees that the functionality of the program satisfies both quality requirements and the expectations of users. It assists in identifying and fixing problems and faults before they are reported by users.

2. **Improving the Overall Performance**

   Performance testing helps uncover bottlenecks and inefficiencies in the program, which paves the way for improvements in efficiency and scalability.

3. **Ensure safety**

   Security testing helps reveal vulnerabilities and weaknesses in the program's code and infrastructure, thereby safeguarding the application from potential threats and breaches that could occur.

4. **Obeying the rules**

   Testing is required for applications that are used in regulated sectors because it ensures that the applications are in conformity with the standards and rules that are particular to the industry.

5. **The Experience of the User**
   Testing, in particular usability and user experience (UX) testing, is an effective method for ensuring that the program in question is user-friendly and straightforward.
6. **Ongoing and Constant Improvement**

Testing generates insights that can be used for ongoing improvement. The results of testing can be used to drive the creation of new features and improvements.

Fundamentals of an Efficient and Effective Test

1. **Begin your testing as soon as possible and continue it frequently**
   It is important to start testing at the earliest possible stage of the development process. Continuous testing should be performed all the way through the software development lifecycle in order to discover problems as soon as possible.
2. **Insurance That Covers Everything**
   Make sure that your tests cover every aspect, including the functionality, performance, and security, as well as the user experience. Make use of a number of different kinds of testing, such as unit testing, integration testing, regression testing, and security testing.
3. **Mechanized Processes**
   Tests should be automated so that efficiency and consistency can be guaranteed. Continuous integration and continuous delivery (CI/CD) procedures can be implemented thanks to the ability to perform automated tests on a regular basis.
4. **Authentic Simulations of the Test Environment**
   Build test cases that are as accurate as possible representations of actual usage. It is important to take into account a variety of user personas and patterns of usage in order to identify problems, some of which may not be obvious in controlled conditions.

5. **Cooperative effort**

   Testing is an activity that requires teamwork. Involve all of the relevant parties, such as users, developers, and testers, in order to get as much input and insight as possible.

6. **Documentation**

   Always remember to keep detailed documentation of the test cases, findings, and problems that are found during testing. The creation of documentation makes it easier to monitor progress and ensures that problems are resolved.

7. **Never Stop Educating Yourself**

Foster an environment that values lifelong education and constant progress. In order to drive iterative development and improvements, use the information gained from testing.

Best Methods and Procedures for Efficient Testing

1. **The Testing of Units**

   Install unit testing so that individual components or units of code may be examined and tested independently. When it comes to unit testing, helpful tools include frameworks such as JUnit, pytest, and xUnit.

2. **Integrity Checking of the System**

   It is important to perform integration testing so that you can examine the interactions and compatibility of the various components or services contained inside your application. Integration testing is made easier with the help of frameworks like TestNG and Postman.

3. **Testing for Regression of Results**

   To verify that new code changes do not result in unanticipated side effects or a breakdown of previously established functionality, regression testing must be performed. Regression testing can be made easier with the help of automation tools like Selenium and Jenkins.

4. **Evaluation of the Performance**

   Make use of performance testing in order to evaluate the performance of the application under a variety of scenarios. Performance testing can include load testing, stress testing, and scalability testing. When it comes to performance testing, having tools such as Apache JMeter and Gatling might be helpful.

5. **Inspections of the Security**

   In order to identify and address potential security flaws, you should incorporate security testing into your overall testing strategy. Testing the security of a system can be made easier with tools like OWASP ZAP and Burp Suite.

6. **Tests of Usability and the Overall User Experience**

Tests should be run to determine the application's usability as well as the user experience it provides, including how easy it is to use and how satisfying the experience is overall. Tools that assess usability, such as UserTesting and Crazy Egg, are beneficial to the UX testing process.

Continuous Integration and Continuous Delivery (CI/CD) is the seventh recommendation

Build continuous integration and continuous delivery pipelines to automate the testing and

deployment process. Testing and deployment operations can be simplified with the assistance of CI/CD systems such as Jenkins, Travis CI, and CircleCI.

Instruments and Methods for the Supervision and Examination of

When it comes to monitoring and testing, there is a vast arsenal of instruments and methods at one's disposal. Your application's unique requirements as well as the technological stack it uses heavily influence the type of tools you should use. The following is a selection of tools and methods that are frequently used:

Instruments for Monitoring

IT RESILIENCE

An open-source monitoring and alerting toolset that was developed with the goals of
dependability and scalability in mind. Prometheus.

Grafana is a popular open-source platform that allows users to create dashboards that are both interactive and customisable, and they can use these dashboards to monitor data.

Datadog is a monitoring and analytics platform that is hosted in the cloud. It provides users with real-time visibility into how applications and infrastructure are performing.

New Relic is an application performance management (APM) platform that offers in-depth insights into application performance, including diagnostics at the code level.

Elasticsearch, Logstash, and Kibana are the three components that make up the ELK Stack, which is a mix of open-source tools that allow for centralized logging, log analysis, and log visualization.

A monitoring and observability service called AWS CloudWatch is made available by Amazon Web Services (AWS) for the purpose of monitoring cloud resources and applications.

Nagios is a free and open-source monitoring system that identifies and fixes issues with computer networks and physical infrastructure.

Dynatrace is an application performance management (APM) solution that provides AI-driven observability and automation for cloud infrastructure and cloud-based applications.

Instruments for Testing

JUnit is a popular testing framework that is based on Java and is used for writing and running unit tests.

Selenium is a free and open-source software tool that automates web browsers and is helpful for testing online applications.

A collaborative platform for API development that includes tools for automated testing and monitoring, Postman is also known as.

Burp Suite is an all-encompassing web vulnerability scanner that can be used for testing and evaluating security.

Apache JMeter is a performance and load testing tool that is open-source and may be used for testing applications, especially online applications.

Cypress is a framework for performing end-to-end testing on online applications that offers real-time reloads for the purpose of test development.

TestNG is a testing framework that supports many different forms of testing, including unit testing and integration testing. It was influenced by JUnit and NUnit.

Appium is an open-source automation tool that can be used for testing mobile and online applications on both the iOS and Android platforms.

Problems Associated with Monitoring and Testing

1. **Environments That Are Complicated**
   Monitoring and testing contemporary programs can be difficult since they frequently run in complicated and dispersed contexts that have a large number of components and dependencies.
2. **An Overabundance of Data**
   Monitoring tools have the potential to produce enormous amounts of data, which might result in an overwhelming amount of information. It might be a difficult task to determine which data are the most pertinent and then to rank them in order of importance.
3. **Erroneous positive and negative results**
   Monitoring and testing programs have the potential to generate false positives (indicate problems that do not exist) and false negatives (fail to discover problems that are actually present). These mistakes have the potential to result in a loss of both time and resources.
4. **Choose Your Instruments**
   The abundance of available choices can make it difficult to select the appropriate monitoring and testing tools for a given situation.

It is absolutely necessary to select tools that are compatible with the requirements of your application as well as its technology stack.

5. **Integration That Is Continuous**

   It can be difficult to keep an efficient testing method alive inside of a pipeline that uses continuous integration and continuous delivery (CI/CD). In order for continuous integration and continuous delivery to be successful, it is essential to ensure that tests are fully automated, comprehensive, and effective.

6. **Cost**

Monitoring and testing can both be resource-intensive activities, which can result in higher overall expenses for operations. It is necessary to strike a balance between the costs of testing and monitoring and the benefits that they give.

In the creation of modern applications, monitoring and testing are essential components that cannot be omitted. The functionality, performance, and overall quality of your application may be ensured through thorough testing, while its availability, responsiveness, and safety can be guaranteed by means of robust monitoring. These practices, when combined, create the foundation upon which application reliability and user happiness are built.

You can develop and maintain applications that not only meet the expectations of users but also adapt to meet the ever-changing demands of the digital landscape if you adhere to the core concepts and best practices for monitoring and testing, and if you choose the correct tools for your individual needs. If you do this, you can build and maintain applications that not only meet the expectations of users but also evolve to meet the demands of the digital environment. Accept the necessity of monitoring and testing as a necessary part of making a strategic commitment to delivering applications that are of a high quality, are reliable, and are performance-driven.

7.1 Continuous Monitoring and Alerting

Continuous monitoring and alerting play critical roles in the arena of modern application development, which places a premium on high availability, optimal performance, and robust security. This in-depth guide digs into the relevance of continuous monitoring and alerting, investigates the role that they play in ensuring the safety of applications, and explains the best practices, important principles, tools, and approaches that are necessary for their successful deployment.

The Necessity of Ongoing Monitoring as an Imperative

1. **The Quick Identification of Problems**
   Continuous monitoring enables the early identification of a wide variety of issues, including performance concerns, security breaches, and others. It enables prompt intervention to minimize these issues before they have an impact on the user experience or the operations of the organization.
2. **Preventative Methods of Problem Solving**
   Teams are given the ability to respond proactively to issues as they arise when real-time monitoring is used. This reduces the risk of lost income and damage to the brand by minimizing the amount of time the service is offline and disrupting users.
3. **Making decisions based on the analysis of data**
   Continuous monitoring results in the collection of useful data and new perspectives. It provides visibility into how applications are working in real time and pinpoints areas in which improvements are required, which enables data-driven decision making.
4. **Capacity for Growth and Optimization of Resources**
   Continuous monitoring is helpful in gaining a knowledge of how resources are being used. It enables proactive scalability and resource optimization, which guarantees that applications can effectively manage rising workloads.
5. **Safety and Regulatory Compliance**

IT RESILIENCE

Monitoring that is ongoing is an essential component of both security and regulatory compliance. It assists in the identification of unauthorized access, anomalies, and potential vulnerabilities, and it also ensures compliance with industry-specific standards and regulations.

The Most Important Tenets of Constant Supervision

1. **Visibility in Real Time**
   Your application has to have real-time visibility into how well it performs, how available it is, and how secure it is if you are using continuous monitoring. A delay in data reporting can be expensive in terms of both downtime and potential security risks.

2. **Insurance That Covers Everything**
   Make sure that the monitoring of your application, infrastructure, and security include all of the essential components of each of these areas. This contains things like mistake rates, performance data, security events, and overall system health.

3. **Providing Warning and Notification**
   Establish means for alerting your team as quickly as possible once established thresholds are
   surpassed or anomalies are found. Notifications are absolutely necessary for the prompt settlement of issues.

4. **The Analysis of the Data and Its Retention**
   Keep track of historical monitoring data so that you can analyze and identify trends later. investigation of data over a prolonged period of time can help uncover patterns, which is helpful for both capacity planning and security incident investigation.

5. **Cooperative effort**
   The process of continuous monitoring is one that requires teamwork. Make sure that the appropriate groups and individuals have access to the monitoring data and alarms, and that they are able to collaborate on the problem-solving process.

6. **The Loop of Feedback**

Create a feedback loop for continual improvement using the data from your monitoring efforts.

Review the monitoring data on a regular basis so that you may make educated judgments about how to improve the performance, reliability, and security of your application.

Standard Operating Procedures for Efficient Continuous Monitoring

1. **The Use of Instruments**

   Code, infrastructure, and security systems should all be instrumented so that they can create the data required for continuous monitoring. Utilize monitoring technologies such as application performance monitoring (APM), security information and event management (SIEM), and infrastructure monitoring.

2. **Automatic Notifications**

   Set up an automated alerting system based on previously specified thresholds and the identification of anomalies. The severity of the alerts should be rated, and then they should be distributed to the appropriate groups or persons for fast action.

3. **The Development of a Dashboard**

   Build dashboards that can integrate monitoring data from a variety of sources, giving you a consolidated picture of the performance, availability, and security of your application. For the building of dashboards, you can make use of tools such as Grafana and Kibana, as well as customized solutions.

4. **Emergency Procedures and Plans**

   Create incident response strategies that will direct the actions of your team in the event that significant alerts are issued. Plans for responding to incidents should incorporate escalation protocols and have preset actions for a variety of potential outcomes.

5. **Always Under Consideration**

   It is important to conduct regular reviews of monitoring data and warnings in order to spot patterns, ongoing problems, and bottlenecks in performance. Leverage the understanding you've obtained via monitoring to make continuous improvements.

6. **Evaluation of Scalability**

   Conduct scalability tests on your monitoring systems to see whether or not they can manage an increase in the amount of data and alarms generated as a result of the expansion of your application and infrastructure.

7. **Security and Surveillance**

Include security monitoring as part of your strategy for continuous monitoring. To identify potential security risks and respond appropriately, implement SIEM solutions and intrusion detection systems.

The Necessity of Sounding the Alarm

1. **Problem Solving in a Timely Manner**

   The fast responses that are triggered by alerts to problems or incidents help to reduce downtime and user disturbances. Fixing problems in a timely manner is absolutely necessary in order to keep services available.

2. **The Management of Incidents**

   The process of alerting people is an essential part of incident management. When an issue arises, it gives a clear method for how to respond and how to solve it, and it also guarantees that the appropriate teams are informed of the issue.

3. **Putting a Stop to the Escalation**

   The use of alerts helps stop smaller problems from snowballing into more serious ones. Teams are able to address issues while they are still controllable since early detection and alerting allows for this.

4. **The Reaction to a Security Incident**

   Within the framework of security monitoring, alerting is an extremely important part of the incident response process. Security alerts are messages that are sent to teams to advise them of potential security breaches or anomalies that need to be investigated and mitigated.

5. **Obligation to comply**

In order to maintain regulatory compliance, alerting is frequently required. It is necessary for organizations to provide evidence that they are capable of reacting to incidents and warnings in accordance with sector-specific criteria.

Principles Crucial to an Efficient Warning System

1. **Clearly Defined Criteria for Warnings**
   Define alerting criteria and thresholds that are crystal clear, basing them on the specific requirements of your application and infrastructure. The criteria should be well recorded and discussed and agreed upon by the appropriate teams.

2. **The Ordering of Notifications**
   Determine the order of importance for each warning depending on how severe it is and how it will affect your application. Alerts with a high priority demand immediate response, whilst alerts with a lower priority can be dealt with during the regularly scheduled maintenance windows.

3. **The Procedures for Escalation**
   In the event that the initial response team is unable to fix an issue, you should establish escalation processes that describe how alerts should be escalated to higher-level teams or individuals.

4. **Different Types of Notification Channels**
   It is important to make use of a variety of notification channels, such as email, SMS, IM, and phone calls, to ensure that alerts are communicated to the appropriate individuals as quickly as possible. Take into consideration the implementation of on-call rotation schedules.

5. **Automated Warning Systems**
   Automate the procedures that generate alerts to cut down on

the amount of time needed to respond and to make certain that notifications are given in a reliable and consistent manner.
6. **Documentation of the Incident**

Always make sure you have complete documentation for any occurrence that is generated by alerts. This record ought to include specifics regarding the warning, the activities done in response to it, and the resolutions.

The Most Effective Methods and Procedures for Alerting

1. **Alerts that are Rich in Context**
   Make sure that alerts include enough context that teams can comprehend the problem at a glance thanks to the information provided. Include details such as the component that is being affected, any error messages, and any relevant metrics.
2. **Eliminating Excessive Noise**
   Put noise reduction tactics into place to cut down on the number of warnings that aren't worth acting on. Instead of bombarding teams with noise, alerts should give information that is valuable to them.
3. **An admission of fault and a proposal for a remedy**
   Alerts need to have protocols for acknowledgment and resolution put into place. Members of the team need to confirm that they have received alerts and document the steps they have taken to fix the problem.
4. **Plans for Further Escalation**
   Create well-defined plans for how critical alerts will be escalated. Identify the groups or individuals who ought to be called in the event that the original responders are unable to fix the situation.
5. **A Review of the Aftermath of the Incident**
   Conduct a post-incident investigation to investigate how alerts were managed, determine

whether there is room for improvement, and identify ways that future events of a similar nature might be avoided.
6. **Keeping an eye on the keepers of the watch**
Maintain a constant vigilance over your warning systems to check that they are operating as expected at all times. Both false negatives (also known as missed alerts) and false positives (also known as alerts that cannot be acted upon) need to be addressed.
7. **Instruction**

Your employees should go through training on how to efficiently respond to alarms. Make sure that all of the members of the team are aware of the escalation procedures and the best practices for alerting.

Instruments and Methods for Ongoing Monitoring and Message Notification

Tools for Monitoring and Measuring Performance

An open-source monitoring and alerting toolset that was developed with the goals of dependability and scalability in mind. Prometheus.

Grafana is a popular open-source platform that allows users to create dashboards that are both interactive and customisable, and they can use these dashboards to monitor data.

Datadog is a monitoring and analytics platform that is hosted in the cloud. It provides users with real-time visibility into how applications and infrastructure are performing.

New Relic is an application performance management (APM) platform that offers in-depth insights into application performance, including diagnostics at the code level.

A monitoring and observability service called AWS CloudWatch is made available by Amazon Web Services (AWS) for the purpose of monitoring cloud resources and applications.

Nagios is a free and open-source monitoring system that identifies and fixes issues with computer networks and physical infrastructure.

Notification Instruments

A digital operations management platform that offers alerting, on-call scheduling, and incident management is known as PagerDuty.

OpsGenie is a cutting-edge incident response and alerting platform that offers features such as on-call management, event tracking, and alerting.

Slack is a platform for collaboration that includes alerting and notification tools built right in. It is ideal for managing incidents and facilitating team communication.

The VictorOps platform is an incident management solution that includes on-call scheduling, alerting, and issue response capabilities.

The Prometheus ecosystem includes a component known as Alert-Manager, which is responsible for the administration and routing of alerts that are produced by Prometheus.

Microsoft Teams is a platform for team collaboration that contains tools for alerting and notification. These features are helpful for crisis response and communication within teams.

7.2 Simulating Failure Scenarios

The capacity to anticipate and react appropriately to failures is of the utmost significance in a world that is becoming increasingly complicated and interconnected. Organizations need to have contingency plans in place for a wide variety of potential failure situations, such as a bug in the software, an interruption in the manufacturing process, a natural disaster, or a breach in cybersecurity. The practice of "simulating failure scenarios" is a potent instrument that can help achieve this level of preparation.

In order to assess the reaction, resilience, and adaptability of systems, organizations, and individuals, it is necessary to create simulated failure scenarios, which entails the controlled and artificial creation of conditions that imitate real-world failures. Because it helps uncover weaknesses, fine-tune recovery plans, and build a culture of continuous improvement, this proactive approach to failure management has gained popularity across a variety of industries, including information technology (IT), engineering, healthcare, and emergency response, among others.

Recognizing the Importance of Practicing Different Ways Something Could Go Wrong

Failure simulation enables businesses to learn from their past errors without having to deal with the actual repercussions of those errors in the real world. Teams are able to analyze the issue, determine the underlying causes, and devise solutions to either prevent the failure from occurring in the future or lessen its impact if it does occur. This can be done by modeling a failure scenario. This preventative method of education speeds up the process of improvement and contributes to the formation of a culture of resilience.

It is impossible to foresee every possible setback, but doing simulations can assist in locating weak areas, vulnerabilities, and potential hazards. Risk Mitigation It is impossible to foresee every possible setback. Because they have a better awareness of these potential sites of failure, companies are better able to take preventative efforts to improve their systems, procedures, and infrastructure, thereby lowering the probability that one of these potential outcomes would occur.

Testing for resiliency involves simulating several failure scenarios, which is similar to doing fire drills. It enables organizations to test their resilience in an environment that can be controlled by the organization. In this way, when an actual crisis occurs, teams will be better prepared and will have a greater ability to respond successfully. It is possible that doing so will make the difference between a speedy recovery and an expensive and time-consuming catastrophe.

Innovation and optimization: In order to foster innovation, companies might benefit by knowingly putting themselves in positions where they could fail.

When confronted with difficult circumstances, teams are frequently put to the test and required to think laterally and come up with original ideas. This has the potential to result in greater competitiveness, streamlined processes, and lower overall costs.

The improvement of decision-making can be accomplished by simulating different failure scenarios, which offers a chance to assess decision-making when under pressure. Members of a team can acquire the skills necessary to make crucial decisions, effectively allocate resources, and communicate with one another at a time of crisis. The general capacity of the company to handle unforeseen occurrences is elevated as a result of this expertise.

Illustrations of Mock Disasters and Their Consequences

Cybersecurity: In the field of cybersecurity, penetration testing is carried out by ethical hackers that simulate cyberattacks in order to locate vulnerabilities and weak points in a company's digital infrastructure. Through the use of these simulations, organizations are able to strengthen their defenses and establish incident response strategies.

Healthcare: In order to gauge their level of readiness, hospitals and other medical institutions often stage simulated disasters, such as those involving a large number of casualties or the spread of an infectious illness. Because of this, healthcare teams are able to improve their methods for responding to emergencies, allocating resources, and caring for patients.

Manufacturing: In order to test their downtime recovery plans, manufacturing firms would often mimic the breakdown of various pieces of equipment or supply chains. This ensures that the business can quickly resume normal operations in the event that an unforeseen failure occurs.

Software Development: Teams working on software development make use of chaos engineering to model the breakdown of computer systems and performance decreases. They are able to develop software that is more resilient and reliable as a result of this helping them identify gaps in their apps and infrastructure.

Emergency Response First responders and emergency management agencies regularly practice for catastrophic events by simulating calamities such as earthquakes, hurricanes, and terrorist attacks through the use of disaster simulations. Responders can improve their coordination, communication, and search and rescue techniques by participating in these activities.

The Most Effective Methods for Reenacting Potential Disasters

Begin on a small scale: Before moving on to more difficult scenarios, start with simulations that are more straightforward and easier to handle. Because of this, teams are able to increase their level of knowledge and confidence.

Involve Key Stakeholders: Make certain that the simulation includes participation from all relevant stakeholders, ranging from frontline employees to high management. This helps to cultivate a common understanding as well as a commitment to progress.

Document and Assess: Make sure to keep records of the simulation, noting both what went well and what didn't go so well with it. Conduct an analysis of the findings and use this information to guide your choices for changes to be made in the future.

Iterate and Improve: Utilize the understanding you've acquired through simulations to make observable improvements to your organization's systems, procedures, and responses. Iterate again and over again to build up your resilience.

Maintain Your Knowledge: If you want to make sure that your simulations are accurate, you need to make sure that you are always up to date on the latest emerging dangers and advancements in your sector. Because the landscape of possible failures is always shifting, maintaining a state of readiness demands constant awareness.

7.3 Regularly Testing Resilience Plans

Resilience is an essential quality for individuals and businesses alike in the modern world, which moves at a breakneck pace and is fraught with uncertainty. The development of resilience plans, which lay out strategies for reacting to disruptions and recovering from them, is an essential component of emergency preparedness. However, if they are not routinely evaluated and refined, these plans run the risk of becoming out of date or useless very fast. The key to ensuring that an organization can sustain a variety of shocks and stressors and quickly recover from them is to routinely put their resilience plans through their paces.

The Significance of Having Contingency Plans

Minimizing Downtime Efficient resilience plans can assist in minimizing downtime, which helps ensure that an organization can continue performing its vital operations despite the presence of adversity. This could mean the difference between continuing to operate profitably and experiencing significant financial setbacks.

Reputational Defense: The ability of an organization to mount an effective defense against a crisis is critical to its ability to preserve its good name. This indicates a dedication to stakeholders, employees, and consumers, which has the ability to develop trust and loyalty on their part.

Compliance with Laws and Regulations: Many different types of businesses must fulfill legal and regulatory criteria in order to be adequately prepared for any type of emergency. If a company has a contingency plan, it will be better able to maintain compliance and will have a better chance of avoiding potential legal problems and penalties.

Stability in Financial Matters: Having a resilience plan in place can assist an organization in protecting its financial stability by reducing the amount of monetary damage that is caused by a disaster. This is absolutely necessary to ensure sustainability over the long run.

Protecting Employees and Ensuring Their Safety An organization that is well-prepared can protect its employees and ensure their safety in the event of an emergency. As a result, this helps to cultivate faithfulness and dedication within the workers.

The Importance of Conducting Tests Frequently

Even if it is necessary to have a plan for resilience, the only way to guarantee the plan's effectiveness is to test it on a consistent basis. The state of the world is always changing, and as a result, new dangers and difficulties appear on a regular basis. Because of this, it is absolutely necessary for companies to regularly examine and improve their strategies in order to guarantee that they will continue to be effective and relevant.

Testing Methods for Different Types of Resilience Plans

Tabletop exercises are a type of discussion-based exercise in which members of a team get together to talk through a fictitious scenario while analyzing their own roles and responsibilities. Tabletop exercises are a fantastic tool for ensuring that everyone is on the same page regarding the plan and their respective responsibilities within it.

Functional Exercises are more extensive than tabletop exercises and feature activities that need the use of one's hands and are based on hypothetical situations. For the purpose of testing its incident response plan, a corporation can, for instance, mimic a cyberattack. A more accurate evaluation of the usefulness of the strategy can be obtained through the use of these exercises.

Full-Scale Drills: Full-scale drills are simulations of actual events that take place in real time. The simulation of a fire, an earthquake, or the malfunction of an extensive information technology system could be among these. The most exhaustive type of testing, full-scale exercises give the most accurate evaluation of an organization's resilience plan because they simulate real-world scenarios.

Advantages to Performing Routine Tests

Identifying Weaknesses Organizations can improve their resilience plans by conducting regular testing to help identify any areas of vulnerability. It identifies the areas in which improvements are required and provides the opportunity for corrections to be made before a genuine crisis emerges.

Improved collaboration: Putting contingency plans to the test encourages improved collaboration amongst the members of the team. It guarantees that everyone is aware of their responsibilities and that they are able to collaborate efficiently in times of emergency.

Knowledge that has been recently updated As new dangers and technologies appear, resilience plans need to evolve. Testing on a regular basis keeps firms informed and up to date, which ensures that their strategies continue to be applicable even as the world around them evolves.

Boosted Confidence: When members of a team consistently rehearse their roles in responding to emergencies, it helps them feel more comfortable in their abilities. This boost in self-assurance can result in more effective actions being taken during actual situations.

Trust among Stakeholders: Trust among Stakeholders can be Instilled by Regular Testing and Successful Execution of Resilience Plans. Stakeholders include Customers, Suppliers, and Investors. If these stakeholders perceive that an organization is well-prepared for unanticipated occurrences, then they are more likely to support and interact with that organization.

The Most Effective Methods for Evaluating Contingency Plans

Testing on a Schedule: Create a timetable for doing routine tests on your resilience strategies. Depending on the requirements of the company, this could take place once a year, twice a year, or even once every three months.

When performing tests, it is important to select actual scenarios that are pertinent to the sector in which your firm operates and the location of that organization. A more precise evaluation of the usefulness of the plan will be obtained as a result of this.

Record the Results: Make sure you keep in-depth records of each test, noting what worked well, what didn't work well, and what aspects could use some tweaking. Make use of these records as a guide for updating the plan.

Feedback and Debriefing: Immediately following the completion of each test, feedback from the participants should be gathered, and debriefing sessions should be held. This input has the potential to provide helpful insights into what went well and what may be improved upon.

Cross-Functional Involvement It is important to make sure that the testing process includes participants from a variety of levels and departments across the organization. Having several points of view might be beneficial in locating security flaws that may not be immediately obvious to a single group or individual.

Continuous Improvement: In order to continuously improve the resilience plan, use the insights you've obtained from testing. Maintaining its usefulness requires consistent maintenance in the form of upgrades and improvements.

The practice of routinely putting contingency plans to the test is an essential element of any organization's overall preparedness strategy. It makes it easier to pinpoint areas of weakness, encourages improved coordination, and guarantees that plans continue to be applicable in a world that is continuously changing. The ability to recover quickly and effectively from unanticipated setbacks and crises is a resource that companies simply cannot afford to ignore in this day and age, as the frequency of these kinds of occurrences continues to climb. The resilience of an organization may be developed, honed, and kept up with the help of routine testing. This helps to ensure the organization's continuous performance despite the presence of challenges.

7.4 Incident Response and Recovery Procedures

It is impossible to overestimate the significance of having effective incident response and recovery protocols in place in an era that is characterized by an increase in the number of cybersecurity attacks, natural catastrophes, and other unanticipated interruptions. These protocols are the backbone for businesses and individuals that want to limit the extent of the damage, ensure that business as usual is not disrupted, and get back on their feet as quickly as possible in the face of adversity. In this essay, we will investigate the significance of incident response and recovery protocols, as well as their essential parts and the most effective ways to put them into action.

Acquiring Knowledge about Emergency Procedures and Recovery

Detection and Identification: Determine and validate the presence of an incident as soon as possible, while simultaneously comprehending its breadth and depth.

Isolate the incident to prevent any additional damage from occurring. This might refer to isolating a hacked system in the case of a cyber incident or containing a fire in the case of a physical disaster. Containment is the process of isolating and isolating the incident.

Eradication and Recovery: Find and get rid of whatever caused the incident in the first place, then get to work on getting things back to normal as soon as you can.

Communication: In order to notify stakeholders, employees, and the general public about the occurrence and its consequences, it is important to establish clear lines of communication.

Documentation and Analysis: During the incident response and recovery phase, make sure to document all you do for later analysis and review after the incident has occurred.

Components Crucial to the Contingency Plan for Recovery Following an Incident

In the stage known as "Preparation," one of the tasks at hand is to lay the groundwork for an efficient incident response and recovery. Creating an incident response team, outlining their duties and responsibilities, performing risk assessments, and devising an incident response strategy are all part of this process.

In the first phase, known as "identification," an organization will discover and verify the occurrence of an incident. This includes monitoring system logs and network traffic, as well as utilizing intrusion detection systems, in order to identify abnormal or suspect activity.

The reaction team takes fast action once an incident has been recognized in order to control the problem and prevent it from spreading further. This can require isolating the systems that are affected, altering the credentials used for access, or turning off some pieces of the network.

The fundamental cause of the occurrence is identified and handled during this phase, which is known as "eradication." For instance, if the incident is an infection caused by malware, it requires scanning and cleaning the systems that have been compromised in order to remove the malware.

At this point in the process, "recovery," the objective is to get back to normal business as soon as feasible. It could involve restoring data from backups, repairing or replacing damaged technology, and ensuring that the company is able to continue performing its vital responsibilities.

After the problem has been resolved, it is absolutely necessary to carry out a comprehensive post-incident investigation. This is one of the lessons that we have learned. This helps to determine what went well, what could have been done better, as well as how the business may improve its incident response and recovery protocols in the future.

The Very Best Methods for Dealing with Emergencies and Getting Back on Your Feet

Prior to the occurrence of an incident, construct a detailed strategy for how you will respond to it using proactive planning. This plan must to be revised on a regular basis in order to account for developing dangers and technology.

Team to Respond to Incidents: Put together a specialized team to respond to incidents, and make sure everyone knows their specific duties and responsibilities. Ensure that all members of the team receive training and continue to educate themselves on the most recent security risks and countermeasures.

Tabletop exercises, penetration testing, and simulated incidents are all examples of realistic testing methods. It is important to test your incident response plan on a regular basis. These activities will help you identify areas where you need improvement as well as deficiencies.

Establishing clear communication rules for notifying stakeholders, employees, and the general public about occurrences is an important step in the communication process. It is essential to be transparent in order to keep people's trust and credibility.

Documentation: Make sure to keep meticulous records of everything you do during the incident response and recovery phases. This paperwork is absolutely necessary for post-incident analysis as well as compliance with regulatory requirements.

Collaborate with other entities, such as law enforcement, industry colleagues, and cybersecurity organizations, and encourage them to collaborate with you and share information. During the process of responding to an incident, this can provide helpful insights and support.

Obstacles Facing Emergency Responders and Those in Recovery

Speed is of the essence when it comes to mitigating damage, but there are occasions when the sense of hurry might cause one to make mistakes. It is necessary for organizations to achieve a balance between acting quickly and thinking things through thoroughly.

Incidents can be quite complicated, with a wide range of interconnected problems and factors. It is not always easy to deal with all facets of an incident at the same time.

Allocation of Resources: An effective reaction frequently calls for a large allocation of resources, which can put a burden on an organization's finances as well as its staff.

Adaptability: Because of the ever-changing nature of dangers and incidents, companies and organizations are required to continually update and modify their policies, practices, and tools.

Response to Incidents Involving Cybersecurity

Notifying impacted Individuals And Regulatory Authorities In the case of a data breach, organizations are legally compelled to notify impacted individuals and regulatory authorities in many different jurisdictions. It is essential that you comprehend these regulations.

Digital Forensics: When responding to a cyber incident, it is common practice to conduct digital forensics in order to determine the source of an attack and compile evidence for possible legal action.

Backups and Recovery: To ensure that data can be recovered in the event that a cyber incident occurs, you should regularly back up any critical data and test the process of restoring it.

Developing a transparent procedure for reporting cybersecurity events within the company and ensuring that they are immediately escalated to the incident response team is an important part of the incident reporting process.

Physical Recovery after a Disaster

Planning for Business Continuity: Create plans for business continuity that include how vital functions will be kept running during and after a crisis.

During and after an emergency, it is critical to maintain a high level of physical security in order to minimize the amount of additional damage that may be incurred.

Redundancy: Be sure to set up redundancy for all of your essential computer systems, including off-site backups and alternative power supplies.

The ability of an organization to successfully navigate and endure unforeseen disturbances is directly correlated to the effectiveness of its incident response and recovery procedures. Whether one is dealing with cyberattacks or natural catastrophes, it is important to remember the fundamentals of discovery, containment, eradication, recovery, and ongoing development. In a world that is always presenting new dangers and obstacles, it is essential to maintain the efficiency and resiliency of these procedures by doing routine testing, maintaining open lines of communication, and being flexible. In a digital environment that is becoming increasingly unpredictable and dynamic, organizations can protect their resilience by ensuring they adhere to best practices and are continually working to improve their incident response and recovery procedures.

Chapter 8

Cloud Providers and Services

The management of data, applications, and infrastructure has been completely transformed by cloud computing, which has made this possible for both individuals and organizations. Cloud providers make available a comprehensive selection of services to their customers, which makes it possible for businesses to harness the scalability, flexibility, and cost-effectiveness benefits offered by the cloud. In this in-depth analysis, we will delve into the world of cloud providers and services, investigating the major players in the market, their products, and the impact that cloud computing has had on a variety of different industries.

Principal Cloud Service Providers
AWS stands for Amazon Web Services.

AWS, or Amazon Web Services, is one of the largest and most well-established cloud providers in the world. It is more frequently referred to by its acronym, AWS. A wide variety of services, such as processing power, storage, database management, machine learning, analytics, and many more are all available through AWS. Amazon EC2, which provides scalable virtual servers, and Amazon S3, which provides object storage, are two of the company's most renowned services.

Azure from Microsoft

One of the most important companies in this sector is Microsoft, which offers its own cloud computing platform known as Microsoft Azure. Microsoft Azure offers a wide variety of services, including virtual machines, databases, artificial intelligence and machine learning technologies, as well as extensive support for apps that run on the Windows platform.

(GCP) stands for the Google Cloud Platform.

Google's solution in the cloud computing arena is known as Google Cloud Platform, or GCP for short. Data analytics, machine learning, and container management are the focal points of GCP's offerings. The Google Kubernetes Engine, often known as GKE, is a well-liked option for container orchestration, and BigQuery is a data warehouse service that sees widespread adoption.

The IBM Cloud.

The IBM cloud computing platform was once known as IBM Bluemix. Its current name is IBM Cloud. It provides a variety of cloud services, such as virtual server hosting, container services that are based on Kubernetes, and solutions that are powered by AI. In addition, IBM Cloud is an industry leader in providing hybrid and multicloud solutions for enterprise customers.

Cloud Oracle. Oracle.

Oracle Cloud is the cloud infrastructure service that is offered by Oracle Corporation. It offers several different cloud services, such as computing, storage, and database management, to its customers. Oracle Cloud is well-known for its concentration on database services and enterprise application development.

Different Categories of Cloud Services

IaaS stands for "infrastructure as a service."

IaaS is a model of cloud computing that delivers virtualized computing resources via the internet. Users have the option of renting storage space, networking components, and virtual machines on a pay-as-you-

IT RESILIENCE

go basis. As a result of its adaptability and scalability, this model is well suited for use in establishments whose work loads are highly varied.

PaaS stands for "platform as a service."

PaaS makes available a platform that incorporates infrastructure, runtime environments, development tools, and services for the purpose of constructing, testing, and deploying software applications. It makes application development easier and frees developers from the burden of managing infrastructure, allowing them to concentrate instead on code.

Software as a Service, sometimes known as "SaaS,"

Software as a service (SaaS) is a model that distributes application programs via the internet and charges users on a subscription basis. Users are able to access these programs by means of a web browser, which eliminates the requirement for installations on users' local computers. Email services such as Gmail and productivity suites such as Microsoft 365 are both examples of common SaaS applications.

Deployment Models for the Cloud

Open Cloud Storage

Cloud service companies make their public cloud services available to customers of the general public.

They are hosted and maintained on the infrastructure owned and operated by the provider. Scalability, efficiency in terms of cost, and user-friendliness are three hallmarks of public cloud computing.

Personal Cloud Storage

Private clouds are those that are only used by a single company or organization and can either be hosted internally or by an external cloud service provider. Because they provide increased control, security, and the ability to customize, they are suited for use in businesses that must adhere to particular compliance criteria.

Mixed or Hybrid Cloud

Hybrid clouds integrate public cloud settings with private cloud environments, making it possible for data and applications to move fluidly between the two types of cloud environments. This paradigm offers flexibility, making it possible for enterprises to make use of the scale offered by public clouds while also keeping sensitive data stored in private clouds.

Services in the cloud and industry specializations

Concerning medical care

The use of cloud computing provides healthcare institutions with a secure method to store and manage patient records. Additionally, it enables the practice of telemedicine, the analysis of data for use in medical research, and the formulation of individualized treatment regimens.

The economy

The analytics of data, the management of risks, and the management of client relationships in the financial industry are all handled by cloud services. Fintech companies that operate in the cloud have caused a disruption in the conventional banking and investment processes.

To educate

The education industry has been revolutionized by cloud services because they provide remote learning tools, collaboration platforms, and solutions that are more efficient and less expensive to manage administrative activities.

Electronic commerce

During the busiest times of the year for online shopping, businesses that use cloud computing can profit from its scalability. In addition, using cloud services makes it possible to make personalized product recommendations, manage inventories, and process payments.

Amusement or recreation

The content streaming, video processing, and digital distribution functions used in the media and entertainment business are all handled by cloud services. Additionally rising in popularity are gaming platforms that are hosted in the cloud.

Industrial Production

Cloud computing is utilized by manufacturers for the purposes of supply chain management, predictive maintenance, and quality assurance. When it comes to data processing, industrial Internet of Things (IoT) equipment frequently rely on communication with the cloud.

IT RESILIENCE

Safety and Regulatory Compliance
Within the context of cloud computing, safety and protection are of the utmost importance. Cloud service companies make significant financial investments in various data and application protection mechanisms. Important aspects of security include the following:

The Encryption of Data
In order to prevent unauthorized access to the data while it is both in transit and while it is stored, the data is encrypted. Encryption services and tools are often made available by cloud providers.

Management of Identities and Access Requests (IAM)
Access to cloud resources can be controlled via IAM solutions. They are in charge of user authentication and authorization, which ensures that only those individuals who are permitted to do so can access the data and apps.

Acceptance or agreement
There are statutory regulations for the processing of data in many different businesses. Cloud service providers typically give enterprises with compliance certifications and tools to assist them in meeting these standards.

Detection of Dangers and Action Taking
Cloud service providers make use of sophisticated techniques for detecting and responding to security threats in order to identify and neutralize threats in real time.

Concerns and Things to Take Into Account

Management of Costs
If they are not managed effectively, the costs associated with cloud computing can quickly become out of hand. It is important for organizations to have ways to track, analyze, and improve their spending.

The Transfer of Data and Its Delay
Moving big amounts of data to and from the cloud may be a time-consuming and expensive process, especially if data transfer and network latency are not addressed. This is especially true when moving huge amounts of data to and from the cloud.

Locking in a Vendor

If you select a particular cloud provider, you run the risk of becoming locked into a vendor relationship, which makes it more difficult to switch to another cloud provider or return to an on-premises infrastructure.

Data Confidentiality

Different sectors and localities have different legislation regarding data privacy. Companies have a responsibility to ensure that they are in compliance with any applicable data protection legislation.

Agreements on Service Level (also known as SLAs)

To ensure the availability, performance, and dependability of cloud services, it is necessary to get an understanding of service level agreements (SLAs) and to negotiate these with cloud providers.

Cloud computing's upcoming developments and trends

The world of cloud computing is continuously undergoing change. The future of cloud services is being influenced by a number of trends, including the following:

Computing without using servers

The necessity to manage servers is removed entirely thanks to serverless computing. The cloud provider is responsible for managing infrastructure provisioning and scaling, so developers are free to concentrate on building code.

Computing on the Edge

Through the use of edge computing, computation and data storage may be brought closer to the source of the data. This helps to reduce latency and enables real-time processing. This is especially helpful for applications related to the internet of things.

Computing on the Quantum Level

The ability of quantum computers to solve issues that are currently intractable for traditional computers holds the possibility of bringing about a revolution in the field of cloud computing.

Interoperability and the use of several clouds

Multi-cloud methods are becoming increasingly popular among businesses as a way to circumvent the dangers of vendor lock-in and take advantage of the most advantageous aspects offered by several cloud service providers. It is becoming increasingly important to provide interoperability between different cloud platforms.

Integration of Artificial Intelligence and Machine Learning

Artificial intelligence (AI) and machine learning are currently being incorporated into cloud services, which will make it simpler for businesses to leverage the potential of data analytics and automation.

8.1 Leading Cloud Providers (e.g., AWS, Azure, GCP)

Computing in the cloud has developed into an essential part of today's modern information technology infrastructure since it provides businesses with the ability to scale, innovate, and cut expenses. Amazon Web Services (AWS), Microsoft Azure, and Google Cloud Platform (GCP) are the three cloud providers that have established themselves as market leaders despite the presence of a large number of competitors. In this piece, we will look into these prominent cloud providers, analyzing their services and strengths, as well as the impact they have had on the corporate world and the world of technology.

AWS stands for Amazon Web Services.

Amazon Web Services, sometimes known as AWS, is currently the industry standard bearer for cloud computing and has been for some time. It first went on sale in 2006, and ever since then, it has been considered the gold standard for cloud services. The comprehensive set of services provided by AWS can accommodate a wide variety of software programs and job demands.

Services Provided and Other Options

AWS provides a wide variety of services, which may be broken down into the following categories: computing, storage, databases, machine learning, analytics, and more. The following are some of the most noteworthy services:

Amazon EC2 stands for "Elastic Compute Cloud," and it is a service that offers scalable virtual servers. Users may start and manage instances of various sizes using this service, which helps them satisfy their computing needs.

Amazon S3, also known as the Simple Storage Service, is an object storage service that is highly scalable and has the ability to store and retrieve massive volumes of data. Backups, archiving of data, and content dissemination are typical applications for this technology.

AWS Lambda is a serverless computing solution that enables you to run code without the need to create or manage servers. It works wonderfully for apps that are driven by events.

Amazon Relational Database Service (RDS): RDS makes it simple to set up, run, and scale a relational database. RDS is also known as Amazon RDS. It is compatible with a variety of database engines, such as MySQL, PostgreSQL, and SQL Server, among others.

Amazon SageMaker is a service that offers several tools for the purpose of constructing, training, and deploying machine learning models. Projects using artificial intelligence and data science frequently select this option.

AWS Redshift: Redshift is a fully managed data warehousing solution that enables businesses to execute high-performance analysis on enormous volumes of data.

Positives (strengths)

A Comprehensive Service Portfolio: Amazon Web Services (AWS) offers its customers a wide variety of services, enabling them to select the appropriate instruments and resources to meet their individual requirements.

AWS provides a wide global network of data centers, which enables users to easily deploy their applications and services in close proximity to their target audience. This feature is known as the "Global Presence."

Security and Compliance: Because Amazon Web Services makes significant investments in security and offers a wide variety of compliance certifications, it is a reliable option for businesses.

IT RESILIENCE

A broad ecosystem of partners, tools, and resources that are designed to assist a variety of different use cases and sectors is provided by AWS through its partner network.

Customers are able to maintain a competitive advantage in a technology landscape that is rapidly transforming as a result of AWS's reputation for continuously developing and releasing new services.

Azure from Microsoft

A strong rival to Amazon Web Services (AWS), Microsoft Azure is the cloud computing division of the software giant Microsoft. Microsoft Azure provides users with a comprehensive selection of cloud services, which may be broken down into three categories: infrastructure, platform, and software as a service. It has quickly become the option of choice for many businesses who have already invested in Microsoft technologies.

Services Provided and Other Options

Azure Virtual Machines is a service that, similar to Amazon Elastic Compute Cloud (EC2), offers scalable virtual servers that are compatible with both Windows and Linux.

Azure Blob Storage is the counterpart of Amazon Simple Storage Service (S3) and is used to store unstructured data such as backups, documents, and photos. Blob storage is used by Azure.

PaaS is for platform-as-a-service, and Azure App Service is a product that facilitates the deployment and management of web and mobile applications.

Azure SQL Database is a managed relational database service that offers support for a variety of database engines. These database engines include SQL Server, MySQL, and PostgreSQL.

This service, which is part of Azure Machine Learning, gives data scientists and software developers the ability to construct, train, and deploy machine learning models.

Positives (strengths)

Hybrid Cloud Capabilities: Because Azure was built from the ground up to work in hybrid cloud environments, it is an excellent option for businesses who have already made substantial investments on-premises.

Enterprise Customers Are Azure's Primary Target Audience Due to its Extensive Compliance Certifications and Enterprise-Grade Support, Azure is Particularly Well Suited for Enterprise Customers.

Integration of AI and the Internet of Things Due to Azure's intense focus on AI and IoT services, the platform presents an appealing alternative for businesses interested in developing these technologies.

Tools that Are Friendly to Developers: Azure provides a variety of developer tools as well as a development environment that is already recognizable to Microsoft-centric businesses.

Reach Across the Globe: Microsoft Azure is expanding its global presence and now has data centers located across the world to serve global installations.

(GCP) stands for the Google Cloud Platform.

Google Cloud Platform, abbreviated as GCP, is the company's cloud product. It is well-known for the data analytics, machine learning, and container management services that it provides. GCP is primarily concerned with assisting businesses in utilizing data and AI for innovative purposes.

Services Provided and Other Options

Google Kubernetes Engine (GKE) is an appropriate solution for container orchestration and management. GKE is a managed Kubernetes service.

BigQuery is a serverless, highly scalable data warehouse that allows for the execution of SQL-like queries on enormous datasets in a very short amount of time.

Cloud AI is Google's name for its suite of machine learning and artificial intelligence products, which includes Vision AI, Natural Language AI, and AI Platform.

This Google Cloud Platform service offers scalable object storage for data, and it integrates very well with the other Google Cloud Platform services.

IT RESILIENCE

Users of Google Cloud Platform's Compute Engine have the ability to run scalable and high-performance virtual servers thanks to this service.

Positives (strengths)

Data and Analytics: Google Cloud Platform is well-known for its skill in data analytics; the company provides services such as BigQuery and Dataflow for the processing and examination of massive datasets.

Learning Machine GCP's artificial intelligence (AI) and machine learning services are well acclaimed, making it a popular choice among businesses whose primary focus is on data science and AI.

Containers and Kubernetes: Since GCP offers comprehensive support for both containers and Kubernetes, this cloud platform is a good choice for running containerized applications because of its versatility.

Global Network: The infrastructure of Google's global network ensures that users may access services and data from anywhere in the world with low latency.

Open Source and Interoperability: Because GCP is dedicated to open-source technology, it is an excellent choice for businesses who choose open-source alternatives to existing solutions.

8.2 Cloud Services for Resilience

The ability of a company to endure and recover from disruptions, whether such disruptions are the result of natural disasters, cyber-attacks, or other unforeseen events, is referred to as resilience. Resilience is an essential component of the operations of any business. Cloud computing services have become an indispensable component in the strengthening of resilience strategies for businesses of all sizes. In this piece, we will investigate how the use of cloud services can help improve a company's disaster recovery and continuity of business operations.

The Value of Being Able to Bounce Back

The term "natural disasters" encompasses a wide variety of calamities, including typhoons, floods, earthquakes, and wildfires. They are able to cause disruptions to the physical infrastructure and render data centers and information technology systems located on premises useless.

Cyberattacks: Ransomware attacks, distributed denial of service (DDoS) attacks, and data breaches are all examples of cyber dangers that can put data, systems, and operations at risk.

Data loss and system downtime can be caused by human error in the form of accidental deletion of data, incorrect setups, or improper handling of equipment.

Disruptions in the Supply Chain Recent events, such as the COVID-19 pandemic, have brought to light the importance of resiliency on the part of businesses in the face of potential supply chain disruptions, which can have an impact on the availability of goods and services.

Power Outages: Whether they are regional or broad, electrical outages can have an impact on a company's ability to function, and this is especially true for companies that rely largely on the infrastructure located on their own premises.

In order to ensure the continuity of business operations and reduce the amount of time lost due to disruptions of this nature, businesses need to have a plan in place. The importance of cloud services cannot be overstated in this context.

Services provided by the Cloud to Ensure Resilience

1. **Backing up and recovering of data**

   Cloud-based backup solutions offer a safe data storage location that is remote from the primary location of the business. Organizations are able to easily restore their data from the cloud in the event that their data is lost as a result of a hardware failure, human error, or cyberattacks, which helps to minimize both downtime and data loss.

   Amazon S3, Microsoft Azure Backup, and Google Cloud Storage are three well-known examples of popular cloud backup services. Because of the scalability, automated backups, and versioning capabilities offered by these services, businesses are able to save historical data records.

IT RESILIENCE

2. **a solution known as Disaster Recovery as a Service, or DRaaS**
   Recovery from Disaster Offered as a Service is a solution that is hosted in the cloud that replicates the important information technology infrastructure and data of a company to a secondary location in real time. In the event of a catastrophe, this secondary location, which is typically situated in a different geographic region, is still reachable. It is possible for businesses to maintain their operations by moving their operations to a secondary location in the case of a disruption.
   IBM Resiliency Services, Amazon Web Services Disaster Recovery, and Microsoft Azure Site Recovery are examples of important DRaaS service providers. These services provide rapid failover and recovery, which guarantees that there will be very little downtime.

3. **Computerization in the cloud and virtualization**
   Cloud computing gives businesses the ability to host their own apps and services in the internet's virtual space. This ensures that employees are able to access their work remotely via the cloud even in the event that the physical infrastructure of the company is hacked. Cloud service providers such as Amazon Web Services, Microsoft Azure, and Google Cloud Platform provide a scalable and on-demand computing infrastructure for executing applications and services.
   The technology known as virtualization, which is frequently utilized in cloud environments, grants enterprises the ability to construct virtual instances of servers and the workloads they manage. In the case that a server fails, it is possible to transfer these instances to other physical servers without causing any disruption to business activities.

4. **Providing for Redundancy and Balancing the Load**
   Redundancy and load balancing are frequently included as standard features of cloud computing services. These ensure that workloads are dispersed across numerous servers or data centers,

hence lowering the risk of service disruption caused by hardware failures or surges in traffic.

For instance, Amazon Web Services (AWS) provides Amazon Route 53 for DNS management and Amazon Elastic Load Balancing for distributing incoming application traffic among several targets. Both of these services are part of the Amazon Elastic Cloud Service (ECS).

5. **Tools for Online Communication and Coordination That Are Hosted in the Cloud**

Tools that facilitate communication and collaboration are indispensable in the modern workplace, and without them, it would be impossible to keep operations running smoothly. The use of cloud-based email, video conferencing, and collaboration systems such as Microsoft 365, Google Workspace, and Slack enables employees to work remotely and keep in contact with one another even when there are disruptions.

6. **Capacity to Grow**

The scalability offered by cloud services makes it possible to meet unexpectedly high levels of demand. Both for effectively managing shifting workloads and for coping with unexpected spikes in web traffic, this is an extremely important factor to consider for organizations.

Cloud service providers typically offer solutions known as auto-scaling, which enable resources to dynamically grow or shrink in response to consumption. These kinds of services include, for instance, AWS Auto Scaling and Azure Autoscale.

7. **Protection of Information and Encryption of Data**

Cloud service providers make significant financial investments in information security, providing features such as encryption, access controls, and advanced threat detection. They contribute to overall resilience by assisting firms in protecting their data and infrastructure from being compromised by cyberattacks.

Advantages of Using Cloud Services When It Comes to Resilience

1. **Efficient in terms of costs**
   With cloud services, businesses no longer need to make costly investments in on-premises infrastructure for data backup and recovery in order to take advantage of these services. The majority of cloud-based services follow a pay-as-you-go pricing model, which contributes to their low overall cost.
2. **Redundancy in Geographic Location**
   Cloud service providers typically operate data centers in multiple geographic locations. Because of this geographical redundancy, data and services will continue to be accessible even in the event that a natural disaster strikes just one location.
3. **Make a Speedy Comeback**
   The backup and disaster recovery solutions offered by cloud services are created with the goal of achieving a speedy recovery. Because of this, companies are able to swiftly resume their activities, which lessens the impact that downtime has.
4. **Capacity to Grow**
   Cloud services provide scalability on demand, which makes it easier for businesses to adapt their operations to changing workloads or other aspects of their business environment.
5. **Knowledge and Assistance in Need**
   Cloud service providers have a wealth of knowledge in the administration of data management and the protection of infrastructure. They provide service around the clock, seven days a week, and are constantly working to improve their security and resiliency.
6. **a pliable nature**

Because cloud services are so adaptable, they enable businesses to pick the precise solutions and configurations that are the most suitable for meeting their requirements for resiliency. As their company expands, they have the flexibility to easily adjust and expand their cloud resources.

Concerns and Things to Take Into Account

1. **The Transmission of Data and Bandwidth**
   It may take a considerable amount of time for an organization to transfer huge amounts of data to and from the cloud, particularly if the bandwidth available to the business is restricted. It is absolutely necessary to plan meticulously in order to guarantee fast backups and recoveries.
2. **Safety and Regulatory Compliance**
   When utilizing cloud services, it is of the utmost importance to keep rigorous security procedures and be in accordance with applicable data protection rules. It is imperative that businesses fully comprehend their roles and responsibilities in the process of securing their data while it is stored on the cloud.
3. **Locking in a Vendor**
   If you substantially rely on a single cloud provider, you run the risk of getting locked into a vendor relationship, which makes it difficult to switch to another cloud provider or return to running your infrastructure on-premises.
4. **Evaluation and Instruction**

It is essential to perform thorough testing of the resilience plans and to train staff in order to guarantee that cloud-based recovery and continuity solutions will function as intended.

8.3 Vendor Lock-in Considerations

In cloud computing, one of the most serious concerns is vendor lock-in. It takes place when a customer becomes extremely reliant on a single cloud service provider, making it challenging and expensive for the customer to transition to another provider or revert to on-premises solutions. In the following paragraphs, we will discuss the concept of vendor lock-in, as well as its repercussions and some things for companies to keep in mind while working with cloud service providers.

Comprehending the Concept of Vendor Lock-in

Using a certain cloud vendor's APIs or other proprietary services, which may or may not be compatible with the services offered by other cloud vendors, is an example of relying on proprietary services.

The act of storing data in a format that cannot easily be transferred to or converted into other forms is referred to as data formats.

Building applications with elaborate setups, which makes it difficult to migrate them; this is referred to as "complex configurations."

Integration Dependencies refer to the process of deeply integrating with the ecosystem of a particular provider, which may include databases, identity management, or monitoring systems.

Service-Specific Features refer to the utilization of features and services that are exclusive to a single provider and may not be accessible or compatible with other providers.

Implications in a Positive Direction

Specialized Services: Vendor-specific services frequently provide organizations with access to one-of-a-kind capabilities, which enables these organizations to make use of more advanced features and functionality.

Performance that is Optimized: When used correctly, vendor-optimized services have the potential to give improved performance.

Maintaining a relationship with just one service provider can help ensure consistency and uniformity throughout an organization's IT stack.

Implications of a Negative Nature

Reduced Flexibility As a result of being locked in with a single vendor, there is less flexibility and agility available, which makes it more difficult to adjust to shifting business requirements.

Cost Escalation: There is a possibility that providers will raise their pricing over the course of time, leaving companies with less options for controlling their costs.

Not Having Access to the Latest Technologies and Innovations: If you just use one provider, you could not have access to the most recent technologies and innovations that are offered by other providers.

Loss of Bargaining Power: An organization's bargaining power can be eroded when it comes to pricing and terms if they are locked in with a certain vendor.

Dealing with Locked-In Vendors: Some Things to Think About

1. **Determine the Specific Requirements for Your Cloud Service**
   Evaluate your organization's needs in great detail prior to making a decision on a cloud provider. Learn which types of services are necessary and which ones can be skipped. You can lessen the likelihood of becoming locked in to a particular vendor if you adopt a minimalistic strategy and steer clear of needless vendor-specific services.
2. **Support the use of APIs and open standards**
   Choose cloud providers that support open standards and offer open application programming interfaces. By utilizing open technologies like OpenStack and Kubernetes, one may better ensure interoperability and portability across a variety of cloud settings. Open application programming interfaces make it possible to integrate third-party software and hardware.
3. **Microservices and Containerization of Objects**
   The use of containerization technologies like Docker and Kubernetes can provide an additional degree of abstraction, which in turn makes programs more portable. It is much simpler to switch between different cloud providers if apps are first broken down into microservices and then packaged as containers.
4. **The ability to transfer data**
   You can ensure that your data will continue to be portable if you avoid using storage solutions or data formats that are proprietary. Choose storage alternatives that enable data to be readily transferred to other cloud providers or back to on-premises

infrastructure. This is an important consideration when making storage decisions.

5. **A Strategy for Multiple Clouds**
Take into consideration a multi-cloud strategy, which involves utilizing the services of many cloud providers all at once. This strategy reduces reliance on a single provider while also spreading out potential dangers. In addition to this, it gives you the ability to select the most appropriate services for a given workload from among multiple suppliers.

6. **Automation and DevOps Systems**
Create infrastructure as code (IAC) and deployment pipelines by putting into practice DevOps techniques and automating related processes. Automation makes it simpler to maintain, replicate, and migrate your infrastructure and applications, which in turn reduces the likelihood that you will become locked in to a single vendor.

7. **Analyze Your Available Exit Options**
Always make sure you have a plan to get out of any situation. Determine how you can move away from a specific cloud provider in the event that this becomes necessary. Performing this step may require establishing a backup of your data, having a clear plan for the migration, and regularly testing it.

8. **Keep an eye on the costs.**
Maintain a regular evaluation of your cloud expenses to ensure that they are in line with the spending plan for your firm. Always be prepared for a rise in costs, and evaluate whether the value the vendor provides justifies any additional expenditures.

9. **Keep Yourself Informed**
Cloud service companies are continually innovating and adding new services and features to their offerings. Maintain an awareness of the current state of the cloud computing landscape, and think about how the changes may affect the techniques your company employs and the worries it has with vendor lock-in.

10. Considerations Regarding Legal Matters and Contracts

It is important to do a thorough examination of the service-level agreement (SLA) provided by your cloud service provider. Check to see if there are provisions for data ownership, data access, and exit strategies in case you end up having to transfer service providers.

Lock-in Risk Mitigation Technologies for Vendors

1. **Platforms for the Management of Cloud Resources**
   Cloud management platforms, such as CloudHealth, RightScale, and CloudCheckr, offer a unified user interface for the control of numerous cloud service providers. They include solutions for cost efficiency, security management, and governance, all of which assist enterprises in maintaining visibility and control across different cloud environments.

2. **Architectures that Don't Use Servers**
   Serverless computing systems, such as AWS Lambda, Azure Functions, and Google Cloud Functions, abstract infrastructure administration. This decreases the likelihood of being locked into a single provider. Nevertheless, companies need to be aware of the potential dependencies that could arise from platform-specific capabilities.

3. **Containers and the Kubernetes Network**
   An open-source container orchestration technology known as Kubernetes gives businesses the ability to deploy and manage containers across numerous cloud providers. Kubernetes makes it possible for containerized apps to be managed in a portable and consistent manner.

4. **Data Management for Multiple Clouds**
   Data protection, backup, and disaster recovery are all services that may be provided by cloud data management solutions like Veeam and Rubrik, which work across several cloud platforms.

These tools can assist in ensuring data portability and resilience in scenarios that make use of several clouds.

5. **Networking Across Multiple Clouds**

Automation and protection of a network's connections are provided by networking solutions like Cisco Cloud ACI and Aviatrix, which are used in scenarios with many clouds. They make it possible for enterprises to keep their network policies and security controls consistent.

The risk of becoming locked in to a single vendor is significant with cloud computing, but it is not an obstacle that cannot be overcome. You can limit the dangers associated with lock-in and keep the flexibility to react to changing circumstances if you give careful consideration to the requirements of your company, promote open standards and application programming interfaces (APIs), and give some thought to a multi-cloud approach. In addition, you can negotiate the intricacies of multi-cloud setups more efficiently by deploying cloud management tools and technologies that utilize containerization.

Despite the fact that cloud providers offer valuable services and innovations, it is essential for businesses to be proactive in managing their relationships with cloud providers in order to guarantee that they will keep their control and flexibility in the quickly developing cloud landscape. In the end, a well-thought-out cloud strategy should prioritize the cloud's resilience and adaptability while also mitigating the risks associated with being locked in with a single provider.

Chapter 9

Cost Optimization

The optimization of costs is an essential component of cloud computing, as it enables businesses to effectively manage their resources while simultaneously increasing their rate of return on investment. Given the potential for cloud expenses to spiral out of control in the absence of sufficient oversight, efficient cost management is becoming an increasingly critical component of the cloud computing industry as cloud adoption rates continue to rise. In this all-encompassing book, we will delve into the significance of cost optimization in cloud computing, discuss techniques for attaining it, and present best practices for effectively managing cloud expenses.

The Importance of Optimal Cost Management When Using Cloud Computing

Cloud computing provides flexibility, but it's easy for costs to spiral out of control if they aren't carefully managed. Cloud computing can improve cost efficiency. When you optimize your costs, you can make sure that you are only paying for the resources that you actually utilize, which eliminates resource waste.

IT RESILIENCE

Allocation of Resources Ensuring that costs are properly optimized in order to do so effectively helps with resource allocation. You don't have to over-provision resources; instead, you can bring them closer in line with what your real needs are.

Control of Your Budget: The process of cost optimization enables you to establish and maintain control over your cloud budget, so preventing unanticipated and unmanageable costs.

Agility in Scaling: Making effective use of cloud resources enables scaling that is both quicker and more flexible. You have the ability to scale up or down depending on the requirements of your organization.

Allocation of Resources Ensuring that costs are properly optimized in order to do so effectively helps with resource allocation. You don't have to over-provision resources; instead, you can bring them closer in line with what your real needs are.

Strategies for Optimizing the Costs Involved
Adjusting for Size

The term "right-sizing" refers to the process of picking the appropriate instance types and sizes to correspond with the actual requirements of your workloads. You can cut costs while preserving performance if you avoid over-provisioning and under-provisioning by doing the opposite of those things.

Plans for Reserved Occurrences and Financial Savings

When instances or capacity are reserved in advance with a cloud provider, customers are eligible for savings. Savings Plans and Reserved Instances (RIs) allow you to commit to a specific amount of consumption in exchange for cheaper hourly rates, which results in significant cost savings.

Observed Occurrences

Spot instances can be started up at a significantly reduced cost, but this convenience comes with the catch that they can be shut off at any time if the capacity is required somewhere else. They are well suited for workloads that are tolerant of errors and can function normally despite occasional disruptions.

Automatic Scaling

By putting in place auto scaling, you ensure that your application is able to dynamically alter its resource allocation in response to the needs of the workload. This strategy not only boosts performance but also stops unnecessary over-provisioning from occurring.

Keeping an Eye on Things and Filing Reports

Continuous monitoring of your cloud resources is absolutely necessary in order to achieve optimal cost savings. Insights and statistics on consumption gathered in real time can assist in locating possibilities to save costs and keeping tabs on expenditure habits.

The Most Effective Methods for Price Reduction

The process of tagging and grouping resources

Implementing resource tagging and grouping is an effective way to organize resources into categories and distribute charges. Tags make it easier to identify the purpose of each resource as well as its owner, which in turn makes it simpler to keep track of expenses and distribute them.

Tools for Utilization Analyses and Optimisation

Utilize cloud cost analysis and optimization technologies to achieve better visibility into your cloud-based financial obligations. Cost breakdowns, cost estimates, and ideas for optimization are all provided through tools such as AWS Cost Explorer and Azure Cost Management.

Continuous Monitoring of Expenditures

The process of cost optimization is one that never ends. Maintain a routine evaluation of your cloud computing expenses and make any necessary adjustments. Reviewing your budget on a weekly, quarterly, and yearly basis will help you maintain financial control over your expenditures.

The process of decommissioning resources

When resources are no longer required, they should be decommissioned to save money that would otherwise be wasted. This includes powering down or otherwise terminating instances, databases, and storage that are no longer being utilized in any way.

Governance of Costs and Related Policies

Establish transparent policies for the management of costs inside your firm. Determine who is accountable for the monitoring of costs and give standards for the distribution and utilization of resources.

Optimization of Costs Across Multiple Clouds

Numerous businesses utilize the services of more than one cloud provider for reasons including redundancy, compliance, and cost savings. Managing one's expenditures across many cloud environments is an essential part of multi-cloud cost optimization. In order to avoid unnecessary expenditures or underutilization of resources, this situation calls for the implementation of a unified plan, as well as constant monitoring and allocation of those resources.

Considerations Regarding Compliance and Security

Encryption of Data: Make sure that data is encrypted both while it is at rest and when it is being moved around. A significant number of cloud providers offer encryption services and solutions to safeguard sensitive data.

Identity and Access Management (IAM) requires that solutions for IAM be implemented in order to govern access to cloud services. This guarantees that only authorized users or computer systems can access the data and services that are being protected.

Compliance Certifications: Regulatory regulations for data management can be found across many different businesses. Compliance certifications are something that cloud service providers offer to help businesses and organizations fulfill these prerequisites.

Security Monitoring Cloud service providers utilize sophisticated methods for threat detection and response in order to monitor, identify, and neutralize potential security risks in real time.

Perspectives on the Future of Cost Optimization

The FinOps

FinOps, also known as Cloud Financial Management, is a relatively new concept that concentrates on reducing costs incurred by cloud computing. In order to better control cloud expenditures, it is necessary to make adjustments to not only the technology but also the culture and the processes.

Computing without using servers

The concept of serverless computing, which isolates server maintenance from the process of application development, is becoming increasingly popular. Because you only pay for the amount of time that is really executed, it might lead to cost optimization.

AI as well as Machine Learning

Artificial intelligence (AI) and machine learning are currently being incorporated into cloud services in order to improve cost forecasting and optimization of resource allocation.

Computing on the Edge

Edge computing, which moves computation and data storage closer to the source of the data, has the potential to reduce data transit and processing times, hence optimizing costs.

Interoperability and the use of several clouds

Multi-cloud methods are becoming increasingly popular among businesses as a way to circumvent the dangers of vendor lock-in and take advantage of the most advantageous aspects offered by several cloud service providers. It is becoming increasingly important to provide interoperability between different cloud platforms.

It is crucial for businesses to control expenses, maintain budget transparency, and effectively allocate resources; cloud computing cost optimization is a key component in achieving these goals.

It is possible for businesses to guarantee that their expenditure on cloud computing is in line with their business objectives while still delivering value and flexibility by adhering to industry best practices, putting into action methods for cost optimization, and keeping abreast of developing trends.

It is essential to ensure security and compliance while simultaneously optimizing expenses. This will guarantee that data will be safeguarded and that regulatory obligations will be satisfied. The future of cost optimization has the potential for more breakthroughs such as FinOps methods, serverless computing, and the integration of AI and machine learning. These developments will all contribute to improved cloud expenditure effectiveness and efficiency.

9.1 Managing Costs in the Cloud

Computing in the cloud has completely revolutionized the way in which businesses function by providing solutions that are scalable, flexible, and cost-effective. On the other hand, the simplicity with which resources can be provisioned in the cloud can, if they are not managed in an appropriate manner, result in costs that were not anticipated. In order for businesses to guarantee cost effectiveness and make the most of the benefits offered by cloud services, they need to implement efficient cost management strategies and industry standards. In this guide, we will examine the significance of properly managing expenses in the cloud, talk about important tactics for reducing expenditures, and present effective procedures for gaining monetary command.

The Importance of Keeping Costs in Check When Working in the Cloud

Cloud computing provides on-demand resources, however it is simple for expenses to spiral out of control if resources are not allocated effectively since cloud computing provides on-demand resources. When you effectively manage your costs, you can ensure that you only pay for what you consume, so cutting down on wasteful expenditures.

Assigning Resources: An essential part of effective cost management is assigning resources in accordance with actual requirements. This helps to avoid both over-provisioning and waste.

Budget Control: It is essential for organizations to have control over the money they spend in the cloud. They are able to avert unexpected and unmanageable bills by effectively managing their costs, which enables them to develop and adhere to budgets.

Scalability refers to the ability of cloud resources to be adjusted in response to changes in demand. Effective cost management makes agile scaling easier, which in turn enables organizations to more swiftly adapt to changing customer requirements.

Optimization of Resources The process of cost management ensures that cloud resources are used effectively, so making the most of the capacity that is available.

Techniques for Efficiently Handling Financial Obligations in the Cloud

Adjusting for Size

The term "right-sizing" refers to the process of picking the appropriate kind and amount of cloud resources to correspond with the actual needs of your workloads. It is important to avoid either over- or under-provisioning, as this can lead to greater costs and decreased performance, respectively.

Plans for Reserved Occurrences and Financial Savings

Pre-agreeing to reserved instances (RIs) or savings plans, which include committing to a particular amount of consumption in exchange for cheaper hourly prices, qualifies customers for discounts made available by cloud service providers. These alternatives offer significant cost reductions, particularly for labor requirements that may be anticipated.

Observed Occurrences

Spot instances are offered at a far cheaper cost, but the trade-off is that they can be cancelled at any time if the capacity is needed somewhere else. This comes with the package deal that spot instances come with. They are appropriate for fault-tolerant workloads that are able to cope with disruptions.

Automatic Scaling

The amount of resources allocated is automatically adjusted dependent on the amount of work being done. This process is known as auto scaling. It avoids over-provisioning during times of high consumption and under-provisioning during times of low demand, thereby optimizing the utilization of resources and lowering associated costs.

Keeping an Eye on Things and Filing Reports

In order to effectively manage costs, continuous monitoring of cloud resources is required. Real-time insights, usage reports, and cost

IT RESILIENCE

breakdowns are all helpful in determining where potential for cost savings exist and keeping tabs on expenditure habits.

Guidelines for Optimizing Cloud-Based Expenditure Management

The process of tagging and grouping resources

In order to classify cloud resources and allot expenses in an efficient manner, resource tagging and grouping should be implemented. Tags are used to convey information about the purpose of each resource as well as the owner of that resource, which makes it much simpler to manage expenses and distribute costs.

Tools for Utilization Analyses and Optimisation

Utilize cloud cost analysis and optimization technologies to achieve better visibility into your cloud-based financial obligations. Numerous cloud providers make available cost management tools, such as AWS Cost Explorer, Azure Cost Management, and Google Cloud Cost Management. These tools provide cost breakdowns, predictions, and optimization recommendations for the user's cloud infrastructure.

Continuous Monitoring of Expenditures

The process of managing costs is an ongoing one. Maintain a routine evaluation of your cloud computing expenses and make any necessary adjustments. Reviewing your budget on a monthly, quarterly, and yearly basis will allow you to keep better control over your expenditures.

The process of decommissioning resources

When resources are no longer required, they should be decommissioned to save money that would otherwise be wasted. This includes powering down or otherwise terminating instances, databases, and storage that are no longer being utilized in any way.

Governance of Costs and Related Policies

Establish transparent policies for the management of costs inside your firm. Determine who is accountable for the monitoring of costs and give standards for the distribution and utilization of resources.

Considerations Regarding Compliance and Security

Encryption of Data: Make sure that data is encrypted both while it is at rest and when it is being moved around. A significant number of cloud providers offer encryption services and solutions to safeguard sensitive data.

Identity and Access Management (IAM) requires that solutions for IAM be implemented in order to govern access to cloud services. This guarantees that only authorized users or computer systems can access the data and services that are being protected.

Compliance Certifications: Regulatory regulations for data management can be found across many different businesses. Compliance certifications are something that cloud service providers offer to help businesses and organizations fulfill these prerequisites.

Security Monitoring Cloud service providers utilize sophisticated methods for threat detection and response in order to monitor, identify, and neutralize potential security risks in real time.

Developing Tendencies in the Management of Cloud Costs
The FinOps

FinOps, which stands for "Cloud Financial Management," is a relatively new technique that concentrates on reducing costs incurred by cloud computing. In order to better control cloud expenditures, it is necessary to make adjustments to not only the technology but also the culture and the processes.

Computing without using servers

Serverless computing separates the task of managing servers from that of developing applications. This can result in potential savings for businesses, as they will only be charged for the time it takes to actually execute their code.

AI as well as Machine Learning

Artificial intelligence (AI) and machine learning are currently being incorporated into cloud services in order to improve cost prediction and analysis, optimize resource allocation, and make recommendations for cost optimization.

Computing on the Edge

Edge computing, which moves computation and data storage closer to the source of the data, has the potential to reduce data transit and processing times, hence optimizing costs.

Interoperability and the use of several clouds

Multi-cloud methods are becoming increasingly popular among businesses of all sizes as a means to circumvent the dangers of vendor lock-in and take advantage of the most advantageous characteristics offered by several cloud service providers.

It is becoming increasingly important for cloud platforms to be interoperable with one another, which enables resources to be seamlessly shared and controlled.

It is crucial for businesses to manage their expenditures in the cloud if they wish to effectively control their spending, maintain budget transparency, and properly allocate their resources. It is possible for businesses to guarantee that their expenditure on cloud computing is in line with their business objectives while still delivering value and flexibility by adhering to industry best practices, putting into action methods for cost optimization, and keeping abreast of developing trends.

It is essential to ensure security and compliance while simultaneously optimizing expenses. This will guarantee that data will be safeguarded and that regulatory obligations will be satisfied. The future of cloud cost management has the potential for more breakthroughs such as FinOps methods, serverless computing, and the integration of AI and machine learning. These developments will all contribute to improved cloud expenditure effectiveness and efficiency.

9.2 Cost vs. Resilience Trade-offs

When it comes to planning for business continuity, cost and resilience are two crucial factors to consider. To ensure that their operations can survive disruptions and recover efficiently after they occur, businesses need to establish the optimal balance between these many aspects. This choice between cost savings and resilience can be difficult to make because prioritizing cost savings may reduce resilience, while concentrating only on resilience may result in exorbitant costs. In this post, we will discuss the cost vs. resilience trade-offs in business continuity planning, as well as the reasons why achieving the proper balance is so important, as well as techniques to achieve it.

The Importance of Maintaining a Consistent Business Continuity

The ability of an organization to perform critical services and recover from disruptions, whether such disruptions are caused by natural disasters, cyberattacks, interruptions in the supply chain, or other unforeseen occurrences, is what is meant by the term "business continuity." It is an essential component of effective risk management and making certain that a company will be profitable in the long run. Planning for business continuity entails developing strategies and putting in place procedures that reduce the amount of time an organization is offline and the amount of data it loses. This helps ensure that the business can continue to function normally in the face of disruptions.

The Catch-22 of Balancing Expenses and Benefits

The most economical option

The concept of cost efficiency refers to the practice of cutting costs while simultaneously improving the use of available resources. When it comes to planning for business continuity, cost efficiency is critical for ensuring that investments in resilience are justified by the organization's financial performance. This is also important for sustaining profitability in the process.

Capacity for Bouncing Back

Building strong systems and techniques that can survive disturbances and swiftly get back on their feet is an essential component of resilience. It is necessary to make investments in redundant systems, backups, disaster recovery planning, and cybersecurity precautions. Although these investments may be expensive, they are essential for continuing business as usual in the face of unfavorable circumstances.

Finding a Good Middle Ground

Finding an optimal equilibrium between cost and resilience is a difficult task that must be accomplished. An organization could be left susceptible if it places an excessive amount of emphasis on cost efficiency, which could lead to inadequate protection and recovery systems. On the other side, placing an excessive amount of emphasis on resilience might result in superfluous expenses, which may have a negative impact on profitability.

Ways to Strike a Balance Strategies for Striking a Balance

1. **An Evaluation of the Dangers**
   Carry out a detailed risk assessment in order to gain an understanding of the potential dangers that could affect the organization and the impact that they could have. This study contributes to determining which areas are the most crucial in terms of the need for resilience measures. You will be able to more effectively manage resources if you center your attention on the most serious dangers.
2. **An examination of the effects on the company**
   Carry out a business impact analysis (BIA) in order to evaluate the effects that interruptions will have on several parts of the organization, including as revenue, the level of pleasure experienced by customers, and reputation. The results of this analysis can help prioritize resilience measures depending on the impact such measures will have on essential business processes.
3. **An evaluation of the costs and benefits**
   Carry out cost-benefit evaluations for the many different indicators of resilience. Analyze the financial repercussions of the various tactics, including the initial expenses of implementing them and the amount of money they could save you during a disruption. With the use of this study, decisions regarding which steps are most cost-effective can be made.
4. **A Hierarchy for the Mitigation of Risk**
   Create a hierarchy for risk reduction that separates different types of resilience measures into distinct groups according to the level of importance they hold. For instance, actions that have a direct

influence on the safety of customers or legal compliance should have a greater priority than those that have an impact on operations that are not vital.

5. **The Progress Made in Small Steps**
   Step-by-step, beginning with the steps that are both the most important and the most cost-efficient, resilience measures should be implemented. Eventually, when the organization's financial status improves, additional measures should be invested in to boost its resilience.

6. **Outsourcing and Cloud Computing**
   Make use of cloud services and outsourcing for your particular requirements for resilience. Outsourcing can provide access to specialized expertise without the need for an organization to invest in-house, and cloud providers frequently offer disaster recovery solutions that are both effective and cost-efficient.

7. **Making Contingency Plans**
   Employ scenario planning to mimic a variety of potential disruptions and the effects those disruptions will have on the company. This gives you the ability to evaluate the efficacy of resilience measures and make adjustments to them as required.

8. **Performing Routine Checkups and Maintenance**

It is imperative that resilience measures be tested frequently and maintained regularly. In the event of an interruption, unanticipated costs may be incurred as a result of outdated or inadequately set systems. Testing these measures on a regular basis guarantees that they perform as expected.

Examples Taken From the Real World

1. **A Local Shop or Boutique**
   When faced with the challenge of protecting its point-of-sale (POS) system against the possibility of data breaches and cyber-attacks, a small store operating on a limited budget must make a

IT RESILIENCE

decision. It is absolutely necessary for resiliency to be achieved by the investment in strong cybersecurity measures, such as firewalls, intrusion detection systems, and frequent security audits. However, there is a continuous expense associated with these precautions. The store makes the decision to implement both essential cybersecurity measures as well as insurance for cybersecurity in order to strike a balance between cost and resilience. This strategy reduces the risk of potential harm while keeping the costs within reasonable limits.

2. **Organizations in the Financial Sector**

A sizable financial organization understands the significance of resiliency when it comes to preserving trust and being in compliance with industry rules. Nevertheless, it is under pressure to lower its operating costs. In order to strike a balance between these requirements, the organization makes investments in a highly redundant data center architecture. This is done to ensure that users always have access to financial services, even if there is a malfunction in the system. The organization views this as a long-term investment in resilience and compliance, which will enable them to continue providing uninterrupted services to their clients despite the fact that it comes with hefty up-front expenditures.

When it comes to planning for business continuity, every company has to face the difficult choice of how to strike a balance between cost and resilience. A company leaves itself open to the possibility of interruptions if it places all of its attention on reducing costs, while placing an excessive amount of emphasis on its resilience can result in costs that are not essential. Organizations are able to discover the optimal balance that corresponds with their particular requirements as well as their available financial resources if they carry out exhaustive risk assessments, cost-benefit evaluations, and regular testing. To ensure that the organization can sustain disruptions, recover quickly from them, and keep its profitability while safeguarding its reputation and the faith of its customers, the goal is to ensure that the company can.

9.3 Cost Optimization Strategies

The optimization of costs is an essential part of running a business. It entails using a methodical approach to cut down on expenses that aren't necessary and to increase the effectiveness with which resources are utilized. Because of the increasingly cutthroat nature of the modern business world, companies are always looking for new ways to reduce expenses while keeping or even improving the quality of the goods and services they offer. In this article, we will discuss various cost optimization tactics that can assist organizations in maximizing efficiency, increasing profits, and maintaining a competitive edge in their respective markets.

The Importance of Getting the Most Out of Your Money

Increased Profitability A direct contributor to increased profitability is a reduction in expenditures. It gives businesses the opportunity to reinvest in growth and innovation or to reallocate resources to other areas.

Advantage in the Market Businesses who are able to reduce their operating costs can offer their goods and services at pricing that are more in line with their competitors, thereby attracting and maintaining more customers.

Allocation of Resources: Optimization helps to make sure that available resources are used effectively and with a focus on what is most vital to the accomplishment of an organization's goals and mission.

Efficiency in cost management not only helps to cut down on financial waste, but it also makes a contribution to the sustainability of both the social and environmental systems.

Strategies for Optimizing the Costs Involved

1. **Managing in a Lean Manner**

    The principles of lean management are designed to minimize waste while maximizing value. The reduction of non-essential operations, the simplification of workflows, and the improvement of efficiency are all priorities for organizations. By reducing business processes, this technique has the potential to lead to significant cost reductions.

2. **Automation of the Process**

    The automation of activities that are repetitive and require human work can save time and cut down on labor costs. Robotic process automation (RPA) is one example of a technology that enables businesses to free up their personnel to focus on higher-value activities by taking care of repetitive duties.

3. **Management of the Vendors**

    It is essential to manage connections with vendors in an effective manner. Organizations are able to lower their procurement expenses if they negotiate advantageous terms and take advantage of volume purchasing opportunities. The performance of vendors should be evaluated on a regular basis, and alternative suppliers should be investigated. Both of these practices can contribute to cost reductions.

4. **Computing in the Cloud**

    Scalability and cost savings are two benefitss that come with using cloud services. By just paying for the computing resources that they make use of, organizations can cut down on their capital expenditures. In addition, cloud service providers frequently give solutions for cost control to assist customers in reducing unnecessary expenditures.

5. **Efficient Use of Energy**

    Not only can lowering your energy consumption bring down your monthly power bills, but it will
    also help the environment in the long run. LED lighting and other energy-efficient technologies and practices, such as smart HVAC systems and other such innovations, can result in significant cost savings.

6. **Management of the Inventory**

    When inventory levels are optimized, there is less likelihood of overstocking, which in turn reduces carrying costs and the possibility of items becoming obsolete. At the same time, it guarantees that products will be available when required in order to fulfill the requirements of the customers.

7. **Effectiveness of the Workforce**

   Improving the effectiveness of the workforce requires careful planning of the personnel, as well as training and supervision of performance. It guarantees that personnel are productive, engaged, and employed to the fullest extent possible.

8. **Analysis of the Data**

   Utilizing data analytics helps companies spot possibilities to save costs and improve profitability. Decision-making that is informed by data can be achieved when businesses do data analysis to get insights into customer behavior, the success of their supply chain, and the efficiency of their operations.

9. **Management of the Total Quality**

   The Total Quality Management (TQM) approach places an emphasis on an organization's commitment to quality in all facets of the business. A focus on quality results in fewer instances of rework and greater levels of customer satisfaction, both of which lead to cost reductions over the long term.

10. **The use of third-party services**

The concept of outsourcing functions that are not essential to the operation can be very cost effective. Costs associated with personnel and infrastructure can be cut for businesses if they contract out work to external consultants or service providers.

Implementing Cost Optimization with the Most Effective Best Practices

1. **Clearly define your goals and priorities.**

   Define your goals for your attempts to optimize your costs as precisely as possible. It is important to have a clear understanding of the goals you wish to accomplish, such as lowering overhead expenses, increasing operational efficiency, or increasing profits.

2. **Include Important Stakeholders in the Process**
   Include the perspectives of people working in different departments and teams inside your organization. They are able to provide useful insights into areas in which measures for cost optimization have the potential to have the most substantial impact.

3. **Take Readings and Keep Track**
   It is vital to measure and monitor something in a continuous manner in order to track development and identify areas that require additional attention. Key performance indicators (KPIs) pertaining to cost minimization should be reviewed on a regular basis.

4. **Establish a System of Feedback Loops**
   Create feedback tools that will enable employees to share their thoughts and input on how to optimize costs. An organizational culture that emphasizes continual improvement can be a powerful driver of innovation in cost-cutting techniques.

5. **Adapt to the New Technology**
   Utilize various technological and software solutions in order to assist in the process of cost optimization. The process can be made more efficient with the help of tools for financial analysis, data analytics, and project management.

6. **Engage in Communicating and Training**
   It is critical to have clear and effective communication. Maintain open communication with all stakeholders regarding the cost optimization activities, and provide training wherever it is required. Make sure every employee knows exactly what part they play in the process.

7. **Keep an eye on current market trends.**

Maintain an awareness of the latest market conditions, industry trends, and technological developments, all of which may have an effect on your efforts to optimize your costs. Always be ready to adjust your strategy to fit the new parameters.

Examples Taken From the Real World

1. **Walmart.com**
   Walmart, one of the largest retailers in the world, has been a leader in the field of supply chain optimization for many years. A cross-docking system was implemented by the company in order to cut down on the costs associated with carrying inventory. Additionally, the company integrated advanced inventory management systems and invested in data analytics in order to maximize stock levels. Walmart has been able to keep its prices competitive while simultaneously enhancing its operational efficiency thanks to these techniques.
2. **The Amazon**

Amazon has achieved remarkable success in optimizing its costs by leveraging technology and automation. The usage of robots in the company's warehouses allows for more streamlined order fulfillment, which in turn reduces the need for human labor and improves overall efficiency. In addition, Amazon provides businesses with cost-effective cloud services through its Amazon Web Services (AWS) division, which specializes in cloud computing. These services enable businesses to scale their operations without making major initial investments.

The optimization of costs is a process that is essential for businesses that want to thrive in a highly competitive business environment. Companies have the power to improve their profitability, maintain their competitiveness, and achieve sustainability if they adopt successful strategies and put best practices into action. The most important thing is to take a comprehensive strategy to cost optimization, which means incorporating all facets of the firm and reiterating your dedication to ongoing development. When they do so, organizations may maintain their agility, improve their efficiency, and better prepare themselves for future difficulties.

10

Chapter 10

The Future of IT Resilience and Cloud

In order to meet the ever-evolving requirements of the digital age, the landscape of information technology (IT) resilience and cloud computing is experiencing substantial transformations. Resilience in information technology, which refers to an organization's capacity to adjust to shocks, limit downtime, and continue operations without interruption, has emerged as a crucial component in the modern-day business environment. Cloud computing has simultaneously emerged as a disruptive force, bringing scalability, agility, and cost-efficiencies that are transforming the landscape of both information technology and business.

This all-encompassing book investigates the prospects of IT resilience and the cloud, concentrating on the changing landscape, developing trends, and problems, as well as the roles that these factors will play in determining the future of the business and technological world.

In this day and age, having resilient information technology is essential

The Concept of IT Resilience

IT RESILIENCE

Resilience in information technology refers to an organization's ability to endure and recover from disturbances while still keeping vital processes running smoothly. These disturbances can be caused by anything from natural catastrophes and cyberattacks to malfunctioning gear and faulty software. Resilience in information technology (IT) refers to the use of proactive tactics, redundancy, and recovery procedures to ensure that an organization can continue operating normally even when faced with challenging circumstances.

The Importance of Having a Resilient IT System

Continuous Operations: The resilience of a company's information technology infrastructure ensures that the organization can function without significant interruptions, so preserving both its productivity and its customers' happiness.

Data protection is the safeguarding of essential data, preventing the loss, breaches, or corruption of data, all of which can have devastating effects on businesses.

Reputation in the Market: Customers have come to anticipate that the services they pay for will be accessible whenever they have a need for them, thus an organization's capacity for resilience is important to its ability to retain its reputation.

Compliance with criteria and Legal Requirements Many different types of businesses and jurisdictions have distinct criteria for the protection of data and the continuity of corporate operations, which has made resilience a legal obligation.

The Revolutionary Potential of Internet-Based Services
Comprehending the Concept of Cloud Computing

Infrastructure as a Service, often known as IaaS, is a model that makes it possible to access virtualized computer resources, including as servers, storage, and networking, via the internet.

Platform as a Service (PaaS) is a model that eliminates the need for application developers to deal with the complexities of infrastructure management by providing a platform on which they may design, deploy, and maintain their applications.

Delivers software programs over the internet and enables users to access and utilize software without the need for local installation. This model of software distribution is known as software as a service, or SaaS.

Advantages of Utilizing Cloud Computing

Scalability refers to the ability of cloud resources to swiftly be scaled up or down to fit demand, which enables cloud computing to be more cost efficient.

Agility: Because the cloud enables rapid deployment and adaptability, it shortens the amount of time needed to bring new applications and services to market.

Using pay-as-you-go models allows businesses to lower their capital expenses and eliminate the need to make investments in on-premises infrastructure, which results in improved cost efficiency.

Reach Across the Globe Because cloud services can be accessed from any location, they make global cooperation and growth possible.

Data Redundancy Cloud service providers frequently provide data redundancy and backup services, which together improve the resilience and protection of stored data.

IT Resilience and the Cloud: Two Roads That Are Converging

Backup and Recovery of Data Cloud services provide a wide variety of alternatives for backing up and recovering data, which lessens the likelihood of losing data and improves disaster recovery strategies.

Redundancy: Cloud systems can provide redundancy on a geographic scale, which ensures that essential data and applications are replicated in many regions so that they can withstand calamities that occur in specific regions.

Scalability and Elasticity: The scalability and elasticity of the cloud make it possible for enterprises to adjust their workloads in response to changing conditions while maintaining both performance and continuity.

Automation: Automation in the cloud makes it possible to respond quickly to disturbances by providing the option to immediately switch over to backup systems and resources.

The Prospects for Cloud Computing and IT Resilience
Resilience Across Multiple Clouds

Multi-cloud solutions are becoming increasingly popular among organizations as a means to circumvent the dangers of vendor lock-in and make the most of the distinctive capabilities provided by several cloud service providers. By distributing the workloads and the data across several different cloud environments, this method makes it possible to achieve higher levels of resilience. Additionally, it offers redundancy in the event that a single cloud service provider encounters an outage.

Protection of Data and Resistance to Cyberattacks

The proliferation of online dangers and data breaches has led to a major uptick in the focus on a network's ability to withstand cyberattacks. Even in the face of sophisticated assaults, businesses are making investments in robust cybersecurity measures and data protection policies to ensure that their data will continue to be secure while still being accessible.

Computing on the Edge and Maintaining Resilience

The practice of edge computing, which entails processing data in a location that is physically closer to the source of the data, is becoming increasingly popular. This strategy reduces latency and enhances responsiveness, but it also creates new issues for the robustness of the system. In order to guarantee the dependability of the data processing that occurs at the edge, companies will need to construct edge computing infrastructures that are robust.

Artificial intelligence and automation in resiliency

There has been a recent uptick in the number of IT resilience techniques that incorporate artificial intelligence (AI) and automation. These technologies are able to predict and react to disruptions more quickly and precisely than humans, which helps to cut down on downtime and improves overall resilience.

Several Obstacles Looming in the Future

Concerns Regarding Security In light of the growing prevalence of cyberattacks and the ever-increasing reliance on cloud computing, businesses have an increasing responsibility to give top priority to the implementation of stringent security measures.

Privacy of Data and Compliance With Data Regulations As data regulations become more stringent, enterprises have a greater responsibility to ensure that they are in compliance with data privacy laws.

Interoperability is crucial in multi-cloud systems because it allows for communication and collaboration across various cloud service providers. The efficient management of multiple cloud ecosystems presents organizations with a number of obstacles that must be overcome.

Shortages of trained employees The incorporation of AI and automation into resilience tactics necessitates the employment of trained employees, which might be difficult to find.

Management of Costs It might be difficult to strike a balance between affordability and reliability in cloud systems. Spending on the cloud needs to be optimized by organizations, but this must come at the expense of reliability.

10.1 Emerging Technologies and Trends

The technological landscape is continuously undergoing new and exciting changes. The future is being shaped by new technologies and trends, which are having an impact on every part of our lives, including the way we work, the way we communicate, the way we do business, and the way we respond to global concerns. In this in-depth guide, we will investigate the most significant emerging technologies and trends, their effects on society, business, and innovation, as well as the possibility for a future that is both exciting and revolutionary that these technologies and trends possess.

The Quickening Pace of Technological Progress and Innovation

1. **A Higher Degree of Connectivity**

   A worldwide network has been established as a result of the widespread availability of high-speed internet as well as the proliferation of smartphones and other connected devices. This network makes it possible for information, ideas, and innovations to be rapidly traded across the network.

2. **Access to Large Amounts of Data**

   The collecting and examination of large amounts of data have revealed insights and patterns that fuel the development of new ideas. Decision-making that is informed by data has emerged as an essential factor in the progression of technological advances.

3. **Capability of Computation**

   The development of technologies that are both more complicated and more advanced has been made possible by advancements in processing power. These advancements have been driven by Moore's Law and by inventions such as quantum computing.

4. **Open Source Software and Collaborative Work**

The open-source movement and increased collaboration within the global IT community have made it easier for new technologies to be developed and disseminated quickly.

Prominent New Technologies and Trends in the Industry

1. **Artificial Intelligence, also abbreviated as AI**

   One of the technologies that has the potential to completely revolutionize our world is artificial intelligence. The areas of artificial intelligence that are making the most headway right now include machine learning, natural language processing, and deep learning. The application of artificial intelligence (AI) in a variety of fields, ranging from driverless vehicles to healthcare, is poised to alter how we live and work.

2. **IoT stands for the Internet of Things.**

   The network of interconnected devices, sensors, and other things that gather and share data is referred to as the "Internet of Things." The Internet of Things has found uses in a variety of fields, including industrial automation, smart homes, healthcare, and more. It is anticipated that it would continue to grow and bring about transformations in several industries.

3. **Technology Based on 5G**

    The introduction of 5G technology is going to completely change the way people connect to the internet since it will provide lightning-fast download times and little lag. This technology will pave the way for future developments in augmented reality (AR), virtual reality (VR), and the Internet of Things, which will make it possible to create new apps and services.

4. **A distributed ledger system**

    Blockchain technology was first designed for use with cryptocurrencies like Bitcoin; however, it is already finding applications in a wide range of businesses. It ensures that records are kept in a way that is both secure and transparent, and it has applications in the administration of supply chains, voting systems, and other areas.

5. **Computing on the Quantum Level**

    The advent of quantum computing may herald a sea change in the way computers are used. It is able to solve difficult problems that traditional computers are unable to tackle at this time. The capabilities of quantum computing will be useful in a variety of fields, including encryption, the pharmaceutical industry, and materials science.

6. **The Biotechnology Industry and Genomic Research**

    Breakthroughs in personalized treatment, gene editing, and the prevention of disease have been made possible as a result of developments in genomics and biotechnology. These technological advancements are having a profound impact on healthcare as well as the ways in which we comprehend and manage disease.

7. **Sustainable Development and the Role of Renewable Energy**

    The movement toward renewable energy sources like solar and wind power is pushing innovation in energy storage, grid management, and environmentally responsible practices. Sustainability

is a top priority on a worldwide scale, and the application of technology is essential to attaining environmental objectives.
8. **Mixed reality experiences such as augmented reality (AR) and virtual reality (VR)**

The augmented reality (AR) and virtual reality (VR) technologies are making advances in a number of different areas, including gaming, education, healthcare, and design. They provide experiences that are completely engrossing and are constantly developing in terms of the hardware and the material they give.

Influence on Both Society and Industry

1. **The Evolution of Digital Technology**
   In order to maintain their positions in the market, businesses are experiencing digital revolutions. They are implementing AI, IoT, and data analytics in order to improve consumer experiences, streamline operations, and drive innovation.
2. **Variations in the Workforce**
   The nature of employment is shifting as a result of the impact that automation and AI are having across a variety of industries. In order for the workforce to adjust to these shifts, retraining and additional education are becoming increasingly necessary.
3. **Recent Progress in Health Care**
   Biotechnology, genetics, and telemedicine are all contributing to improvements in patient outcomes through boosting the delivery of healthcare and individualized treatment options.
4. **Long-Term Viability of the Environment**
   The adoption of sustainable practices, renewable forms of energy, and circular economies is being propelled forward by technological advancements, which in turn helps to address global environmental concerns.
5. **Confidentiality and safety concerns**
   Privacy and data security are becoming increasingly important as

a result of the growing interconnectivity of devices and the use of data to drive decision-making. In order to solve these problems, new rules and cybersecurity measures are currently being developed.

6. **Instruction and Acquiring Knowledge**

Education is being transformed by technology, which is also making learning easier to obtain. Platforms for online learning, adaptive learning, and other educational technologies are all reshaping the ways in which information is obtained and disseminated.

Concerns and Things to Take Into Account

1. **Problems of an Ethical Nature**
   In particular, artificial intelligence creates ethical challenges, such as those pertaining to bias, privacy, and the making of decisions. The creation of ethical frameworks is an essential step in the process of guiding the development and application of technology.
2. **Safety and privacy online**
   Cyberattacks and data breaches are becoming increasingly likely to occur as the use of technology becomes more pervasive in our everyday lives. The defense of digital infrastructure should be a top concern.
3. **Legal and Regulatory Structures**
   The swiftness with which technology is advancing necessitates regulatory adjustments on both the national and international levels. This includes tackling challenges like data privacy, governance of artificial intelligence, and digital currency.
4. **Disruption in the Workforce**
   The loss of jobs that can be attributed to automation and AI necessitates the development of policies for the retraining of the workforce as well as an emphasis on the creation of jobs in emerging industries.
5. **Availability of Access**

The task of ensuring that the benefits of technical advances are available to all people, irrespective of considerations such as economic standing or location, is a continuing one.

Opportunities for the Future and Emerging Technologies

1. **The Investigation of Space**
   The improvement of technology will make it possible to conduct more extensive space exploration, which could eventually lead to the establishment of space tourism, the settlement of the moon, and the discovery of extraterrestrial life.
2. **A Revolution in Energy Use**
   Innovations in energy storage as well as in the use of renewable energy sources have the potential to completely transform our energy systems, making them both more sustainable and effective.
3. **Recent Advances in Medical Care**
   Genomic medicine and drug development that is driven by artificial intelligence have the potential to lead to improved customized healthcare and new treatments for difficult diseases.
4. **Internet on the Quantum Level**
   The creation of a quantum internet may one day make possible highly protected communication, as well as improvements in data transport and encryption capacities.
5. **Enhancement of the Human Condition**

Human augmentation could be achieved by the use of technologies such as brain-computer interfaces and wearable technology, which would increase our cognitive and physical capacities.

The future of up-and-coming technologies and fashion trends is both thrilling and transformational in equal measure. Technology continues to have a tremendous impact on society, industry, and our day-to-day lives, and this trend is only expected to continue. In order to successfully navigate this constantly shifting terrain, it is essential that we address difficulties such as ethical considerations, cybersecurity, and regulatory frameworks, while at the same time remaining open to the opportunities that emerging technologies have to offer.

The future holds the potential for amazing advancements in the fields of space travel, healthcare, the energy sector, and human enhancement. The quickening pace of technical innovation is the primary force behind modern advancement and is providing answers to many of the most important problems facing the globe today. It is a future that will be characterized by the capacity for adaptation, ethical responsibility, and the limitless potential of human inventiveness.

10.2 AI and Machine Learning in Resilience

The influence that Artificial Intelligence (AI) and Machine Learning (ML) are having on resiliency is significant due to the fact that these two technologies are transforming a variety of different industries. In a world that is becoming more linked and unpredictable, the capacity to respond effectively to disturbances and quickly recover is absolutely necessary. AI and ML offer advanced tools that can boost resilience by detecting and reacting to disruptions, automating operations, and delivering real-time insights. These techniques can also be used to streamline procedures. In this book, we will look into the role that AI and ML play in resiliency, explore their applications across a variety of different industries, and evaluate the benefits and problems that these technologies bring to the table.

The Crucial Importance of Resilience

The ability to tolerate stresses and recover efficiently after they have been experienced is what we mean when we talk about resilience. These disruptions can be caused by a variety of events, including natural catastrophes, cyberattacks, pauses in the supply chain, or even pandemics in some cases. Resilience is an important quality for companies, governments, and organizations to have in order to keep their operations running smoothly, keep their trust and reputation intact, and protect the well-being of their stakeholders.

The Contributions of AI and ML to the Concept of Resilience

1. **Analytical Predictions and Modeling**
   Algorithms based on AI and ML can examine past data in order to recognize trends that indicate impending problems. Because of this predictive capabilities, firms are better able to prepare for anticipated problems and take preventative action to limit risks.
2. **Systematic Approach to the Problem**
   In areas of the world that are prone to the occurrence of natural disasters, early warning systems driven by AI employ data collected from a variety of sources, such as meteorological forecasts and seismic sensors, to issue alerts in real time, thereby facilitating both evacuation and preparation.
3. **Resilience of the Supply Chain**
   Artificial intelligence has the ability to improve the efficiency of supply chains by assisting with demand forecasting, the identification of potential interruptions, and the suggestion of alternative suppliers or routes. The capability of a corporation to adjust to unanticipated occurrences is improved as a result of this.
4. **Protection of Computer Networks**
   When it comes to detecting cyber risks and devising effective countermeasures, AI and ML are indispensable tools. Models that use machine learning can identify anomalies in network traffic and user behavior, which enables real-time identification of threats and lowers the risk of data breaches.
5. **Recovery from Natural Disasters**
   In the event of a system breakdown or an outage at the data center, disaster recovery solutions that are powered by AI are able to duplicate data and applications to remote sites in an autonomous fashion, thereby assuring minimal downtime.
6. **The Resilience of the Infrastructure**
   Maintenance and monitoring of essential infrastructure, such as electricity grids, bridges, and highways, that is driven by AI can assist discover potential problems before they become severe enough to cause disruptions. These technologies make predictive

maintenance possible and improve the overall performance of infrastructure.

7. **Resilience of the Healthcare System**

AI and ML have applications in the medical field, including the early diagnosis of diseases, the triage of patients during emergency situations, and the predicted allocation of hospital resources. During the COVID-19 epidemic, these technologies have shown to be of incalculable use.

Using AI and ML to Improve Resilience and Its Benefits

1. **Instantaneous Reaction**
   Artificial intelligence (AI) systems are able to rapidly evaluate and respond to interruptions, which reduces downtime and lessens the effect of disasters.

2. **Mechanized Processes**
   Artificial intelligence and machine learning automate routine operations, freeing up human resources to concentrate on making crucial decisions in the face of disruptions.

3. **Making decisions based on the analysis of data**
   Machine learning models examine enormous volumes of data in order to present enterprises with actionable insights, which in turn assists these organizations in making educated decisions.

4. **Improvements to the Predictions**
   The more accurate forecasting of prospective problems that is made possible by predictive analytics enables better planning for disruptions to occur.

5. **An increase in productiveness**
   Increasing the effectiveness of processes like the management of supply chains and the upkeep of infrastructure leads to increased productivity in day-to-day operations as well as in resilience initiatives.

IT RESILIENCE

6. **Reductions in Expenses**

   The costs that are associated with downtime, unscheduled maintenance, and inefficient resource allocation can be reduced with the assistance of AI and ML.

7. **Capacity for Change**

The ability of machine learning models to adapt to shifting conditions and learn from previous disruptions enables businesses and other institutions to continuously improve their resilience plans.

Difficulties Associated with the Implementation of AI and ML in Resilience

1. **The Quality of the Data**

   When it comes to training and making accurate predictions, AI and ML models require high-quality data. Data that is inconsistent or biased can result in the production of erroneous results.

2. **Knowledge and experience**

   A staff with the necessary skills is required in order to implement AI and ML in resilience tactics. The recruitment and retention of data scientists and AI professionals is a challenge for many different types of enterprises.

3. **Moral and Social Considerations**

   The use of artificial intelligence (AI) in crisis decision-making may give rise to ethical problems, particularly in circumstances where human lives could be at risk.

4. **Expenses**

   Initial investments in artificial intelligence and machine learning infrastructure, as well as training, can be large; therefore, businesses need to examine the cost-benefit ratio very carefully.

5. **Incorporation of**

The incorporation of AI and ML into pre-existing processes and systems can be a challenging endeavor that calls for significant investment of both time and resources to ensure a smooth transition.

Applications in the Real World

1. **The Prediction of Hurricanes**
   Artificial intelligence is being utilized by the National Oceanic and Atmospheric Administration (NOAA) in order to enhance storm predictions. In order to improve predictions of hurricane tracks and intensities using machine learning models, historical data is analyzed. This results in more accurate and timely warnings.
2. **Reactions to Natural Disasters**
   The World Food Programme (WFP) of the United Nations employs artificial intelligence to aid in disaster response. In the aftermath of natural catastrophes, AI algorithms analyze satellite imagery to determine the extent of damage and determine the order of priority for help distribution.
3. **Resilience in Financial Matters**
   Artificial intelligence is being used by financial institutions to detect fraudulent activities and real-time cyberattacks. Anomalies in transaction data can be spotted using machine learning models, which can then cause warnings to be generated for urgent action.
4. **Readiness of the Healthcare System**

During the COVID-19 pandemic, AI and ML were utilized to make predictions regarding the transmission of the virus, analyze medical data in search of possible cures, and improve the distribution of resources inside hospitals.

The Role that AI and ML Will Play in the Future of Resilience

1. **Improved Capabilities in the Area of Prediction**
   The continued development of machine learning models will

result in more accurate predictions, which will allow businesses to more confidently prepare for the effects of disruptions.

2. **The Reaction of the Body on Its Own**
   AI systems will grow more capable of responding independently to disruptions and making quick judgments to lessen the impact they have.
3. **Collaboration Between Humans and AI**
   Together with human decision-makers, AI and ML will increasingly collaborate to offer insights and recommendations for more effective resilience tactics.
4. **Resilience to Change and Adaptation**
   Machine learning models will adapt to changing situations and dynamically change resilience tactics based on real-time data and emerging risks. This will allow the models to better protect against future dangers.
5. **Cooperation on a Global Scale**

The worldwide response to natural disasters and man-made disruptions could be improved with the help of international collaboration in the research, development, and implementation of AI-driven resilience solutions.

The landscape of resilience is undergoing a transformation as a result of the rise of AI and ML, which offer new tools and capacities to foresee, respond to, and recover from shocks. These technologies offer a wide range of advantages, such as improved speed of response and decision-making, increased automation and productivity, and enhanced reliance on data.

However, in order to properly exploit AI and ML in resilience, obstacles such as data quality, knowledge, ethical concerns, pricing, and integration need to be solved. Applications in the real world highlight the discernible influence that these technologies are having across a variety of industries.

The future has the potential for even greater advances in autonomous response, adaptive resilience, and predictive capacities. In a world that is becoming more unpredictable, AI and ML will continue to play a crucial part in guaranteeing the resilience of businesses, communities, and societies.

10.3 Sustainability and Resilience

The ideas of sustainability and resilience are becoming increasingly interwoven in an era that is characterized by climate change, the depletion of natural resources, and the expansion of environmental concerns. The foundation for resilience is provided by sustainability, which places an emphasis on the responsible management of resources and environmental stewardship. Resilience refers to the capacity to adapt, endure shocks, and recover from disruptions. In this book, we investigate the essential connection that exists between sustainability and resilience, as well as their consequences for a variety of different industries and the ways in which they, collectively, form a more robust and environmentally friendly future.

The interdependence of sustainable development and strong communities

1. **Administration of Resources**
   Managing our planet's resources in an ethical manner is the cornerstone of sustainability. It entails producing less waste, preserving resources, and having a less overall impact on the environment. These environmentally responsible behaviors immediately contribute to resilience by assuring a consistent resource base even in the face of disturbance.

2. **Actions to Reduce the Impacts of Climate Change**
   The effects of climate change, which include both extreme weather and natural disasters, are
   substantial contributors to the occurrence of disruptions. Both the negative effects of climate change and our ability to withstand them can be mitigated via the adoption of sustainable practices

such as cutting emissions of greenhouse gases and shifting to the usage of renewable energy sources.

3. **Biological variety and the robustness of ecosystems**

   It is absolutely necessary for the continuation of sustainable practices that biodiversity be protected and ecosystems be kept in good health. Ecosystems that contain a greater variety of plant and animal species are more capable of withstanding the effects of shifting conditions in their surrounding environment and continuing to deliver important goods and services such as pollination and clean water.

4. **Reliable and Ethical Supply Chains**

   The use of supply chain procedures that are sustainable helps to ensure that an organization's sources of raw materials and components remain robust in the face of stresses such as political instability, natural disasters, or a lack of resources.

5. **Social Resistance to Disruption**

Beyond environmental considerations, sustainability also takes into account societal elements, such as the general welfare of a community and the distribution of available resources fairly. A society that is resilient is one that is sustainable on all fronts: economically, socially, and environmentally.

Implications for a Number of Different Sectors

1. **Agricultural Practices**

   The use of sustainable farming practices, such as crop rotation and organic farming, contributes to the preservation of the soil's natural quality and decreases the demand for man-made chemicals.

   Resilience can be achieved by diversifying agricultural operations and crop production in order to assist farmers in adapting to changing climate conditions and withstanding the effects of severe weather.

2. **Vitality**
   Transitioning to renewable energy sources such as solar and wind power, for example, lowers emissions of greenhouse gases and has a less overall impact on the environment. This is important for the sake of sustainability. Decentralized energy networks that are fueled by renewable sources improve energy resilience by minimizing the vulnerability of the energy system to centralized power generation and distribution.
3. **The underlying framework**
   The design of sustainable infrastructure, such as environmentally friendly buildings and transportation networks that use less energy, lowers the amount of resources used and the amount of damage done to the environment.
   Resilience: A resilient infrastructure has elements that can resist extreme weather disasters and other disturbances, which ensures that services will continue uninterrupted.
4. **Health care services**
   The reduction of medical waste and the implementation of healthcare procedures that are less harmful to the environment both contribute to environmental sustainability.
   Resilience refers to the ability of a healthcare system to withstand shocks in patient demand and to make contingency plans for unforeseen circumstances, such as those that may arise in the event of a pandemic.
5. **Modern methods of production**

Reducing technological waste, using environmentally friendly materials, and developing energy-efficient devices are all components of sustainable technology development.

Resilience: Technological resilience requires the implementation of cybersecurity precautions in order to protect against data breaches and interruptions.

Creating a Future That Is Both Sustainable and Resilient

1. **Efficient Use of Resources**
   The promotion of resource efficiency through environmentally responsible behaviors, such as recycling, trash reduction, and water conservation, adds to the resilience of both the environment and its resources.
2. **Transition to Renewable Energy Sources**
   Increasing the rate at which we migrate to renewable energy sources, such as wind, solar, and hydroelectric power, cuts emissions of greenhouse gases and improves our ability to withstand disruptions in the energy supply.
3. **The Restoration of Ecosystems**
   Increasing biodiversity and resistance to the effects of environmental change can be accomplished through protecting and restoring ecosystems, particularly woodlands, wetlands, and coastal zones.
4. **Adaptation to the Climate**
   In order for communities and organizations to better deal with the effects of climate change and become more resilient, it is essential for them to develop climate adaptation plans and strategies.
5. **Reliable and Ethical Supply Chains**
   Building resilience against interruptions and a lack of resources can be accomplished by implementing sustainable supply chain procedures. These activities should include ethical sourcing and responsible production.
6. **Spreading Knowledge and Being Aware**
   The cultivation of a culture of responsible resource management and readiness can be accomplished through the education of individuals, communities, and organizations on the topics of sustainability and resilience.
7. **Working Together and Creating New Things**

Innovation and the creation of sustainable and resilient solutions are both driven by encouraging collaboration between governments, corporations, and non-governmental organizations (NGOs), as well as between communities.

Obstacles & Obstacles along the Way

1. **Thinking Only in the Near Term**
   Many businesses place a higher value on near-term profits than on the long-term viability and resiliency of their operations, which hinders investments in critical improvements.
2. **An Absence of Conscience**
   It is possible for forward movement to be hampered by a lack of awareness and comprehension of the interrelationship of resilience and sustainability.
3. **Restricted Access to Resources**
   It may be difficult to put sustainable and resilient practices into place due to a lack of available resources and financial restrictions.
4. **Obstacles Caused by Regulations**
   Regulations that are inconsistent or insufficient can be discouraging to actions that are sustainable and resilient.
5. **Opposition to New Experiences**

The adoption of sustainable and resilient solutions might be hampered by individuals' reluctance to change and a preference for methods that have been around for some time.

Sustainability and resilience are closely intertwined, and together they offer a route to a stronger and more stable future. These ideas direct us toward a more responsible and well-prepared world at a time when the globe is confronted with a variety of difficult challenges, such as the effects of climate change and the depletion of natural resources.

We may lay the groundwork for resilience by embracing sustainable behaviors that help us save resources, cut down on waste, and alleviate the effects of our actions on the environment. Organizations, communities, and governments that place a priority on sustainability and resilience are better equipped to adapt, better able to endure shocks, and more likely to continue their operations, even in the face of unanticipated problems.

Efficient use of resources, transitioning to renewable energy sources, ecological restoration, climate adaption, ethical supply chains, education, and innovation are all necessary components in the construction of a future that is sustainable and resilient. It is essential to triumph over obstacles and hurdles in order to make progress, such as thinking in the short term and being resistant to change.

10.4 Ethical and Societal Considerations

Ethical and societal considerations have never been more important in a world that is defined by rapid technological breakthroughs, globalization, and cultural shifts. These considerations span a wide range of subject areas, including environmental stewardship, social justice, and responsible technical development, among others, such as privacy and social justice. In this guide, we will analyze the problems and possibilities that ethical and societal concerns bring as we navigate the complex landscape of the 21st century, explore the importance of ethical and societal considerations, study their impact on many elements of our lives, and look at how they affect various aspects of our lives.

The Obligatory Nature of Ethics

Ethical concerns constitute the moral basis that directs human behavior. They serve to ensure that people, organizations, and society behave in a manner that is fair, just, and accountable. These factors take on an even greater level of importance when seen in the perspective of the rapid advancement of technology, the economy, and culture.

The Configuration of Society

Considerations pertaining to society take into account a wider range of topics, such as the social, economic, and cultural facets of human existence. These factors are essential to a society's health and advancement, as they mirror the collective well-being and harmony of the society as a whole and contribute to it.

The Dynamic Relationship Between Ethics and Society

1. **Moral Compass in Leadership**
   Leaders who uphold ethical standards provide examples for the rest of society to follow. The actions and choices that they make have an effect on the ethical standards of a company, a community, or a nation.
2. **Legal Procedures and Procedures**
   rules and regulations are frequently used to codify societal ethics. These rules and regulations specify what kinds of behavior are acceptable and what kinds of behavior are not acceptable, so directing and managing society.
3. **Shared Principles and Ideals**
   The ethical principles of a society are shaped by the collective values of that community. Culture, history, and the obstacles that society has experienced throughout its existence all contribute to the formation of these values.
4. **Social Struggles and Uprisings**

Ethical considerations have the potential to motivate social movements as well as changes in the conduct of society. For instance, the movement for civil rights has actively advocated for ethical ideals such as fairness and equality.

The Effects That It Has On Many Different Aspects Of Life

1. **Modern equipment**
   Ethical Considerations Ethical decisions in the creation of technology include concerns such as privacy, data security, bias in artificial intelligence, and the responsible application of emerging technologies.
   The introduction of new technologies has had a profound effect on society, altering the ways in which people work, communicate,

and gain access to information. Concerns concerning digital inequality and the digital divide are included in the societal impact.

2. **Commercial Activity and Economics**

   Ethical Considerations Ethical decisions in the business world entail corporate responsibility, fair labor standards, environmentally sustainable supply chain management, and ethical management of supply chains.

   Impact on Society Unethical business activities can have a negative impact on society, including increased wealth disparity and deterioration of the natural environment.

3. **The environment and its sustainable development**

   Ethical Considerations: Ethical decisions surrounding the environment entail things like conserving resources, using them in an ethical manner, and taking climate action.

   Impact on Society Unsustainable activities, such as deforestation and overfishing, have substantial repercussions for society, including the reduction of biodiversity and the disturbance of ecosystems.

4. **Health care services**

   Ethical Considerations The ethical principles that govern the healthcare industry include patient autonomy, informed consent, equal access to healthcare, and the ethical application of medical technologies.

   Implications for Society Disparities in healthcare and unequal access to medical services can have severe repercussions for society, having an adverse effect on public health and overall wellbeing.

5. **Instruction**

Ethical concerns Ethical concerns in education include ensuring that all students have equal access to high-quality education, developing curriculum that is free from bias, and creating learning environments that are welcoming to all students.

The impact on society is that unequal access to education can make existing socioeconomic inequities worse and reduce the number of possibilities available to disadvantaged communities.

The Obstacles to Overcome and the Potential Benefits

The Obstacles:

The rapid progression of technology has prompted the emergence of new ethical concerns about the application of developing technologies such as artificial intelligence, biotechnology, and genetic engineering.

The term "globalization" refers to the process of connecting different communities and cultures, yet it can also result in cultural conflicts and ethical conundrums.

Environmental Challenges: Confronting climate change and the destruction of the environment needs collaboration on a global scale and making moral decisions for the conservation of resources.

Inequalities in Society: Inequalities in society continue to be a major ethical and societal concern, regardless of whether they are based on gender, race, or socioeconomic background.

The advent of the digital era has raised worries regarding the protection of personal data, the safety of online transactions, and the limitation of individual liberties.

Occasions to seize:

The progress made in technology and research has led to the development of new solutions to a variety of global issues, such as climate change, sickness, and social inequality.

Exchange of Cultures: Globalization makes it easier for people to share their ideas and cultures with one another, which enriches civilizations and promotes mutual understanding.

Movements in Society: Grassroots movements, which are propelled by moral concerns, have the potential to bring about constructive change and bring attention to important problems in society.

Education and Awareness: Education is one of the most important factors in bringing about an increase in societal and ethical awareness as well as in motivating responsible actions.

Collaboration: Working together to find ethical and societal solutions, such as coming to an international accord to address climate change, can be accomplished through collaboration between governments, organizations, and individuals.

In this quickly evolving world, taking ethical and societal concerns into account is absolutely necessary. They point us in the right direction when it comes to making responsible decisions, promoting justice, and tackling global concerns. The complex relationship between ethics and society has deep implications for many facets of our lives and a myriad of other spheres.

To address problems, whether they are brought about by advances in technology, globalization, environmental concerns, social disparities, or the transition brought about by the digital revolution, it is necessary to have ethical awareness, innovation, teamwork, and a dedication to the overall well-being of society.

We, as individuals, businesses, and nations, have the potential to set an example for others to follow by incorporating ethical and societal considerations into our actions and decisions. In doing so, we can help shape a society that is more just, inclusive, and sustainable for all.

www.ingramcontent.com/pod-product-compliance
Lightning Source LLC
LaVergne TN
LVHW010155070526
838199LV00062B/4368